THE EDITORS

Sian Rhiannon Williams was born in Rhymney, Monmouthshire and educated at Ysgol Gymraeg Rhymni, Ysgol Gyfun Rhydfelen, Pontypridd and the University College of Wales Aberystwyth where she read History. She was awarded a Ph.D. in 1985 for her study of the social history of the Welsh language in industrial Monmouthshire, which provided the basis for her volume, *Oes y Byd i'r Iaith Gymraeg* (University of Wales Press, 1992). She taught at Rhydfelen and worked as a Radio Producer in the Education Department of BBC Wales before taking up her current post of Senior Lecturer in History at the University of Wales Institute Cardiff. She lives wit her family in Rhoose.

Carol White was born in Ferndale in the Rhondda Valley and educated at Ferndale Grammar School. She took a Fine Art degree at Cardiff College of Art and went on to work as a theatre and television designer. She was a founder member of Red Flannel, the women's film and video workshop that made *Mam*, the Channel Four documentary on the history of women in the South Wales Valleys. Her recent directing work for television includes *All in the Game* – the story of Welsh women's football; *In Praise of Older Women* – which looks at the lives of three inspirational women, all over sixty; and *Starstruck in Aberdare* – which follows the trials and tribulations of a group of Aberdare women as they put on a local fashion show. She presently works as a freelance director with Teliesyn Production Company and lives with her family in Taffs Wells.

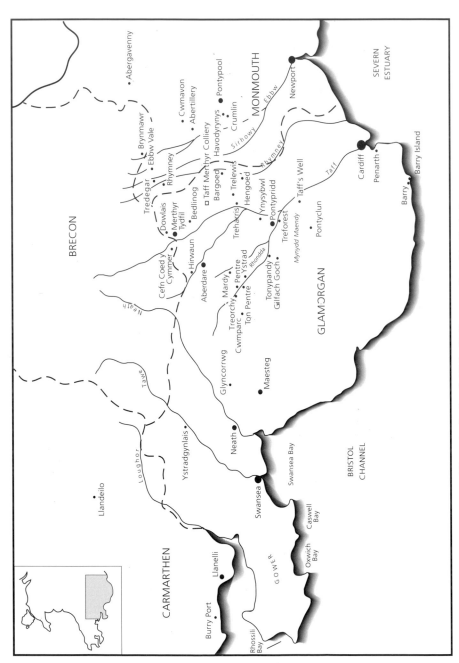

Places in the South Wales Valleys mentioned in the text.

STRUGGLE
OR STARVE

Edited by

Carol White & Sian Rhiannon Williams

honno

Published by Honno
'Ailsa Craig', Heol y Cawl, Dinas Powys,
CF6 4AH

First Impression 1998
© The Contributors

British Library Cataloguing in Publication Data
A catalogue record for this book is available from the British Library

ISBN 1-870206-25-8

Published with the financial support of the
Arts Council of Wales

Cover photograph – courtesy of Iris Roderick Thomas from her book
Remember When. The Photograph was taken by Joe Short, a miner who
developed an interest in photography in the early 1920s.
The photograph, taken on a Kodak autographic, show his sisters – Rosie is in
the bath and Emily, who has already bathed, reads in the background.

Designed by Debbie Maidment

Typset in Gwasg Dinefwr Press, Llandybïe

CONTENTS

PROLOGUE

Olive

~

Elaine Morgan

There is always a danger, in describing the lives of women in earlier times, of making them sound like stereotypes. I thought it would be easy to counter this by writing about one individual that I knew well – or ought to have known well – my mother. The attempt to do this has only shown me how little I really understood.

To begin at the beginning: around the year 1900 my English grandmother received a letter from her estranged husband suggesting a fresh start; he had found well-paid work in the pits and offered a home to her and their two children in Pontypridd. It was a fast-growing town in the grip of the Coal Rush. She arrived late on a Saturday as the pubs were closing and was shepherded down Taff Street through alarming scenes of drunken brawling, flying fists, blood and broken glass.

Back home in Somerset she had worked as nursery maid in the squire's mansion where she had picked up some pretensions to gentility. That (plus her English 'twang') did not endear her to her new neighbours so she quickly grew lonely and very depressed. Within five or six years all the bright hopes lay in ruins. Her husband had taken to gambling and she had taken to gin. There came a dark day when she lay in the grip of *delirium tremens* on what was assumed to be her death-bed, with the landlord threatening to evict the feckless widower and his offspring straight after the funeral.

That was the low spot of the family's fortunes. The fact that they climbed out of it was entirely due to their daughter Olive, a winsome child with brown ringlets, big blue eyes, bags of filial loyalty and considerable strength of character. At the age of ten she took charge of events. She nursed her mother through her self-inflicted

3

illness. She pleaded with the landlord, swearing a Bible oath to bring him the rent each week plus a small sum off the arrears. On pay days she waylaid her father outside the colliery and wheedled rent and housekeeping money out of his docket before the bookies could get hold of the rest. She cooked and cleaned and washed and mended and got her young brother off to school.

My grandmother was so terrified by the hideous creatures that had haunted her d.t.'s that she promptly got herself Saved, and turned into a teetotaller, by the very next Revival that swept through the valleys. But she never resumed her household duties. She found it much easier and more genteel to leave all that to Our Oll, who had proved herself so capable. A message was sent to the school saying that Olive Neville's education must be considered at an end, as her services were indispensable at home. The teachers were indignant, because Olive's compositions had regularly been read out in front of the class, but there was nothing they could do.

When she was fourteen, Olive was allowed to sit in on sewing-machine lessons given to four sisters in the house across the lane, and their brother Billy (my father) would enter the room and gaze at her. He was a popular lad with a mind full of mischief and practical jokes and ingenuity. When Olive was laid up for a few weeks after an accident, he rigged up a pulley across the lane from his bedroom window to hers, so that he could send secret messages which her mother could not intercept. In the Great War, he sent her letters from the Western Front beginning 'Dear little English sweetheart', and later a gold ring which he forged himself out of molten sovereigns.

After the war they married, agreeing to share a home with her parents while they saved up for a deposit on a house. Olive at that time was strikingly beautiful. (It is not just my opinion. Last year in an HTV dubbing room a producer was sorting through family photographs I had lent for a feature programme, and when Olive's picture was flashed on the screen one of the crew stared and pointed and exclaimed 'Who is that woman?') Billy was handsome too. A qualified engineer like his father, he had secured a good job driving the van at the Great Western Colliery, and there seemed every likelihood that they would live happily ever after.

That was where the iron forces of geography and economics

came in and shattered the dream. They were living in the wrong place at the wrong time. In South Wales, the effects of the Great Depression that followed the Wall Street Crash were particularly severe and long-lasting. They never did get a home of their own. My grandfather lost his job and never worked again. My father lost his job and was unemployed until 1938. He was seldom idle, since he acted as odd job man to the whole neighbourhood. He would mend burst pipes and broken watches and windows, put new tiles on roofs and new soles on boots and run a doll's hospital for broken toys in the days after Christmas – but since his clients were all in the same financial bracket as we were, the average reward for his labour varied from 'thank you very much' to two-pence – the price of a packet of five Woodbines.

I have sometimes been asked whether the traditional picture of the Welsh Mam – the backbone of her family, the peace-keeper, the self-sacrificer, the tower of strength – was just a romantic myth. I don't think so. Olive's own mother was certainly no rôle model but she had a better one in her Welsh mother-in-law who was all of those things – and Olive followed her example. My childhood memories of a household of four adults and a child, run on two dole packets, are of a life of comfort and ease and harmony.

There was not much ease for Olive, as for most of the women in that place and time. Mondays were the 'long weary workday' that Gracie Fields used to sing about. It was a back-breaking job – repeatedly filling a heavy cast-iron boiler with water and heaving it on to the coal fire, steadied with the knee, then staggering out with it to the back yard, to the zinc bath and the washboard and the wooden rinsing tub and the starch bowl and the mangle and the clothes line. It was all taken for granted as part of the job. Olive did everything. Feather-brained grandma occasionally washed a dish or peeled a potato; the men never lifted a finger either. Olive was a dynamo of energy, and if I tried anything in that line she grew impatient with my 'half-soaked' efforts: 'Oh get out of the way, let me do it.' Besides, she had a fierce determination that in this generation, the writer of praised compositions was not going to be conscripted into black-leading the grates.

Through it all she kept smiling. I remember her singing around the house, playing the piano, laughing at Billy's jokes and planning little treats. Starting in August every year, she squirrelled away enough weekly pennies to enable Santa Claus to do his stuff and to put a chicken on the table – tasting all the better for being the first one for a twelvemonth. She was the strongest character in the household and within those walls could have got her way over anything she set her heart on; but what she set her heart on was keeping the peace. I realise now that that was no small achievement, with a clever atheistic husband, a smugly pietistic old woman, a fat morose old man and an excitable child, all cooped up in one small room for 365 days in the year. But she swung it, most of the time. I remember very few rows.

At the time it never occurred to me that she had money worries, or that for someone with her looks it must have been a grief not to be able to make the most of them. She would wear a dress until it fell apart before squandering on herself the price of the material to make a new one. I remember one cross-over apron that got so threadbare the iron went through it and tore it. To my astonishment, she threw the thing on the floor and danced on it, to celebrate the fact that she would never have to put it on again.

Years later, when I got a summer job in London and invited her up, I took her to the matinée of a drawing-room drama by, I believe, Dodie Smith. There was a short scene between two below-stairs characters who wept in each other's arms because the man could not find a job. At the interval, she wiped her eyes and marvelled that a playwright could understand so well what life was like for other people: 'Daddy and me used to do that sometimes, when there was nobody about.' Full marks for perception to Dodie Smith – and nought out of ten for me. I lived with them, and I never dreamt that that sort of thing was going on.

The old idea of the 'good woman' – good daughter, good wife, good housekeeper, good mother – has become outdated, and sometimes derided as a symbol of subservience and wimpishness. But the past is a different country, and there were far fewer options open for women then, or for men either. Olive was never meek; she was dauntless. She took the cards that life dealt out to her – on the whole it was a pretty lousy hand – and played it by the rules and made the very best of it. On the centenary of her birth, I remember her with love and gratitude and with pride.

INTRODUCTION

INTRODUCTION

About three weeks after Jim and I were married the glorious
news broke on the world that the war was at an end and an
armistice would be signed. The colliers had a day off work
and Jim and I went to Llandeilo Fair. What a load seemed
suddenly to be lifted from all our hearts, and with what hope
we all said 'never again!'[1]

Winifred Griffths' recollection of the end of the First World War
vividly captures the spirit of hope of Autumn 1918, and, like many
other works included in this volume, describes a significant event
from the perspective of a woman's personal experience. This collection of autobiographical writing by women brought up or living
in the South Wales mining valleys during the 1920s and 1930s
focuses on the inter-war years with occasional earlier childhood
memories and reflections on the changes brought about by the
coming of the Second World War. (Honno Press has already published a volume on Welsh women's war experiences.[2]) The inter-
war period is one which has left us with some of the most powerful
and memorable images of the area in prose and verse, picture and
sound. That time of depression, dislocation and dramatic industrial
and political struggle holds a fascination for everyone who is
interested in the society of the valleys and continues to provide
historians, literary critics and film makers with questions of
interpretation. *Struggle or Starve* is new in that it brings together a
range of experiences against this historical backdrop from a female
perspective. The focus is on the women's struggle at once part of,
and separate from, the men's.

To date, the portrayal of the South Wales mining communities
in literature has depended largely on the writings of male authors
with the result that a one-sided picture has emerged. As Angela V.
John comments:

> The women's sacrifice has been noted yet not questioned.
> Autobiographies are the classic example of this . . . Time and
> again women enter autobiographies only at the point where
> they are about to marry the narrator . . . They tend to feature,
> if at all, as the miner's wife, at one possible stage in the life
> cycle. We hear little of them as young girls . . . Sources can of
> course be a major problem. For a number of reasons women
> have tended not to write the stories of their lives in mining
> communities.[3]

The problems encountered in unearthing material for this book have
underlined the scarcity of written works by women, for although
women's lives in the 1920s and 1930s are fairly well documented in
oral history accounts, comparatively few valleys' women have put
pen to paper to record their histories. As editors, our main source
for unpublished material has been local women's writing groups,
while other works were voluntarily sent to Honno Press to be
considered for publication. But we have also had to depend heavily
upon previously published works (many having been published
privately or now out of print) and are grateful to the authors and
publishers for their co-operation. We have confined ourselves to
works written in English (although one contribution by Heulwen
Williams was originally written in Welsh), so similar Welsh language
material remains an untapped source. As regards language, the
contributions generally reflect the anglicisation taking place in the
valley communities in this period and some extracts raise points
related to women's rôle in linguistic transition, yet it might be that
the Welsh speaking element has been under-represented here.
Given the limitations, it has been difficult to be totally comprehen-
sive and representative, but our main aim has been to present an
enjoyable and readable literary document of the time.

We are, nevertheless, conscious of the complexities of using
autobiography to present an historical period. Questions of repre-
sentation and memory are immediately posed. For example, as
Margaret Lloyd, in her poem 'Childhood Poverty' (Chapter 2) says:

> I didn't know we were poor when I was a child,
> no one told me as I dreamed my dreams.

I only remember the gleaming brass fender,
a chariot of fire in the flickering flames.

The majority of the authors are older women recalling their childhood and youth, and to a considerable extent, we are exploring these years through the eyes of little girls. By its very nature, therefore, this material involves the reader in a discussion of the relationship between autobiography and history and of the way in which the very act of re-telling personal stories reconstructs an historical past which is continually being recreated. It also invites consideration of the particular nature of women's autobiographical writing, a genre which, according to some feminist critics, has a character all of its own.[4]

The book is organized thematically, a structure to which the available material lent itself. Yet, as editors, we have also attempted to adhere to a broadly chronological outline. Our aim, in this respect, has been to strengthen the sense of period while also enabling the reader to follow the life stories of individual women from childhood in the 1920s, through the 1930s, to adolescence and womanhood during the Second World War. This is particularly true of the extracts taken from the autobiographies of Maggie Pryce Jones, Mair Eluned McLellan and Beatrice Wood, whose personal histories unfold with the book. The extracts as presented are, in many instances, selections from longer works. Editing has been undertaken with a view to avoiding repetition and overlap while also illuminating the interrelationship between themes and experiences and ensuring that the narrative flows easily. (For a full list of authors see Appendix page 271.)

The areas which form the backdrop to the extracts are mainly the steam coal producing valleys of the Glamorganshire coalfield, with some pieces set in the anthracite area to the west and in Gwent. The single industry (coalmining) village is, therefore, dominant throughout, although it must be remembered that steelmaking and other related industries were also seriously affected by the depression. Another feature of the area reflected here is the proximity of woods and moorland, and the continued presence of agricultural smallholdings which played a part in the life of many families in the period. The extracts mostly reflect the common experience of those communities entirely dependent upon coal, yet we are also reminded that the valleys were by no means homogeneous. Differences existed in culture and language and in the nature and quality of life depending upon background and economic circumstances. Similarly, the valleys' women themselves were not necessarily a uniform group. Their responses to their circumstances varied according to personal and cultural factors, a consideration which has often been overlooked in historical representations of the time.

The dominant image of the women of the mining valleys during this period has been that of the matriarch or 'Welsh mam' (wife, mother and neighbour) as traditionally portrayed in literature and films, the most enduring example of which has been Richard Llewellyn's *How Green was my Valley*, first published in 1939. Little has been written about the inner life and individuality of these women, nor of the experiences of girls, young women or the many widows of the valleys. More recently however, this image has been scrutinized and questioned by historians, writers and film-makers.[5] The voices of the women writing here help to remedy this question of image, giving testimony to the diversity and complexity of women's lives while also encapsulating a common experience. Their stories reflect the experiences of both generations of the inter-war years; meaning, for the editors at least, our grand-mothers' generation who saw their hopes of new opportunities after 1918 dashed by the onset of the depression, yet struggling to build a better future for their daughters, and our mothers' generation, children during the years of hardship, who, as young girls experienced not only the losses of the Second World War, but also the changes and new opportunities it brought. They too were touched by another post-war spirit of hope for an improvement in women's lives which, in South Wales after 1945, centered upon the nationalization of the coal industry, the establishment of the Welfare State and increased educational opportunity.

For many women, the end of the war in 1918 held out particular aspirations for the future, in addition to the hopes for peace and prosperity which they shared with men. It was felt that women had successfully challenged tradition during the war, and that increased equality and freedom would follow. The winning of the vote for qualified women over thirty had established the principle of women's suffrage, and the Sex Disqualification Removal Act of 1919, opening the professions to women, seemed to augur well for the future. Margaret Haig, Viscountess Rhondda, daughter of the coal magnate and landowner D.A.Thomas, wrote in her auto-biography:

> We found ourselves in an utterly changed world . . . The war had broken down barriers and customs and conventions and had left us curiously free.[6]

Yet, the experiences of the women of this book, all (unlike Margaret Haig) from working class backgrounds, testify to the fact that opportunities for self-development remained limited by economic circumstances and by the norms of social and gender relations. The overriding theme here is not freedom, but constraint and sacrifice. As Winifred Griffiths, quoted earlier, discovered when she became active in campaigning in South Wales for the further extension of the franchise in that first post-war election, her all male audiences 'did not seem at all enthusiastic about demanding any more freedom for their women folk'[7] (see Chapter 11).

Due to the dominance of heavy industry in the area, the lives of most women were centered upon the home. Despite women taking up jobs traditionally done by men during the war, the majority soon found themselves unemployed when hostilities ended, and were soon to be denied benefits as the government pressurised women back into the home or into domestic service, particularly after 1921 when women had to prove that they were 'genuinely seeking work'. A notable characteristic of employment patterns in South Wales in the period, mentioned by several social commentators and Government reports, was the low level of participation of women in the workforce. Some employment opportunities existed in the metal trades, but these were few, and the vast majority of jobs for women, (circa 80% in 1931), were in the 'Personal Service' sector, that is, domestic service, catering, laundrying and so forth, or in shopwork and clerical work. Only 13.6% of females over 14 were employed in the County Borough of Merthyr Tydfil in 1931, 10.3% in Rhondda Urban District, and 14.3% and 14.2% respectively in Glamorgan and Monmouthshire (Administrative Counties).[8]

It was generally expected, and often actively insisted upon, that a woman would cease to work outside the home once married. Indeed, marriage was looked upon as a means of release from paid work and the period between leaving school and marriage was, therefore, a 'waiting' period rather than the beginning of a career. Most paid work for working class women was transitional, undertaken at particular points in the life cycle; before marriage, during early widowhood or after the children had left home, particularly if the husband was unable to work. Economic necessity rather than any career aspirations seems to have been the main motivation for women entering the job market at this time. Few married women took paid work outside the home, although 'unofficial' employment such as childminding, cleaning or washing in other people's houses, or taking in washing or sewing were common means of supplementing the family income in times of need, and hundreds of women whose husbands were unemployed for several years were forced to do this. This work (not reflected in the census figures) would be undertaken in addition to the responsibility of caring for the household, although some help would be expected from daughters.

Given the imbalance of the sexes in the mining communities, (964 females per 1000 males in South Wales in 1921 and 982 per 1000 males in 1931), girls not migrating could generally expect to be married locally. Openings to train for careers such as teaching or nursing were still extremely limited for working class girls for financial reasons, and those who did manage to follow professional training realised that marriage would have to be forfeited if they wished to continue working because of the operation of the marriage bar (see Chapter 10). Most women, therefore, became housewives and spent the main part of their lives rearing children and caring for their families. This lifelong occupation was hard, dangerous and difficult, required wide-ranging skills and was heavily burdened with financial and moral responsibilities.

A Woman's Work is Never Done (the title of the Labour Party campaigner Elizabeth Andrews' autobiography featured in Chapter 11) is undoubtedly an apt summary of the daily lives of the women of industrial south Wales, particularly the women of mining families (the largest group) who had the added burden of coal dust and miners' baths. All aspects of the organisation of the home, including financial management and childcare were solely the responsibilty of the wife, widow or daughter (the latter particularly if the family had been left motherless). With the South Wales coalfield having 271,000 miners at the height of employment in 1920, it can be appreciated that the experiences described by the women in this book were very common indeed.[9] Although men would undertake some chores, such as blackleading the grate, or cutting coal or sticks to assist their wives, 'women's work' was clearly defined. It seems that men in mining communities rarely helped with the less pleasant aspects of childcare for example, and, in general, avoided becoming too involved with household matters. Oral evidence of their reluctance to be seen to be helping with housework underlines the gendered division of labour which characterised home life in the period, although it might also suggest that some men helped more than they were willing to admit.[10] (For further evidence see Chapter 3.)

Many accounts of valley life have drawn attention to the constant struggle of the women to keep their homes, pavements and back yards spotlessly clean despite the adverse environment and coal dust, and this again has been heavily emphasised in oral accounts.[11] Cleanliness was an integral part of the culture which proved that a woman was a good wife and was one aspect which contributed towards the clear delineation between the 'respectable' and the 'rough' families. It was expected of a young wife that she would be competent at her job, providing her family with good food, clean, well made or neatly mended clothes and a well organised and comfortable home. This, particularly in view of the inconveniences and lack of basic facilities in many valley homes, required her absolute commitment literally 'full time'.[12]

While the miners were working a seven-hour day, (won in 1919 and lengthened to eight hours in 1926), their wives' working day was nearer seventeen, perhaps even longer, depending on the requirement to get up to make breakfast for husbands, sons or lodgers on the early shift. In the absence of labour-saving devices it was essential that women's work at home was carefully organized in order to be able to complete the necessary tasks. It can be said that the women's work in their homes was as well regulated and as rigidly structured as the men's in the collieries and works. Particular days were given over for specific tasks, for example, washing on a Monday, ironing and cleaning on a Tuesday, baking and shopping on a Wednesday, cleaning the upstairs on a Thursday and so on. Their work would involve scrubbing the floors, picking up and beating the mats, cleaning the walls and windows, polishing the brass, blackleading the grate, scrubbing the front door step, window sills and pavement, baking bread and cakes, in addition to the constant routine of preparing for and clearing away meals and nursing and caring for babies and infants. The especially heavy and dangerous work of carrying and boiling water for baths was undertaken at least twice a day by miners' wives and daughters. It is noteworthy that the investigators of the Pilgrim Trust who undertook a sample study of 76 families in the Rhondda in 1934 described 86% of the houses as 'clean' and 88% of home management as 'good' (the highest categories) despite the fact that 37% of Rhondda families at the time were wholly or partly dependent upon unemployment benefit.[13] Although some contrasting examples were presented, when compared with other areas, the Rhondda statistics testify to the fact that, in general, the women took great pride in keeping their homes and children spotlessly clean. As Maggie Pryce Jones says of her mother, 'Tidy was the most important word in mam's vocabulary' (Chapter 5). To be 'tidy' ('decha' in colloquial Welsh)[14] was to be decent and respectable, and despite the impoverished circumstances, the concept of 'tidy women' was certainly a reality.

In addition to their own, often large families, a large proportion of women took in lodgers to add to the family income. Numbers were usually limited to one or two because of cramped accommodation, but occasionally there were more, and they would be accommodated by ensuring that they worked different shifts, or by using both ends of the bed, sleeping 'top and bottom'. Lodgers either paid for full board which included washing, ironing and darning or for lodgings only, buying and cooking their own food. Many lodgers were relatives or close family friends, often single men or widowers, who stayed with the same family for many years. These 'uncles' often played a prominent part in the lives of valleys' women, as the work of several of the authors testify. (See Chapter 3.) Although many of these lodgers created a 'helping' rôle for themselves within the family and sometimes contributed financially over and above their fees, their presence, nevertheless, added considerably to the burden of work borne by the women.

The poor condition of valleys' housing was another factor which made the work of the housewives of South Wales particularly hard. The low quality of the housing stock, and problems of over-crowding, infestation and a lack of facilities were reported through-out the period, but, due to the depressed state of the economy, very few council houses were being built in the areas which needed them most. It was recognized that housing was a woman's issue given the fact that the greater part of her life was spent in the home and it became apparent that women were suffering as a direct result of the condition of their houses. For example, the high incidence of tuberculosis amongst women between 15 and 30 years of age was partly attributed to this. In her article on women in the Rhondda between 1881 and 1911, Dot Jones demonstrates how miners' wives suffered because of their working practices and conditions of work. Her evidence starkly illustrates how, like the miners themselves, their lives were constantly in danger.[15] The absence of a census in 1941 makes a comparative study of the next thirty years difficult, but conditions remained very unsatisfactory and may even have worsened as the strain and suffering placed on families, because of poor standards of housing, was intensified by the particular cir-cumstances of these years.

The experiences of women, therefore, need to be set against the economic and industrial background of the time. While the war years had been difficult ones in many ways, they had, nevertheless, brought growth and comparatively high wages to the South Wales mining industry, particularly to the central and eastern valleys which specialised in high quality steam coal for export. The miners felt that because their coal was much sought after and especially dangerous to extract, they should be entitled to a higher standard of living and this had caused disputes both before and during the war. The majority report of the Commission on the Coal Industry, known as the Sankey Commission (to which the Labour activist, Elizabeth Andrews, gave evidence regarding the need for better housing and pit-head baths) advocated the nationalization of the industry in 1919. The government's failure to implement the proposals, together with the sudden end to the post war boom and deregulation, (the return of the pits to the owners), led to the Lock Out of 1921, which came soon after a strike of the previous year.

Sometimes described as a dress rehearsal for 1926, this four month Lock Out (April-July) caused great hardship. The strikers were not entitled to Poor Relief, and although wives and dependents received some support, families failed to keep up with outgoings and ran up debts which they were unable to clear for many years afterwards. The miners were forced to return to work on reduced wages. Yet hard as things were, much worse was to come.

Despite the advent of the first Labour government in 1923 and a temporary boom in coal exports, by the summer of 1924 the crisis of heavy industry was already imminent. A sharp slump, intensified in 1925 by the detrimental effect of the return to the Gold Standard meant that contraction was now inevitable. Again, the miners, who felt that they had not benefited from the boom of 1923-4, were required to take a drop in wages. The threat of a General Strike was narrowly averted in July 1925 as Baldwin's government played for time by commissioning another enquiry into conditions in the coal industry. But the terms put forward by the Samuel Commission in March 1926 were rejected by the miners and it was this which led to the major event of South Wales in the period, the six month Lock Out which followed the collapse of the nine day General Strike.

'That summer of soups and speeches' has become legendary in the history of the mining communities; famous for the solidarity and determination of their people in the face of hardship. The resourcefulness of the women in struggling to keep a semblance of normality on very little money and in holding families together was a key element in the ability of the miners to hold out for so long, as was their great effort in organising fundraising and the provision of relief (See Chapter 11). While the men idled on street corners, the women's job became even harder, and the personal sacrifice of miners' wives in terms of health during both the 1921 and 1926 Lock Outs is starkly illustrated by the increase in infant mortality in 1922 and 1927-8, for as they struggled to feed their families, they starved themselves of the nourishment they needed during pregnancy.

The end of the 1926 Lock Out was the beginning of even more hardship, for the strikers returned to work on harsh terms and with union power reduced and international markets lost. The fact that they were now working an extra hour meant that workers could be shed without affecting the output. Many never regained their jobs and so started the increase in unemployment which was to continue until the war. By 1928, the plight of the 'stricken coalfield' was becoming a grave public and political issue. A government report of that year drew attention to the increase in child mortality, deaths due to TB and the high incidence of 'languor and anaemia' among the young women caused by inadequate diets.[16] When it is considered that this was commented upon even before the onset of the deepest depression, the long term and intense nature of the hardship suffered can be appreciated.

The increase in unemployment and the problems of inadequate benefits, together with the effort to re-establish the position of the South Wales Miners Federation (SWMF) (which had suffered a marked decline in membership) dominated valleys' politics during the 1930s. As well as the contraction in coalmining, the decline of the iron and steel industry in the heads of the valleys area led to the closure of all but one of the main works by 1930 creating extremely high unemployment rates. The fall of the second Labour government in 1931 heralded a particularly memorable period of hardship for the families of South Wales. The new National Government cut benefit rates and introduced a much despised Means Test. While benefits were reduced, male unemployment in South Wales rose to its highest point of 42.8% in August 1932 with fourteen areas having levels of over 50%. The scale of the problem was vast; for example, there were more than 13,000 men unemployed in Merthyr Tydfil alone.[17] Unemployment figures reflected the fact that those areas which had been the main benefactors of the buoyant export markets up to the 1920s were now the areas which were suffering most. In 1934, the year which saw the first Hunger Marches organised by the National Unemployed Workers Movement (NUWM), 44.5% of insured men were unemployed in the eastern coalfield and 28.6% in the western area. It was not merely the scale of the problem but also its permanent nature which made it so intractable. The Portal Report of that year drew attention, not only to the high percentages, (74% male unemployment in Brynmawr and Dowlais, for example) but also to the fact that many of the unemployed were never likely to obtain work locally. There was, therefore, no hope of recovery. At this time, 75% of the unemployed in the coal industry and 90% in the steel industry had been unemployed for two years or more, and 55% and 80% respectively for three years or more.[18] It is little wonder that the incidence of mental illness increased and that the wives of the unemployed, mindful of their husbands' sanity, would struggle to find the money for them to continue to be able to buy a drink or cigarettes, often sacrificing their own needs to do so.

The various government reports of the 1930s initially saw 'transference', the removal of the unemployed to the more prosperous areas of south east England and the Midlands, as the only solution to the coalfield's problems. Yet, even though many thousands left the area, it was not easy for a family in debt with strong local ties to move. Some efforts were made to attract new industries, particularly under the Special Areas legislation which created approximately 10,000 jobs in South Wales between 1934 and 1939, including the reopening of Ebbw Vale Steel works and the establishment of Treforest Trading Estate, which provided some jobs for women locally. Yet this was minimal in relation to the number of jobs required. It was, of course, the coming of war which eventually solved the problem of unemployment in the coalfield.

An investigation into women's history in the inter-war years is intricately bound up with the facts and figures of the depression since their lives were dramatically affected by it. But this cannot be separated from the prevailing nature of gender relationships, men's and women's attitudes towards each other and expectations of the female rôle. An example of this is the responsibility of women in managing the family budget. Possibly the most important factor in the image of the valleys women as authoritarian rulers of their households, women's responsibility for the household economy has been cited as evidence of empowerment. It has been argued that the men's practice of handing over their wage packets to their wives or mothers meant that, despite their deference to their menfolk, revered for being the wage earners, it was the women who were in control. However, in reality this practice often allowed the men to renounce all responsibility for household management and, in some instances, to avoid facing the fact that their wages were failing to provide the women with sufficient income. Moreover, it was unlikely that the whole wage would be handed over. At the very least, most men had 'pocket money' handed back for extras and leisure which enabled them to keep hold of their privileges as wage earners, while their wives had no release from the responsibility. When wages were replaced by unemployment benefit, the women could at least be sure of a regular income, but the inadequacy of the sums they received negated this advantage. Poverty could still be blamed upon the wife's failure to manage the budget effectively, and the pressure to 'manage' weighed as heavily on the women as the pressure to earn did on the men. 'Managing' therefore has a dual meaning here, as the mothers' lives in these stories, continually struggling to make ends meet, illustrate (see in particular Chapter 6).

In many instances we are party to the survival strategies employed by the women as we read these extracts. One obvious strategy was to 'go without' themselves. Several stories illustrate the deprivations of mothers who had 'already eaten' at mealtimes. Beatrice Wood's tale, quoted in Chapter 6, of a neighbour who rubs her drunken and sleeping husband's lips with mackerel grease in order to disguise the fact that she has, in desperation, eventually eaten the supper she had originally kept for him, is an illustration of the intensity of the wife's hunger, although not typical in the fact that the majority of wives would probably not have succumbed to the temptation. Certainly all the evidence points to the self-sacrifice of the women. As Eli Ginzberg, an American visiting the depressed communities of South Wales at the time observed:

> The children are hungry, the men are hungry; but most hungry of all are the women who deprive themselves so that their husbands and children can eat a little more. The wives and mothers must live on spirit more than food and that probably explains why they succumb so rapidly once their spirit is broken.[19]

Keeping the children 'tidy' invariably involved personal sacrifice. In the words of one of Diana Gittins' Rhondda informants referring to her response to her son's teacher on hearing that he would not be receiving a free pair of boots despite the fact that his father had been on the dole for six years:

> 'Yes', I said, 'I do keep him tidy. I'm going short', I said, 'it's I got to go short, not the children'.[20]

The extracts also illustrate how many married women resorted to taking low paid work when times were particularly bad, being unable or too proud to ask relatives for help. Others were forced to depend on parents or other relatives, sometimes to take long term care of one or more of the children. The rôle of relatives and lodgers, in helping to supplement family income is clearly borne out here. This would sometimes cause friction since it suggested that the head of household was incapable of supporting his family. John in Maggie Jones' *Kingfisher of Hope* and Dat in 'Shadows on the Wall' by Mair Eluned McLellan provide clear examples of this.

Although not wage earners until fourteen years of age in the inter-war years, younger children's skills were often utilized to help supplement income, and the examples cited here of girls working in shops, doing piecework at home, caring for siblings, or scavenging for scraps of food can also be seen as a part of women's survival strategies at a time of dire poverty, and provide too an illustration of the expectations and exploitation of young girls. 'Make do and mend' was a way of life in South Wales long before the coming of the Second World War made it a slogan, and the stigma of being poorly dressed weighed heavily on many young girls at this time. Their hopes of earning independent incomes were remote, with domestic service, much hated and resisted, being the only source of employment offered to the majority. Lucy Arundell and Beatrice Wood's experiences were typical of many (See introduction to Chapter 8). Even when local employment was secured, most, if not all of the daughter's earnings would be handed over to the mother. The operation of the Means Test from 1931 meant that the earnings of children living at home were taken into account before benefit could be paid, and many daughters were, therefore, supporting their parents on their low incomes.

A family's ability to 'manage' on a low income depended to a considerable extent on the number of mouths there were to feed. The inter-war years saw a particularly dramatic decline in the birth rate in the South Wales valleys, not least because it had been higher in the area in the first place. For example, Rhondda Urban District experienced a drop of -53.7% between 1911 and 1931, while the figure for England and Wales as a whole was -38%.[21] There were various reasons for this, but poverty, the migration of women of marriageable age together with increased accessibility to birth control information were significant factors. Yet although families of more than three children became the exception rather than the rule, nevertheless there were still many large families in the mining areas, and, economically, children were a liability rather than an asset.

Several of the extracts relate stories of pregnancy and childbirth and testify to the dismayed reactions of women on discovering that they were pregnant again. It would be rare for a new baby to be expected without a genuine fear for the mother's well-being, in addition to worries as to how an extra child would be fed, clothed and, possibly, educated. Young girls received very little information about sex, and were often almost completely ignorant of birth control methods on marriage, while pre-marital pregnancy was quite common. As Diana Gittins[22] has shown, most information was obtained via women's networks of neighbours, female relatives or work colleagues, although official information about birth control became more accessible during the 1920s (due mainly to the efforts of feminist campaigners). Local Welfare Clinics were allowed to give information on birth control to women considered to be at risk from further pregnancies from 1930 but it was not statutory for them to do so. The failure of the first hospital birth control clinic at Abertillery in 1925-6 illustrates the strength of opposition from the chapels and the continued association of birth control with immorality which served to keep women away despite the fact that the local miners' union lodges had voted in favour of it.[23] There was also a belief that birth control was 'up to the men' in the same way as sex was considered to be their right, and many women found it impossible to take initiatives in order to control family size. Needless to say that the result was a large number of unwanted pregnancies, as the evidence of self-induced abortion practices (from pills advertised in newspapers and slippery elm to extremely dangerous home operations with knitting needles or crochet hooks), together with the presence of untrained local abortionists illustrates. According to Lady Juliet Williams of Miskin Manor, a prominent campaigner for maternal welfare at the time, illegal abortion accounted for the deaths of 35% of the mothers who died in the Rhondda in 1935-6. Government statistics record an increase in deaths due to 'criminal abortion' during the worst years of depression, but it is extremely unlikely that all cases were recorded as such.[24]

Continual childbearing had very serious consequences for women's health, as the Women's Co-operative Guild's publication, *Maternity* (1915) and Margery Spring Rice's work based on the Womens Health Enquiry Committee evidence (1939) demonstrated.[25] Young women whose health was already below par because of inadequate diets became even more worn down by successive pregnancies. Childbirth still posed a great danger to women and, for most of the period, as Deirdre Beddoe has said, became more rather than less dangerous.[26] In Wales, the rate of puerperal deaths was higher than in other parts of Britain, a fact which gave rise to a Ministry of Health investigation in 1936[27]. It reported that many babies were still delivered in cramped or unsanitary conditions by local untrained midwives, and that aftercare was very lacking. Although the high rate of infant deaths in the valleys was successfully reduced (overall) by the end of the inter-war period, the maternal mortality rate remained scandalously high, and despite the establishment of a network of Maternity and Welfare Clinics which considerably improved the health of pregnant women, the depression hindered the development of an effective service. In addition to deaths directly due to childbearing, the 1936 report also commented upon the high incidence of deaths from other causes where childbirth was a contributory factor, for example, deaths from influenza, heart disease and tuberculosis. As previously mentioned, the effects of poverty on women's health were also borne out by statistics on TB which affected young women particularly. Despite the efforts of the Welsh National TB Association between 1912 and 1948, and the fact that deaths from TB were in decline in Britain as a whole, the 'white scourge' continued its grip on the valleys with, for example, a 30% increase in the Rhondda between 1932 and 1937.[28]

It was, therefore, not uncommon for a young family to lose its mother. Under such circumstances, the eldest daughter was, almost invariably, expected to take over the mother's rôle. It was taken for granted by all concerned, women as well as men, that these 'little mothers' would dutifully sacrifice their futures to tend to the needs of a growing family and widowed father, often to the detriment of their own health. Early widowhood was also common in the valleys given the particularly dangerous nature of the men's work. Although the granting of widows' pensions in 1925 eased the difficulties of widows and possibly enabled some to discontinue working outside the home, pension levels were low. Furthermore, compensation payments to widows of miners killed in pit accidents were also small, and not easily granted.

The devastating effects of unemployment and of poor living and working conditions are clearly demonstrated by the statistics. It is rather more difficult to measure their impact on the internal workings of family life. The fact that women often struggled against all odds to hold families together must not lead us to romanticise the harmony of working class homes. Undoubtedly, tensions were exacerbated by poverty and unemployment which undermined accepted patterns and routines. Men's pride as wage earners was destroyed by unemployment and conflict over money was common, particularly if drink was involved. Ginzberg observed that men's loss of status through unemployment was leading their wives to treat their husbands as they would their children, thus increasing friction in relationships, although his conclusion was that marital relations were 'substantially unimpaired' by the depression. A study of Mardy in the period states that domestic violence and wife desertion were ever present, although not necessarily widespread.[29] The apparent acceptance by wives of their subordination to their husbands, demonstrated by their readiness to 'give tendance', to submit their chairs, to eat separately from the men or to hold back from arguing had its roots in historical image making, but it may also, in some cases, have been symptomatic of an underlying fear of the threat of male violence despite the more popular image of the Welsh 'mam' of the valleys as a confident ruler of her household. In this book the experiences and recollections of Beatrice Wood and Maggie Pryce Jones provide examples of male violence within families.

Given the adverse circumstances of their lives, it is, perhaps, understandable that a picture of sacrifice and suffering is the one generally presented of the women of the valleys in the inter-war years. Yet, although many, if not most, women were constrained by family commitments and were too involved with day-to-day survival to become actively involved in campaigning for improvements in their position and quality of life, a considerable number did take part, motivated by the events and circumstances of their times.

During the years which followed the winning of the first stage in the long struggle for the vote in 1918, working class women in Britain thronged to join local branches of labour and socialist movements, as if making up for lost time.[30] This may have been related to the changes which were taking place in the nature of the feminist movement, where more emphasis was being placed by some groups on the rights of women as mothers, as opposed to their equality with men in public life. Socialist groups dominant in the valleys were mainly concerned with issues of class and employment, but they now needed women's support, and by appealing to women as wives and mothers, were successful in securing it. From 1919, the Women's Labour League, which had only three branches in South Wales at that time, was transformed into a network of Labour Party Women's Sections in the Parliamentary wards with the aim of organising the recently enfranchised women into the Labour Party. These local organisations provided an important channel through which women could become active, and increased in number and influence during the 1920s, and, together with the Women's Co-operative Guild (a part of the Co-operative movement), had the greatest proportion of politically active women. Both groups aimed to educate and inform working women on topics relevant to their lives, and became a source of inspiration to many, as Mrs Smith, a Rhondda miner's wife testified in 1931:

> The women most steadily support their men in their Trade Unions . . . and also the Women's Co-operative Guild is a

great help, and I would not miss going for anything, as we have such very beautiful lectures . . . that it seems to uplift us and help us to carry on from time to time.[31]

Although Gillian Scott, in her article on the Guild, argues that the movement lost its radical edge as a feminist 'trade union' for married women after 1921 when it shifted away from the principle of an autonomous working women's movement and avoided confrontational issues like abortion and birth control, nevertheless, it remained, with the Labour Party's Women's Advisory Councils and local Sections, at the forefront of the campaigns for maternal care and related issues.[32] The Communist Party, including the Young Communist League, committed (in principle, at least) to the equality of the sexes, was also attractive to women, and Communist women played a prominent part in organising in the National Unemployed Workers Movement (NUWM) and in several local political campaigns. Sue Bruley, who has researched the part played by women in the NUWM, describes the wives of unemployed South Wales miners as the most militant activists.[33]

The industrial struggles of the inter-war years are invariably recorded in terms of the miners and unemployed men working through the unions or political party organisations with some acknowledgement of the support of women on the periphery. The fact that women were almost entirely excluded from heavy industry and had no work-based channel through which to lobby meant that it was difficult for them to move beyond the rôle of sideline supporters and make their voice as women heard. As Chris Williams, referring to Rhondda politics writes, 'Male activists paid little attention to the concerns of their womenfolk'.[34] Yet it should not be assumed that women were passive in standing loyally by their men. Many did take initiatives to motivate the male dominated organisations to campaign on issues which they may not otherwise have stressed. For example, arguing for better housing and the need to establish pit-head baths in her evidence to the Sankey Commission in 1919, Elizabeth Andrews declared:

It was the women of the Rhondda who renewed this agitation by asking the Executive of the South Wales Miners

Federation to urge the lodges to take this matter up . . . I have addressed 25 meetings since March in mining areas in South Wales . . . and both men and women have realised what it means to them in raising the standard of life all round . . . I have been organising among the miners' wives for five years, and have during that period been in touch with thousands of miners' wives in South Wales, and at various meetings and conferences the women have very strongly expressed their desire for better conditions . . . [35]

As previously mentioned, during the Lock Out of 1926 particularly, the initiatives taken by the women's organisations proved indispensable in the continuation of the miners' struggle. As the writers in Chapter 11 mention, the relief effort, a huge undertaking, was managed by working class women who were themselves suffering as a result of the strike.

Despite (or, possibly, because of) the worsening of the depression, women continued to be active in various campaigns during the 1930s. From 1934 there was more co-operation between the various women's political groups and an upsurge in activity, due, in part, to the proposal to cut relief scales under the new Unemployment Act. Although women's political meetings were, in general, less well attended than the men's, mass mobilization of women was possible in the valleys in the inter-war years as was proven in 1935 when thousands of women took part in protests to demand an end to the Means Test. Despite having less leisure time than men to attend meetings and with fewer acceptable places to meet, women were at the forefront of several crusades, in particular, in fighting for social welfare reforms such as family allowances, improved maternity and child welfare, nursery education and the increased availability of birth control information. As Mari A. Williams has shown, it was the *women* of South Wales who ensured that the issue of maternal and child mortality was brought centre stage and tackled by charitable organisations, local authorities and central government.[36] Women also became prominent in the Peace Movement of these years.

It should not be assumed that women's activities, for example, in chapels and social organizations, were necessarily of a passive nature. Although women did most of the fundraising and the organising of social events, the work required both formal and informal organisational skills. The 'public' skills of those women who took part in religious services or addressed women's missionary, temperance or philanthropic gatherings should not be underestimated. The women's clubs, (organised by the National Council for Social Service from 1932 in parallel with the men's unemployed clubs) were also run by the women themselves once established. These became an important source of social contact and instruction for the wives of unemployed male workers and others, despite the fact that they were not universally welcomed. There were 260 women's clubs in South Wales by 1939.[37]

It is true that, to a considerable extent, men and women's interests within families and in the wider community in the South Wales valleys were mutual and intertwined. Given the circumstances of the inter-war years, class and conjugal solidarity often took precedence over the unity of women. Yet the women's 'struggle' within the home and in the wider community needs to be more fully appreciated in relation to the working class campaigns of these years. Women's networks, centred upon the home, were as strong as the men's in the pits and it was largely women's efforts which held families and communities together. It could be argued that, far from being peripheral, women's contribution was central in that they provided the backbone of the men's more public struggle for justice.

In the recollections of this volume, the resilience and steadfastness of the women shine through. Mothers hoped for a better life for their daughters, for improved medical services and release form enforced childbearing. Their daughters, (not always supported by the older generation of women) strove for economic independence, education and freedom from domestic toil. The question of whether the Second World War brought gains for women's emancipation has been shown to be a difficult one to answer straightforwardly, but for those women who had been brought up in the South Wales valleys in the inter-war years, the end of the war and the coming of a Labour government heralded a new era, and with it, the hope that they would be accorded opportunities which had been denied to their mothers' generation.

NOTES

1. Griffiths, Winifred, *One Woman's Story* (Rhondda, 1979) p 75.
2. Verrill-Rhys, Leigh and Beddoe, Deirdre (eds.), *Parachutes and Petticoats: Welsh Women Writing on the Second World War* (Honno Press, 1992).
3. John, Angela V., 'Miner's Struggle, Women's Protests' in *Llafur*, Vol. IV, 1, 1984 pp 72-89.
4. For a discussion of these issues, see for example, Steadman, Carolyn, *Past Tenses: Essays on Writing Autobiography and History* (Rivers Oram Press, 1992); Benstock, Shari (ed.), *The Private Self: Theory and Practice of Women's Autobiographical Writings* (Routledge, 1988); Spender, Dale (ed.), *Personal Chronicles: Women's Autobiographical Writings, Women's Studies International Forum Special Issue*, Vol 10, No. 1, 1987; Stanley, Liz, 'Moments of Writing: Is there a Feminist Auto/Biography?' in *Gender and History*, Vol. 2, No. 1, Spring 1990, pp 58-67.
5. See for example, Beddoe, Deirdre, 'Images of Welsh Women' in *Wales: The Imagined Nation: Essays in Culture and National Identity* Curtis, Tony (ed.) (Poetry Wales Press, 1986) pp 227-238, also 'Women between the Wars' in *Wales between the Wars* Herbert, Trevor and Jones, Gareth Elwyn (eds.) (U.W.P., 1988) pp 129-160 and the film *Mam* Red Flannel Films, 1988.
6. Viscountess Rhondda, *This Was My World* (Macmillan, 1933) quoted in Alberti, Johanna, *Beyond Suffrage: Feminists in War and Peace 1914-28* (Macmillan, 1989) p 137.
7. Griffiths, Winifred, *op.cit.* p 76.
8. Census of Great Britain 1931 *General Report* (H.M.S.O., 1950) and *Industry Tables* (H.M.S.O., 1934).
9. Davies, John, *Hanes Cymru* (Penguin, 1990) p 109.
10. Crook, Rosemary, 'Tidy Women: Women in the Rhondda Between the Wars' in *Oral History Journal* Vol. 10, 2, Autumn 1982, pp 40-6.
11. ibid. Also Williams, Eurwyn, *Rhyd-y-car: A Welsh Mining Community* (National Museum of Wales, 1987).
12. Tibbott, S. Minwel and Thomas, Beth, *O'r Gwaith i'r Gwely: A Woman's Work* (National Museum of Wales, 1994).
13. Pilgrim Trust Report, *Men Without Work* (Cambridge University Press, 1938) p 422. N.B. the figures referred to were 'put forward with reserve' by the researchers.
14. 'Tidy' has an added meaning in South Walian English usage. In addition to neatness it is associated with notions of respectability, decency and clean living.
15. Jones, Dot, 'Counting the Cost of Coal: Women's lives in the Rhondda, 1881-1911' in John, Angela V. (ed.), *Our Mothers' Land: Essays in Welsh Women's History* (U.W.P., 1991) pp 109-133.
16. *The Report of Ministry of Health on the Investigation into the South Wales Coalfield*, (Cmd. 3272) viii 689, 1928-9.
17. Davies, John, *op.cit* p 553.
18. *Report of Sir Wyndham Portal in Ministry of Labour Reports of Investigation into the Industrial Conditions of Certain Depressed Areas*, (Cmd 4728) xiii 313, 1933-4.

19. Ginzberg, Eli, *A World Without Work : The Story of the Welsh Miners* (Transaction Publishers, USA, 1990) (2nd Edition) 1st published by Harper, New York, 1942, p 37.

20. Gittins, Diana, 'Women's Work and Family Size between the Wars' in *Oral History*, Vol. 5, 2, Autumn 1977, p 94.

21. Beddoe, Deirdre, *Back to Home and Duty: Women between the Wars 1918-39* (Pandora,1989) p 104.

22. Gittins, Diana, *op.cit.*, pp 84-100.

23. Douglas, Margaret, 'Women, God and Birth Control: The First Hospital Birth Control Clinic, Abertillery 1925' in *Llafur*, Vol. 6, 4, 1995, pp 110-122.

24. Gittins, Diana, *op. cit.* Also *Women in Inter-War Wales Project Grace*, Unit 9 (Bangor, 1994), p 12 and Williams, Mari A., 'Yr Ymgyrch i "Achub y Mamau" yng Nghymoedd Diwydiannol De Cymru, 1918-39' in Jenkins, Geraint H. (ed.), *Cof Cenedl XI*, (Gwasg Gomer, 1996) pp 117-146.

25. Davies, Margaret Llewelyn, *Maternity: Letters from Working Women* (1st published 1915; reprinted by Virago 1978); Rice, Margery Spring, *Working Class Wives* (1st published 1939; reprinted by Virago, 1981).

26. Beddoe, Deirdre, *op.cit.* 1989, p 3.

27. *Report of the Ministry of Health on Maternal Mortality in Wales in Reports of the Commissioners*, (Cmd. 5423), xi ,1936 pp 367-524.

28. Davies, John, *op.cit.* p 557.

29. Ginzberg, Eli, *op.cit.*, p 184, Macintyre, Stuart, *Little Moscows: Communism and Working Class Militancy in Inter-war Britain* (London, 1980).

30. Graves, Pamela M., *Labour Women: Women in Working Class Politics, 1918-39* (Cambrige University Press, 1994).

31. Davies, Margaret Llewelyn (ed.), *Life as We Have Known it by Co-operative Working Women* (1st published 1931; reprinted by Virago, 1977) p 72.

32. Scott, Gillian, 'A Trade Union for Married Women: The Women's Co-operative Guild 1914-20' in Oldfield, Sybil (ed.), *This Working Day World: Women's Lives and Cultures in Britain 1914 45* (Taylor and Francis, 1994) pp 18-28.

33. Bruley, Sue, 'A Woman's Right to Work? The role of Women in the Unemployed Movement Between the Wars' in Oldfield, Sybil (ed.), *op. cit.*, p 50.

34. Williams, Chris, *Democratic Rhondda: Politics and Society 1885-1951*, (UWP, 1996) p 17.

35. *Royal Commission on the Coal Industry, Second Stage, Reports and Evidence*, (Cmd. 360) xii.1. 1919, pp 1019-22.

36. Williams, Mari A., *op. cit.*

37. Ginzberg, Eli, *op. cit.*, p 180-1.

CHAPTER 1

SETTING THE SCENE

SETTING THE SCENE

Nessie Williams' atmospheric description in the opening extract of this chapter, evocative of the scenes and centres of valley life, provides the backdrop to the experiences and events which follow in the course of this book. With a heightened awareness of the valley itself as a real presence, she leads us through the ribbon-like streets with their crowded, cosy homes, their front room shops, public houses, workmen's halls, cinemas and chapels to the colliery itself, the focus of most valley communities. Yet for the women home was the place where they spent by far the greatest proportion of their time, and this, despite the cramped conditions and lack of facilities, was also their palace, as described by Edith S. Davies in the second extract.

Outside of the house, the chapels were the main social centre for the chapel-going section of the community, and they fulfilled an important rôle for women who had few opportunities to develop their own knowledge and interests and to be of service in the public arena. Despite the overall decline in the popularity of the chapels during this period, the scope and influence of the work of the sisterhoods within these institutions increased. It was also during these years that female deacons (chapel officers) became more common, yet they remained in a tiny minority, and gender rôles continued to be largely segregated. For the majority of those women who did not attend chapel, the pubs were ordinarily 'out of bounds', being almost exclusively male domains, and although many women worked as landladies and barmaids, it was not until after the Second World War that the pub became a more acceptable centre of leisure for women.

Although the workmen's halls and miners' institutes were, like the chapels, pillars of valley society, providing a base for community identity, action and education, they did not belong to the women in the same way as they did to the men. For example, the running of the Institute was an exclusively male undertaking. Despite many institutes having a 'Ladies Room' and a few having separate libraries and reading rooms for women, evidence shows that whereas men would spend hours at the Institute, women would visit for specific activities, suggesting that they were not completely at ease there. In some cases, women were barred from using specific facilities and were rare visitors.

Yet it was in the Institutes that many of the first cinemas were established as the new film industry made inroads into the valleys cultural life. It is significant that by far the majority of regular cinema goers in South Wales in the 1930s were women. The cinema, with its ability to project the viewer into a world of romance far removed from the reality of daily life, had a special appeal to young women in particular. The magical thrill of the pictures became a necessary 'fix'.

Shopping was another activity which took up a fair proportion of women's time, although it could not be regarded the 'leisure' activity it is today. Money being so scarce, the weekly shopping was a heavy responsibility with the challenge of stretching resources as far as possible. Yet, shopping was also a means by which women as consumers could, to some extent, exercise control using their purchasing power. This was a strong element in the culture of the Co-operative movement, which, although not described here, was another pillar of society in most valley towns. It is the small front room shops which are most commonly described in this book, although the all-important Co-op, the grand 'Emporiums' and lively local markets also feature in other chapters.

My Childhood in the Valleys

~

Nessie Williams

I was born in the curve where the mountain merged into the hollow of the valley. When I climbed up the mountain and looked down on the valley, I thought it was very beautiful and, like roes in the belly of a herring, the houses nestled together, warm and snug. When it rained, the slates were navy blue with long wet dark shadows and the smoke rose like a conjurer's chiffon scarf from the chimneys. The tram lines, the train lines and the river, like silver snakes – when the sun shone – wended their way down the valley, and the trams like large red beetles moved along slowly.

There were noises peculiar to the valley. Sometimes I would wake at night and hear the tramp of feet heavy with boots: like a mighty army marching to war the men went on the night shift. Tin jacks and food tins clinked together in their black pockets, and in that world of sleep they spoke softly, and mouths were busy manipulating the cigarette stumps so that they lasted until they reached the colliery. I remember a little shop with a lighted candle on the counter and they sold Woodbines. I can see now the colliers bending their capped heads to light a cigarette and inhaling deeply. This usually on their way home.

There was pathos in the valley. How often I would hear the sound of hobnailed boots treading more softly than usual and a small sad procession moving slowly down the street. On a stretcher a covered body. People stood silent in sympathy – not a word. Men removed their caps and women wept quietly, and the tramping feet went on to the sad stricken home.

There was much consumption and the young often faded away in their teens. Old men with coal-encased lungs coughed away their remaining days. There were men old before their time, worked out like the coal seams below ground . . .

There was much talk of Bolsheviks, Russia, the red flag, capitalists and economics. There were lodge meetings, fiery speeches, and talk of pooling wages. There were workmen's clubs and institutes and I often heard the collision of billiard balls on the green baize tables. And there was always Lloyd George.

The minimum wage was a pittance and there were many children and great poverty. Small boys covered the seat of their pants with their hands to hide the peeping shirt and sometimes there were patches covering the whole of their backsides. Parish pay was ten shillings and there was much unemployment. People often lived in apartments, one or two rooms, often in cellars, and like divers coming to surface for air, they would sit on the window-sills. Many of them would marry on the dole, have children and die, never having had a regular job. The men loved babies and would often nurse them in a shawl, Welsh fashion.*

At the end of the street stood the defiant pubs and sometimes I could smell stale hops and strong tobacco and there was sawdust on the floor and cloudy glass on the window and big letters 'Saloon Bar', and there were side entrances where women with long bags entered furtively and would come out, look both ways, grateful to the darkness for devouring them . . .

The grocers' shops were enchanting places and had a smell of their own, a blend of coffee, floor polish, tea, and smoked bacon. There was butter from Carmarthen in a tub and, with greaseproof paper on the left hand, the grocer would adroitly plunge a wooden pat into the tub, place it on the waiting paper and slap it and pat it. How often my face was splashed and I would push out my tongue and lick the briny water from my lips.

I loved the parlour shops where one would ring the bell and sometimes the door was locked, and the shop-keeper, usually a woman, like a wardress, would put her hand into her apron pocket, produce a key and open the door. I would stand on a wooden box and there were wooden bars around the window. I would gaze at the wonderful array of sweets – toffee on a tray and a little hammer to crack it into small pieces, large gob-stoppers, pink, mauve and blue. Triangular bags containing sherbet, with a tube of what I think

---

* The practice of wrapping a shawl around the baby and carrier alike.

was called Spanish inserted into the neck, and what delight when the sherbet fizzed in the mouth! On the floor were bottles of lemonade and soda water with a glass marble on the top and when with much difficulty the marble was pushed down into the bottle, the contents spurted out like a fountain. The ice cream was pressed into the cornet with great care and sometimes my mouth would water because she was so long pressing it down. I remember bars of chocolate and on the wrappers five boys in various stages of ecstasy.

The shops which fascinated me were the drapers' shops. They were like caverns of darkness. There was a cascade of wonderfully named materials to greet you as you entered therein – picquet, voile, georgette, foulard silk, crepe-de-chine, luvisca, flannelette. There were little drawers labelled in gold, and rolls of ribbon and rolls of material on the shelves, and a brass measuring tape fitted into the counter. The draper would welcome the customer at the door, offer a chair, rub his hands and with perfect timing would undo the material – measure it – snip – rip, and fold it – set reels of cotton on top. I can smell the unbleached calico now as it was ripped, a fine powder would invade my nose and make me sneeze. When everything was ready, the draper made the bill out and called 'Check, Miss Evans please!' I have never known the first reckoning to be wrong, but this palaver gave integrity to the performance. Joy of joys was when the bill with the money was put into a little brass cup, screwed up and placed on some overhead trapeze, finally to come back with the change. The parcel was a work of art, packed and stringed with a little loop and the draper with great aplomb handed it to you as though he was presenting you with a certificate of merit. The whole performance was perfect and one had the impression that particular transaction had rescued the draper from bankruptcy.

The cinemas were magic places. For one shilling and three pence, and on Saturday afternoons twopence, Ronald Colman's smile beguiled you. Herbert Marshall limped into your heart, and Greta Garbo lured her lovers to destruction, and long kisses filtered through the darkness. Bullets cracked and hissed, and hit and missed, and the sheriff's posse rode on, encouraged by the piano, and there was a loud stamping of feet from the front seats. Sometimes the cinema manager would appear on the platform to tell us about the next picture and in a loud voice he would say 'Synopsis! –

A maid and a lad, fire and water, love comes creeping in. Carry on with the show.' This never failed to amuse the audience. He stuck posters on the board with a long handled brush and there appeared, in lurid colours, film stars puffed out with air bubbles and blobs of paste . . .

Sunday morning was a very special morning and the smell of dinners hung in the air. It was a time for street singers. I have seen a whole family – mother with babe in arms and father clutching the hand of another child – and they would sing sad songs as the pennies clinked into the proffered tin. I have often thought the collection boxes in the chapels must have suffered as the result of this diversion of funds before the people arrived. Sometimes, we would give the singers a little paper bag containing a cake and some bread and cheese. Very often the voices of the singers were drowned by the Salvation Army, who held their service on the corner of the street and with drums and tambourines would march victoriously, singing their stirring hymns and followed by many small children beating imaginary drums, their feet unconsciously following the beat of the music.

The Nonconformists, discreetly dressed, walked to the various places of worship, Bethesda, Horeb, Noddfa, Jerusalem. A few, like black sheep, belonged to the Church, but the Salvationists marched on . . .

Babies were often brought to chapel and sometimes taken out when they cried. I often longed for some such excuse and I watched the mothers rocking them to and fro through the glass window leading to the church porch. Sometimes, during the service, the babies were fed at the maternal fount and there were loud inter-mittent sucking sounds during the sermon, very disturbing, to say the least, to the adult congregation.

There were great church teas. The cutters sat on the platform wearing white aprons and cut stacks of bread and butter and cake dotted with great red cherries. There were those who kept trays at each end of the table and who brought lovely teapots and cosies knitted in bright colours to keep the tea hot. There were quivering jellies and pyramids of coconut – brown on the top – and little doughnuts dipped in sugar and maids of honour cakes, and sticky fingers and demanding mouths, and tea was spilt, and spoons were dropped, and there was the ceaseless chatter of happy children . . .

I think now of the valley at night. The chapels and the schools empty of sound and full of darkness. The mountains black against the moving clouds, and the sound of the colliery like a giant breathing. The great colliery wheel, black now, with its great rope like an umbilical cord having the power to resurrect the men below, or to create a sepulchre.

The Innocent Years

~

Edith S. Davies

Every terraced house lacked that essential requirement, a bathroom, and pit-head baths were, as yet, many light years away. As the miners came off shift large iron kettles were put on the fire to boil while the huge zinc bath was carried in and set before the hearth. First bowls of cold water were tipped into the bath and afterwards boiling water was added until a suitable temperature was reached. Many toddlers were scalded to death in these zinc baths when the simple precaution of putting in cold water first had not been taken. When everything was ready my father, who had taken off his filthy 'top' clothes out of doors, removed his grimy singlet and kneeling on the floor soaped himself all over and thoroughly scrubbed off the dirt. My mother washed his back clean as my father was a stickler for cleanliness. Some miners did not wash their backs regularly as they believed that too frequent washings gave them back trouble. Satisfied that he was clean from the waist up my father dropping his soiled drawers stepped into the hot bath, washing himself from the waist down. All this time we children were playing in the same room which was our living room. We called it the back kitchen. Bath time for my father was a ritual which was so familiar that we took no notice of it. As I grew older, however, I became aware that my father took great pains to conceal something with his left hand while he vigorously scrubbed away with his right. Young as I was

I had an undefined feeling that this concealment was not a matter for discussion. One day my curiosity got the better of me, and while my father was upstairs dressing, I asked,

'Mammy, what is Daddy hiding in his left hand?' My mother looked at me in a thoroughly vexed manner.

'Mind your own business!' she snapped, adding darkly, 'Them that asks no questions don't get told no lies.' Thereafter, I was banished during my father's bath-time into the cold middle room where there was no fire.

I suppose we were a typical miner's family in that we used the back kitchen as a living room cum dining room, bathroom, laundry room and play-room rolled into one. Simply furnished, it contained a scrubbed kitchen table, a sofa along one wall placed behind the table where we children sat for meals, a wooden armchair and one kitchen chair. The focal point was the fireplace where burnt a cosy coal fire and around which we sat as a family in the evenings . . .

The middle room was a room for 'state' occasions and contained a dining-room suite upholstered in a dark leatherette, a polished table and a Welsh dresser filled with best china. This dresser was the pride of my mother's heart. In contrast to the scrubbed flagstones of the back kitchen, the middle room boasted a linoleum floor covering and a piece of coconut matting in front of the fireplace. The brass fender, stand, fire-irons and rod across the mantelpiece gleamed from constant applications of Brasso. The armchairs on either side of the fire boasted hand-crocheted antimacassars . . .

The front room was a small narrow room often furnished and frequently let to another family, as people were too poor to pay the few shillings rent for a whole house. Living in apartments comprising one bedroom and the small front room was common practice at this time. Even if furnished the front room was seldom used except for courting or laying out the dead . . .

Upstairs there were three small bedrooms. In the largest bedroom the washing stand, complete with jug and basin, remains vividly in my memory although I cannot remember it being put to any use. Possibly it was used at births because babies were born at home then. Decorously concealed beneath each bed, behind the valance, was the essential chamber pot, as a trip to the *Tŷ Bach** in the

---

* *Tŷ Bach* (little house) – the outside toilet.

middle of the night was unthinkable. Feather beds were the height of luxury and making the bed was a real performance with much pummelling and punching of pillows and mattresses with feathers flying everywhere.

Each bedroom had a small fireplace and coal fires were lit in cases of serious illness, when the patient had to be kept in a constant temperature. Pneumonia was common then and without antibiotics extremely life-threatening. I must not omit the pantry in this description of a miner's terraced house. Situated immediately behind the kitchen it was large and had plenty of shelf room for dishes and food. An important feature of the pantry was the 'stone' which was cold enough to salt down a home grown pig, or keep butter from melting and the milk from going sour, provided they were placed in earthenware containers filled with cold water.

There was no gas or electricity during my early childhood but oil lamps with shades of great beauty stood on tables or were suspended from ceilings. When at last electricity came to Ynysybwl we could not afford to install it throughout the house so we had electric light downstairs only. Upstairs I read in bed against all the rules, by candlelight . . .

The majority of miners' wives were extremely house proud, vying with each other in keeping their houses spotless. It is true that in some instances there were exceptions, and poverty and dirt understandably went hand in hand. Such houses, one or two only in a street, would be frowned upon and the lackadaisical mothers would be described as *didorath* or *igamogam** to use the local vernacular. However clean a house was, it was impossible to get rid of the cockroaches which came home in the miners' clothes, the pit props of Norwegian pine being infested with them. After lights out in the houses they emerged from their nooks and crannies in their hundreds and if perchance a light were suddenly switched on, there they were scurrying in every direction with a light metallic rustling sound seeking refuge behind skirting boards, under floor boards, and behind the bricks of the fireplace. It is strange that a cricket on the hearth is a charming insect but even one cockroach is loathsome. We children called them 'black pats' and shuddered at the sight of

---

* *didorath*: from 'didoreth', meaning lazy and disorganised. *Igam-ogam*: the Welsh word for zig-zag.

them. There was no glimpse of them by day, so we conveniently forgot all about them . . .

Despite the presence of nocturnal beetles most houses were kept spotlessly clean. Hearths were whitened daily and grates shone after being polished with black lead. Steel fire-irons were cleaned with 'whiting' until they gleamed like silver. Brass fire-irons glittered like gold after applications of Brasso and much elbow grease. Front door steps were scoured with sand and stone until they assumed a blue hue and the wrath of the housewife would descend upon whoever was careless enough to leave a dirty footprint on its unsullied surface. Golden rays of light radiated from the brass knockers and letter boxes.

For the self-respecting housewife, Monday was always washing day. Clothes were rubbed on a washing board standing in the kitchen sink, sometimes called the 'bosh', full of soapsuds, with vigorous applications of household soap. After being washed in clean water two or three times they were thoroughly rinsed several times. The 'whites' were then starched and 'blued', for long before the days of Persil, which according to the advertisement washes 'whiter than white', local housewives were proud of the *grain** of their clothes as they fluttered on long lines in the back gardens. Pit clothes were washed separately using a wooden tub and dolly in the back yard. Washing day took almost all day so when we children walked home from Trerobart School at the end of the morning session, lunch would be either stew or fry-ups, something ready or quickly prepared. White Windsor soap, stew, and fry-ups are aromas pleasantly mingling in my memories of washing day. If Monday was a good drying day, Tuesday would be ironing day. Whites were lightly sprinkled with water, rolled up, and when sufficiently dampened, were ready for the iron which was heated on the bars of the grate. To test the temperature of the iron the housewife spat on the surface where it sizzled with the heat. It was then inserted into a shiny metal cover so that the clothes would not be soiled. After the clothes were ironed they were folded and placed upon lines strung around the kitchen for airing overnight.

Sweeping and dusting were a daily must as coal fires created a

---

* Whiteness and brightness of the washed clothes. Derived from the Welsh 'graen' meaning lustre, gloss or condition.

great deal of dust especially when the ashes were shovelled out of the grate. Furniture was polished to a high gloss and for those who could afford linoleum, floors were polished also. A miner who worked hard with pick and shovel at the coal-face had to eat well so a cooked dinner was a must every day. With washing, ironing, cooking and cleaning together with caring for the children, a miner's wife too worked incredibly hard. Yet I never remember my mother or any of her married friends complaining that they were 'shattered' or 'bored', common complaints today. My mother sang as she worked and was always busy. She could sew, knit, crochet, cook (her pastry was as light as a dream), paper and paint, repair our shoes, and feather and dress a fowl to perfection . . .

There were some housewives who were so houseproud that they carried things to extremes. Some of their homes were described as being so clean that one could 'eat off the floor'. One such housewife used to take her duster and walk all the way down the garden path before shaking it – over the wall of the house next door! Many covered up their coco-nut mats with clean sacks and one lady of my acquaintance had two sets of coco-nut matting, one for morning and the other for afternoons. The husbands of such women led cheerless lives, not even being allowed to enjoy a smoke indoors. Such women polished the linoleum to such an extent that it was as dangerous to negotiate their homes as it is to cross the north face of the Eiger.

CHAPTER 2

CHILDHOOD

CHILDHOOD

Not unexpectedly perhaps, three of the six extracts in this section describe games and play, and in that respect they are typical of many childhood reminiscences from various areas and eras. Yet the particular geographical and social character of the community within which the play takes place, is immediately apparent. The surrounding streets and tips are part of it, and, in the memory, become inseparable from it, as in 'Penydarren Flyer' by Dorothy Craig in the second extract.

The opening extract, taken from Mair Eluned McLellan's hitherto unpublished autobiography, 'Shadows on the Wall', is the first of several selections. The third extract, which explores childhood relationships, rivalries and fears in the context of a game of skipping, is an early scene from a novel by the internationally renowned author, Menna Gallie. Set during the 1926 Lock Out, *Strike for a Kingdom* was published by Gollancz in 1955. The village of Cilhendre, revisited in Chapter 4, is based upon Menna Gallie's home area of the Neath valley.

In this section too we are introduced to Beatrice (or Beatie) Wood whose story of childhood poverty provides much of the material on the hardships of a valleys' upbringing in the 1920s and 1930s in this volume (see, in particular, Chapters 6-9). The stigma of being so poor as a child is brought home to us in this extract, but her charm shines through here as it does in future extracts, despite the fact that she has to grow more streetwise.

The parents of E. M. Mitchell, author of 'Oddities' kept a smallholding, and, as such, she and her sister were not typical of the majority of valleys' children. The taunts they suffer selling their radish illustrates this, and their activities underline the fact that contact with the land continued to be a feature of life in the area even in the inter-war period.

The final story, 'Pearls for Mammy', has a Christmas feel to it. It illustrates the necessity to save for even very cheap items, the rôle of the unemployed work clubs and the joy of a family Christmas despite the hard times.

Childhood Poverty

~

Margaret Lloyd

I didn't know we were poor when I was a child,
no one told me as I dreamed my dreams.
I only remember the gleaming brass fender,
a chariot of fire in the flickering flames.

We mottled our legs as we sat huddled close
and travelled the world in the red of the coals.
I only remember toast speckled with soot
and sliced lambs' hearts lace-curtain thin.

Yellowed wool blankets covered with patches
love-quilted with needle and thread.
I only remember the whispers and laughter
as we three sweated, in summer, in bed.

No one told me we were poor when I was a child
as I sat on my golden seat.
I only remember sleighing on teatrays
and days that were summer sweet.

Shadows on the Wall

~

Mair E. McLellan

It seems to me that we were street children in a very real sense of
that phrase. In the heat of summer we spilled over into the street,
children and grown-ups alike, the children to sit on the edge of the
pavements, the mothers to stand in the doorways, the men to cluster
in groups, usually around the pub we knew as 'The Alec'. Perhaps
it was the heat of the coal fires, kept burning through the summer

and winter alike that drove us out. All the cooking was done over this fire. A teapot was always kept on the hob, and meats and cakes cooked in the oven on the other side. Even stews were cooked in this way, although only in the winter time which was the one thing, perhaps the only thing, I liked about winter.

We did not only play in the street, the mountains then were open to us, the Maindy mountain in particular. Coming back in the dusk of early evening I would hear the sound of a flute being played by someone who sat just inside the doorway, almost at the top of the street. It was a sound that still reminds me of those days, even though I did not know what tunes this stranger played, or even what it was he played, until I asked. Then the player left the street, or for all I know, the entire valley. It was like that then, people came and went; were part of the life of the street for perhaps only a short while, then went on their way. I know now that part of this pattern which I accepted as natural was a hunt for work. If the man found work, the family would stay on. If he failed, they would leave. It was as simple as that.

The street *was* our world, and I toppled out into it eagerly. It seems to me now that I almost never walked, but ran. I ran over the tarmac that covered the top half of the street, and over the cobblestones that covered the bottom half. The one break in the uniform pattern of the street was The Alec. It was built on a bit of a rise, and surrounded by iron bars. We all played on the bars, met and talked on the bars. On these bars we were all unknown and undiscovered Olga Korbuts, and who cared if we showed our knickers to the world!

Penydarren Flyer

~

Dorothy Craig

When I was a child, all too long ago, I think my favourite playground was the grassy Penydarren tip near my home. And what I liked best to do there was to fly my kite. For me it even beat the intricacies of ball games like sevensies and tensies, as well as the delights of communal skipping with the orange rope, whip and top and scotch.

Our house on the Penydarren High Street could not have been better placed. I just had to cross the road, go down the steps of the 'gwlly',* cross the Morlais Brook, aptly nicknamed Stinky, and there I was. A scramble up brought me to a fine flat area for running.

Of course my kite wasn't a bit like the magnificent plastic objects sometimes seen today, in brilliant translucent colours and all manner of shapes. But thanks to the tip it was a bonny flier. A blue sugar-paper job it was, made by my Dad, with crossed thin strips of wood for a skeleton, and a long string tail with gaily coloured bows all the way down. These were scraps of material my mother gave me and let me cut up to the right size with her big scissors.

When I went up the tip alone or with the boys next door, Mammy had no need to worry about safety. There was little traffic, and thoughts of anything more sinister never occurred to us. But in any case, she could keep an eye on me from time to time from the front windows – which she probably did!

When I reached that flat area, kite in hand, a run, a throw and up she'd go. At the right moment I'd start to let out from my ball of twine. *Then*, the power of wind transmitted to my hand, taking her up and up. Thrilling! What greater enjoyment could I ask?

Unless perhaps to slide back down that black scree-like slope by Waterloo House on an old japanned† metal tray, whose pattern of roses had been scratched by years of use before being demoted to this more sporting function.

So much for childhood pleasures in the thirties! Disappeared, like 31 High Street. Like the tip.

---

* *Gwlly/gwl*: narrow alleyway between the houses.
† *japanned*: laquered – usually in black.

Strike for a Kingdom

~

Menna Gallie

'Chewing-gum, chewing-gum ma-adc of wax,
Brought me to my grave at last.
High upon the mantelpiece,
There you'll find a ball of grease
Shining like a thripenny piece
And out goes she.'

Six or seven small girls were skipping with a long rope held across
the August road. One of the children, holding the far end of the rope,
stood almost inside a dusty hawthorn hedge, while the other stood
on the doorstep of 'Cartref', a small semi-detached house standing at
the end of Cilhendre village street. As the rope was turned, heavy
and rhythmic, the other children jumped into the twirl of it and
chanted,
'Chewing-gum, chewing-gum ma-ade of wax.'
The art was to keep skipping until the end of the stanza and then
to leap gracefully away without disturbing the rhythm of the rope.
Most of the little bouncing girls succeeded, but one hung back to
the very end of the line and when at last it was inevitably her turn,
she set her projecting teeth well into her lower lip, blushed, prayed
and doggedly ran at the rope. She jumped up, far too high, far too
determined, and at once tangled her feet and long doe's legs and
stopped the rope.
In silent acceptance of what having Nan in the skipping always
meant, the children changed the turners and started again,
'The wind, the wind, the wind blows high,
The rain comes scattering from the sky;'
while Nan, her faith in God once more destroyed, leaned on the
window-sill of Cartref. There she was joined by Blodwen Bevan,
her friend, whom she hated almost as much as, at the moment, she
hated God.

Blodwen was full of the pursed-in confidence of an elderly gossip.

'My mother said Gwen Evans in there is very bad in bed and sure to die.'

'Will they have a funeral?' Nan said, looking into the setting sun, away from the skipping.

'Yes, sure to be. We had a lovely funeral, remember, when Uncle Willie died. I had one of the ribbons off a wreath for Sunday. Sitting on the stairs, we were to hear the singing and Mammy was crying out loud. And after, we had a big tea with cook-'am. Have you ever been to a funeral, Nan?'

'No.'

'Come you, I expect you'll have one. Have you got anybody old?'

'I don't know.'

'Of course you have. You got your Grannie.'

'My Grannie can't have a funeral.'

'Why?'

'Well, she's my Grannie, that's why.' Nan was gripped by her terrible despair which was becoming almost habitual; she wanted to cry, from the soles of her feet. She knew they'd never have a funeral or anything unless perhaps she died, but then she wouldn't have a ribbon. But they might all be nicer to her if she did die, if only for a little while.

'Are you going to the Carnival, Nan?'

'I 'spect so.'

'What are you going as, then? You won't be a fairy for sure, nor a bride. Your teeth spoils you, don't they? P'raps they'll fall out. Our Dai's did.'

'No. They won't, they're my second teeth and they feel strong, like two big rocks. There's not much chance – unless I can get knocked down by a bike.'

'Well, I'm going like a fairy, whatever. I got a wand too, with a star on it.'

Nan looked at Blodwen with desperate, despairing envy, at her ringlets, made every night with rags, at her doll's eyes that looked like china, at her sharp, small, pointed teeth that hid properly behind her lip. Nan's eyes, that her mother called 'her redeeming feature,' filled with ever-ready tears and went pink around the rims as Blodwen pushed herself off the window-sill and jumped to take her turn in the skipping. Nan turned her head to follow the pattern in the lace curtains behind her and pretended not to notice when it was her turn to skip.

She pushed her tears away with her fist when her face was out of sight and decided to give God another chance. Tomorrow, before anyone at home could find her and shake their heads over her, she would look for a good hiding-place, somewhere nice and light, and if God didn't let them find her before the Carnival, she'd give Him one more try. Before she had to face the indignity of that rope again, a man came out of Cartref and asked the little girls, in a funny choking voice, if they'd go and play somewhere else because they were making a bit too much noise for Gwen. The owner of the rope, Blodwen of course, quickly lapped it around her middle.

'All right, Mr. Evans. We was going home. Our Mammy will be shoutin' for me. Carnival tomorrow, must have a bath and go to bed early tonight.'

The shrill children went their separate ways. Nan and Blodwen, who were neighbours, went together and Nan announced that she was going to the Carnival dressed as a queen, that they had a real queen's dress in their house and a real gold crown and she would wear it tomorrow. She didn't for a moment expect Blodwen to believe her, but her lies, as she consciously thought of them, came pouring out of her mind as though of their own volition. She was not aware of thinking them before they were out, and was sometimes amazed herself by the glories of her lies. They arrived at their doors, and as Blodwen called 'See you tomorrow' Nan went on with her plans. She went into her own house, sulky and guilty and resentful, unable to accept the love and welcome there because she mistrusted it all. Who could love her with those teeth? She sought revenge in impertinence and sulks and went to bed in disgrace.

Wednesday's Child

~

Beatrice Wood

Doreen was having a birthday party. She was telling me all about it. She was going to have a big doll that said, 'Mama'. She even showed me the invitation cards they were sending out, but I wasn't invited. It was to be held in a Hall not far from where I lived. The day of the party came. I desperately wanted to go. I went over to the Hall and hung about outside. I could hear all the fun and games going on. I had never been to a birthday party, not ever.

I knew if you went to a birthday party you had to give a present, but we couldn't afford a present even if I was invited. I went back home and got my treasure box down from the lavatory shelf, where I kept it. It was a shoe box, really, but all my treasures were in it. I emptied them onto the table and spread them out. There was a pair of skewers the butcher had given me to knit with (but I never had any wool); two small curtain rings; an alley* of my brother which he didn't know I had; a piece of slate I used for my scotch†; a piece of limestone for my chalk, and bits of coloured glass I had collected from the road. I don't know what I was going to do with them, but the colours were beautiful: the green and the white from glass bottles, the blue from medicine bottles, the reds from fancy bottles – I picked them all up. Then there was my piece of tar I picked up when the men were repairing the road, which we used to chew; a cotton reel with four nails in it for my corkwork, and a large wooden curtain ring from a big wooden pole I used to wear as a bangle.

'Now, let me see, what shall I give her?' I didn't want to part with any of them really, but I did so want to go to the party. 'I think I will give my curtain ring bangle.' Yes, my mind was made up. I put all the other things back into my box and got a sheet of newspaper and wrapped it up, and off I went. But I didn't have an invitation card, so I stood by the door of the passage in the Hall. I could see

---

* *alley*: large marble.
† *scotch*: hopscotch.

all the children in their party dresses. How I wished I could have joined them. Then one of the ladies who had been helping asked me what I wanted. So I handed her my present and asked, 'Please can I come to the party?' She said, 'Oh, love, they have finished eating – but come here'. She took me into the back kitchen where they had cut up all the sandwiches, and put some jelly and custard into a dish with some cream and sat me down by the table, saying, 'Look at the lovely present she brought'. I thought, 'Well, I made a good choice, anyway'. They all liked my present. One lady even said, 'It's the thought that counts, isn't it?' But by now I was having second thoughts about my bangle. I wanted it back. You see, I was full now, but I remember my sister saying, 'Once you give something, you can't have it back'. She even had a saying for it.

'Give a thing,
Take a thing,
Dead man's plaything.'

It didn't mean a thing to me but I couldn't ask for it back after that, could I? . . .

Doreen came to school one day with a brown paper parcel. Teacher had asked the better-off children if they had any old clothes to bring them to school. She gave it to teacher. Teacher asked me to stay behind playtime. The bell rang for play and teacher called me to the Headmistress' room. They opened the parcel Doreen had brought to reveal a beautiful blue velvet dress and a pair of buttoned up black boots, and a pair of gaiters. It didn't matter that the dress was faded. It felt all warm and soft to touch. I took them home. My mother was delighted, so she made some lace to go on Doreen's knickers.

I wore the dress next day and I swear everyone was looking at me and saying, 'Look at that pretty little girl! Isn't that a beautiful dress?' I was so proud, my very first dress that I can remember, and lucky, too, because if it had fitted my sister I wouldn't have had it. I used to wear all her hand-me-downs. Anyway, I saw a group of girls looking at me, so I did a bit of showing off. I did a twirl and kept on looking back to see if they were still looking and thinking to myself, 'I bet they wish they were me now'. Then bang I walked right into a lamp-post. That brought me back down to earth.

Funny what a dress can do. I felt different. Everything seems brighter and lighter. I wonder if it is a magic dress. I wonder if I am really a princess who had got lost, and my mother and father found me and brought me up. I straightened myself up to my regal position, head held high. Why, I could even feel the crown on my head . . .

Doreen was having another birthday party now. She was five years old – the same age as me – and would you believe it, I was invited. They really must have liked my curtain ring bangle the last time, and her mother had come to know me better now, especially after my mother making that lace for Doreen's knickers.

This party was a smaller one. It was to be held in their front parlour. She had what my mother would call a three-piece suite, a settee and two armchairs, not like our wooden one, but upholstered. I had only seen these in catalogue books. She had lovely velvet cushions with working in silk on them. On the floor was a big red square carpet. It was lovely to walk on. I had put my gaiters on to hide the hole in the knee of my stockings. The furniture was put to one side to make room for the table. On the table was a white tablecloth and the birthday cake with five candles on it. There was jelly and custard, cakes and everything. But I went too early – I couldn't wait for the tea to start. So when the rest of the children were playing, I just stood by the table, drooling over all that food.

I had my best blue velvet dress on, and I wrapped my corkwork reel in a newspaper for a present. I didn't use it much because I never had any wool. At last it was time to sit down! I had been all around the table to see which dish had the most jelly and custard. I stood by the one I thought looked the fullest, so as I could sit there. But when we were all told to sit down, I was pushed from the place where I stood. I was galloping the food as fast as I could: I was afraid it would all go. Then I thought of my mother – what wouldn't she give to see all this food? So I sneaked a bit of cake and was putting it into the pocket of my best blue velvet dress when Doreen's mother saw me. She got a paper bag and said 'Give me that cake that is in your pocket. I will put it in a bag for you'. I stammered, 'I wasn't taking it, honest! It just fell into my pocket'. (A lie, if ever there was one.) By now the roots on my hair stood on end. I went on, 'I was getting it out when you saw me'. I thought sure I would go to jail. You see, my father had never failed to tell us about stealing and of the hell-fire we would go to if we did. I was very frightened. She was very kind, though, and said 'I will give you some in a bag for you to take home'.

After tea Doreen's mother asked us who would give thanks to God for our tea. Well, as I had taken the cake, I thought I had better make my atonement, so I said I would. They all bowed their heads in reverence and put their hands together and I said the only after-dinner prayer I knew.

> 'We thank the Lord for what we had.
> If we had more we would be glad,
> But as the times they are so bad,
> We thank the Lord for what we had.'

My uncle had taught me that one on his knees. Doreen's mother looked up and I saw a smile on her face. I went to bed that night with a full belly. My sister and brothers enjoyed the cakes Doreen's mother gave me.

I was wondering how it was that God gave a lot of food to some people and not to others.

'Mam, why has Doreen's mother got all that food?'

'God only knows,' my mother said. That elusive God again. I will ask him in my letter. How do you address a God? Is it 'Dear God,' or 'Dear Sir God,' or 'Dear Your Majesty God'. I will ask my sister, she will know.

I still wore my best blue velvet dress every day. It was in the wash every Saturday night after we had our bath. My mother would wash it in the bath water.

On Monday the inkwells were due to be filled in school. One of the older girls used to come and fill them from a large square bottle. She came to my desk but had to take my inkwell away because someone had put blotting paper into it and it had to be washed. She brought it back, but didn't put it in the hole provided for it, so she knocked it over, all over my desk and, horror of horrors, all over my best blue velvet dress. I howled and screamed. Teacher came running up to me. She thought I had hurt myself. But this was worse, much worse, my best blue velvet dress was ruined. Teacher sponged it with blotting paper and got most of it off, and she was very angry with the girl for being so careless. I was afraid to go home when school was over, so I went to the stable to hide. All my dreams of being a princess gone, with my best blue velvet dress all stained.

Then I saw a black pat,* and another, so I started to play with them. I wasn't afraid of them – we had them at home. Why, I used to have to turn my boots upside-down every morning in case one had got into them during the night. I started to count them: one, two, three: one in the corner, four. The next thing I remember is hearing voices all around me, someone was picking me up and saying, 'Thanks be to God – he was with her'. I looked up and saw my father and I said, 'No, he wasn't, Dad, I didn't see him.'

I must have been to sleep because it was dark when I was found. My mother gave me one penn'orth of chips because I hadn't had any tea, then she put me to bed. The dress was put to soak in cold water and the stain came out.

Oddities

~

E. M. Mitchell

My hatred of radish is as strong today as it was at eight years old. Radish is a quick-growing crop, seed planted and ready for pulling within six weeks. So it was decided by my father that the money to buy him a new suit from the 30/- tailors would be raised from crops of radish. The variety chosen was 'Red Icicle', approximately five inches long, similar to a young carrot. Dad planted row upon row upon row, we weeded and pulled them, backache upon backache. Whilst my sister and I washed every trace of soil off them in buckets of ice cold water my father busied himself cutting white hairy cord into 8" lengths. As it was three strand cord he would then untwist each length to form three separate cords. We now bunched nine radishes together under my father's critical eye. 'Change that one, it's too short for the rest. Keep the lengths even, they look much tidier.' 'Yes Dad.'

---

* *Black pat*: cockroach

He then tied them, double knots and the end of the knots cut neatly with the scissors. My next job was to cut all the tails off. My sister, who had a better eye and was three years older, trimmed the green tops to a 1½" flat surface. Tomato boxes were then filled with about sixteen bunches.

Up until now my sister and I had worked quickly and methodically (which continual practice had made possible), but now we had reached the dreaded stage – the delivery of baskets.

The drop-off point was a house in a row of terraced houses at the bottom of our mountain. The lady of the house bought all the radish at 1½d a bunch and sold them at 2d per bunch. Unfortunately to reach this house we had to walk the length of the terrace. Opposite the house was a three tiered railing as long as the terrace and every tier seethed with the children of the street, an average family in those days was seven children. The leaders were the older boys supported admiringly by the girls and younger boys. One horrible boy would shout 'here's the radish kids coming' and the cry would be taken up by this mass of children 'Give us a radish then . . . carry your basket? . . . bet you don't go to school or play games, only grow radish . . . your house is like a radish!' I just stared at them and poked my tongue out but my sister had reached the sensitive stage and had developed boy awareness. She blushed continually and even this likened to radish red! The return journey with empty baskets was peppered with new insults. As we did four journeys every day, my father couldn't understand our delight on the day he said 'I've enough money to buy the suit'.

It was a dark brown double breasted suit with a feint line through it; the money even ran to a light brown tweed cap, and with burnished brown boots we thought he looked so distinguished.

The Radish Suit, as it was always called, was only worn on Saturday evenings, when he went for a drink and a stroll around the market which was open until quite late. He would buy fruit for the week and from the sweet stall two quarters of coconut ones only, picked out of liquorice allsorts by the stall assistant. They were our favourites.

When he returned we were bathed and ready for bed. After saying goodnight, our last act would be to pat the pockets of the Radish Suit jacket checking if Sunday's treat was there.

Pearls for Mammy

~

Eunice Hughes Thomas

As I passed the shop window, I saw it, the pearl necklace. If only I had the money! But I didn't have any. Still the man in the shop wouldn't know that, so in I went. The floor-boards creaked as I walked across the wooden floor and he leaned over the counter to look down at me. 'Please can I see the necklace of pearls that you have in the window?' I asked nervously. 'Why?' he asked back. 'Because I would like to buy it for my mother for a Christmas present,' I said, 'for she always says that one day, when she is rich, she will buy a pearl necklace, but if it isn't too dear, I will buy it for her now.' I waited as he went to the window and, putting the necklace into a green cardboard box, he brought it for me to take a closer look at. It was beautiful, small little pearls. 'How much, please?' I asked. 'Well,' he said, 'cash or weekly payments? It costs sixpence.' Well it had to be weekly. 'Right then,' he said, 'halfpenny now and I'll put it away.' 'Please don't put it back in the window,' I said, 'will you wait until I run home to see my father.' 'Alright,' he said, 'but mind you, if you're not back by this afternoon, back in the window it goes.'

I raced across to the Workingmen's Hall where all the ex-soldiers and colliers who were too ill to work anymore had wood and nails given to them and were taught to make different things. My father was making me a dresser but of this, I was unaware. There was always a man on the door. 'Please can you tell Mr Tom Hughes that I am here because it is very important,' I said. My father soon appeared and gave me a whole penny to give to the man in the shop. Every week we went to the shop and paid a halfpenny each, until the card was marked 'paid'.

All the preparations were done in the weeks leading up to Christmas, we hung holly, home-made garlands and handmade Christmas crackers. The chicken cooked with stuffing, and smelling to perfection, the yeast cake baked in the oven by the coal fire, the

Christmas pudding boiled in a basin with a white cloth tied on tight, inside an iron boiler on top of the coal fire. Home baked mince pies and jars of beetroot, pickled cabbage, home made onions and sweet pickle. Whinberry tart, apple tart and home made pop made from stinging nettles. The smells and sights of a by-gone age. For weeks before Christmas, the preparations and the smells coming from our kitchen were magical. A new nighty to wear to go to bed on Christmas eve and Daddy bringing up all the fresh vegetables from the allotment. 'Please God, it it's fine, let me have a doll and pram, if it rains, please let me have a new red mac and a red umbrella.'

Christmas morning came and my mother was laughing, smiling, and hugging me, saying that she thought she would have to wait years until she was rich enough for her pearls. I had a lovely wooden dresser with a tin tea set on it from Father Christmas, and a Christmas stocking, one of Mammy's lisle ones, that was full to the brim. We played ludo and draughts, I knew they would let me win.

After tea, I noticed Mammy's necklace. 'You have lost some pearls,' I said. She put her hands to her neck and to my dismay, those beautiful wax pearls had melted. I sat on her lap and she cuddled me tight. 'Don't worry,' she said, 'it was the best Christmas present I ever had'. So I put on my red mac, opened my red umbrella and sat outside on Mammy's white doorstep in the rain. It was a very happy Christmas day.

CHAPTER 3

UNCLES
AND LODGERS

UNCLES AND LODGERS

As noted in the introductory chapter, long term lodgers, many of them male relations, played a central part in the early family life of many women in the mining communities. Each of the three uncles portrayed in this chapter, Uncle Dick, John and Dat, illustrate the rôle of the lodger-uncle in supporting the miner's wife and family, both emotionally and in practical ways. All three regularly helped with household chores and child minding, (as did the father in the final extract). Their stories may lead us to reconsider the assumption that the miners, during this period, were not concerned with helping within the home (see Introduction).

In the first story the setting is the 'black kitchen', the hub of family life in a mining household. Family relationships and gender rôles are drawn out through the story of Uncle Dick. In the second extract we are introduced to the family of Maggie Pryce Jones, one of the three authors whose personal stories are followed throughout the book. John is a very special person in Maggie's life, and in her case, as in the case of Dat in the final extract by Mair Eluned McLellan, the rôle of the lodger illuminates the relationships and tensions within mining families.

Mair McLellan, the apple of her uncle's eye, suffered from asthma as a child and never went to school. Her contact with other children was limited, but she became an avid reader, resulting in her subsequent involvement in politics and her ambition to write.

The Back Kitchen

~

Barbara Walters

He stood all six foot of him in the back kitchen doorway, the peak of his Dai cap almost touching his left ear. That Dai cap and his eyes tell my mother and I that Dick has had more than his usual two pints.

With difficulty, he manoeuvres his long arms and stooped shoulders out of his heavy overcoat. Loosening his muffler, he announces ceremoniously, 'Well, I have reached my half-century!' Looking at me, he places his thumb and fore-finger together – flicks them, and says, 'Gone those years, like that!' And I, in my green years think – 'Duw Dick, there's old'. I was just fourteen.

He pegs his muffler, Dai cap and heavy overcoat on a hook on the back of the kitchen door.

My mother asks, 'Have you seen Evan?' The kitchen misses the sound of her knitting needles, as she prepares Dick's supper, a culf of cheese and bread and butter. Pouring the tea into a basin-sized cup, and receiving no immediate reply, she begins to talk her thoughts aloud.

'He really doesn't sleep enough hours in the day for his night shift.'

My mother's on pins – waiting for my father. Why is she so worried? I don't know – he's always last lap or cutting it fine, as my Uncle Dick would say.

My mother places the tea-pot to sit snuggly under the woollen cosy. There it will await the inevitable second cup.

My mother continues with her thoughts, 'I know he tells us about that swankey job he's had since his accident, but . . .' My mother nearly always leaves sentences unfinished.

A swankey job to my mother is when you can dress like the Co-op manager to go to work, when you can eat your food with clean hands, where there's a WC, and when it's not necessary to bath every time you come home from work.

'Press a button, I do Peg.' (That's my father's special name for my mother.) 'Tap a wire with my knocker and watch all the others do the donkey work.'

Now the pit has become more mechanised, he is minus two fingers and has a busted ankle. Now he hasn't got to strain every muscle in his body to put coal trams back on rails, he has promoted himself by calling his job a swankey one. What he won't admit to himself or anyone else, because he's still a young man, is that he's not able to do the donkey work any longer.

My mother is the cook, the dressmaker, the patcher of colliers' clothes and the one whose crochet needle would travel faster than the speed of light, looping one loop into another, creating patterns as intricate and as fine as any spider. Through the years I watched those weblike patterns grow, loving her selfishly, as children will.

Dick is intent on resuming the conversation he started on his entrance. He pauses while he takes a chair to the table. 'In all probability, I'll not see another half-century for sure.'

Fifty years is miles away from me. I couldn't understand what he was making all the fuss about. My only wish, at that time, was that grown-ups would say when their birthday is due. My mother must have had a similar thought.

'Bit late Dick, I know,' she said 'but a Happy Birthday, and may you have many more!'

'Me too Dick.' I chime in. My Uncle is my best pal. He used to take me everywhere, to cattle marts, fairs and once to a posh cinema where the shimmering silk of golden curtains was made splendid by theatrical lights, and I was convinced that in my whole lifetime I would never again see anything as glamorous as this.

He grins, my Uncle, as if reaching fifty has become a big joke!

'Have you seen Evan, Dick?' My mother is trying to curb her impatience. My Uncle calls my father Ianto – as most people do but my mother only ever calls him Evan.

'Ianto,' says Dick. 'O aye, I've seen him. He *is* cutting it fine. Him and Dai Quiet Wedding have a game of dominoes on. You'd swear they had a hundred quid on it, not a pint. They both have the whole bar wrapped around their every move.'

I smile to myself. I know my father. The excitement he could whip up around the back kitchen table when playing with friends of mine.

Over the shaking of a dice, before and after the dice revealed its number, we knew, my friends and I, he wasn't adverse to cheating, but a game of Snakes and Ladders or Ludo could become so boring without my father's involvement. So, it's Dai Quiet Wedding who's my father's opponent. I learned in the back kitchen that he was called that because he got married in daps.

'You know Maggie, I think Ianto has been studying some kind of time and motion the way he puts the working clothes on, only he would think of putting working boots on before trousers and get away with it.'

My mother has placed my father's working clothes around the hearth exactly the way he has taken them off.

His long pants have stockings dangling from the legs, his singlet, shirt, pullover are as one. He reckons it's like the North Pole where he works – him and his swankey job! His moleskin trousers are under the stool with the boots. The stool is only used when taking off working clothes and putting them on. His two waistcoats and jacket are also as one – the pocket watch in a brass case hangs on its chain from the mantlepiece, and a kerchief is knotted ready to slip over the head and around the neck. It was worth buying a ticket to watch my father dress for work.

'My Best Suit,' that's what he called his working clothes. He'd shoot out of his clean clothes and just as quickly don his working clothes. 'Not to lose any heat, see Peg.'

My father is what you'd call a born teaser. 'Best Suit,' he'd say and his eyes would look for me. He knows I hate those clothes dulling the hearth. He would pause, so that his words would take effect. 'Without these there wouldn't be any others.'

Then the front door bangs. He's made it! It's ten minutes to ten. At ten o'clock the colliery bus will beep its horn. He enters the back kitchen doorway. He's beaming, the buttons of his coat and waistcoat are already undone. My mother asks the question that is on Dick's and my lips:

'Well Evan, who won?'

'No-one Peg,' he says with a wink. 'You can't rush a game like that.'

He's rushing now though, arms and legs setting a pace in the changing of clothes.

He's timed everything to the last minute. The bus beeps its horn. My father grabs his jack of water that has been filled ready for him, shouting as he goes 'Goodnight, keep the bed warm Peg!'

My uncle fetches his working clothes from the *cwtch** under the stairs. His working belt makes them into a neat bundle. When he loosens the bundle, a black pat scurries away from the clothes to escape under the skirting board, back into the darkness from whence it came. 'Dash those things!' My mother never seems to miss the sight of an escaping cockroach! 'I'll put some Keatings powder down before I go to bed.'

Dick is engrossed in setting the alarm on his clock for four-thirty in the morning. He doesn't need to be on top of the pit before six o'clock. That's when the pit hooter will sound and the cage will start taking men underground. He won't let my mother get up to put his breakfast. 'I can manage Maggie. Have a lie in. I like walking to work from the village.'

By now the black leaded grate has accepted my Uncle's working clothes and takes second place once more to that sweet-sour smell.

'You know,' Dick carries on, 'Your father would tell that horse 'Monday', if it didn't behave he would *clec†* about him to other horses in the stable. And it would behave.' I thought, 'That's a tall one!', but I put my book down on the sofa, I'll not offend my Uncle. He's taking me to the Rhondda this Saturday to see his sister. My aunt owns a sweet shop and because I'm an only child and my cousins are all older boys, I'm spoiled rotten! Now he has my attention he starts again. 'Yes, a man's living as a haulier depends on how well him and his horse understand each other.' He reels off horses' names – Monarch, Rebel, King, Arab and Abel – as if their very names would give me an insight to their characters.

Dick was a popular man with my mother on weekends, he would beat hell out of her coconut mats. Getting up at the same time in the morning as if he was going to work, Dick would scrub the floor, black lead the grate and shine the brass, but he would leave the brass knocker and the front steps to me, not to show the outside world he was doing a woman's work.

---

* *Cwtch*: cupboard.
† *Clec about*: carry tales/'split on'.

Dick was always teaching himself something. Once he had a craze for mending watches and clocks. I can see him now, bent over the back-kitchen table, with his eye-glass and tweezers, his huge hands manipulating small springs and screws.

Years hence my Mother faithfully dusted those clocks, displaying them on mantleshelves and chests of drawers while their insides lay inside an old biscuit tin.

He was also our street barber. Men would wait to have their hair cut on a wooden chair just outside the kitchen door. Clippers, comb and scissors, cutting everyone's hair in the same style. Sometimes, he'd cut mine, when I'd let him. Why he wanted to cut mine, I don't know! I guess it was because I was a girl and it was a kind of challenge. My Uncle liked a challenge! After he'd cut it, he would give me sixpence and then I'd go into the house, burst into tears and turn all the mirrors to the wall. My Uncle professed to be a jack of all trades and master of none! After having a haircut I was inclined to believe him! He tried to teach me the mandolin, but was daunted when he found I was only using three fingers instead of four. 'Like making three men do the work of four,' he would say.

He was known to be a fair workman. I often heard this said of him by boys of my own age starting work at fourteen. 'Dick Evans always buys the chalk to mark the trams.' It meant a lot, buying that chalk when you're on small money. He always paid good trumps (tips) on good or bad weeks. I heard my Uncle explain this in the back kitchen. Talking to other men, he would say, 'When we work the hardest, we're often paid the least. But boys' trumps should stay the same.' Being a girl, thank goodness, I didn't have to go down the pit but I understood what he said. When coal was hardest to hew, less trams were filled therefore, less pay. So he accepted the loss himself and always paid his boys the full wage.

'Dick was the scholar,' I heard my father say in the back kitchen. 'And to prove it, the old woman bought him a bookcase and writing desk on the never-never.* She fitted it with encyclopaedias, Dickens and Shakespeare, but Dick collected all the books of the political Left he could find and put those red-covered books on a special shelf.'

When Dick's mother died, he came to live with us, bringing with him the desk and bookcase. Pointing to his shelf of red books he said

---

* *Never-never*: hire purchase.

to me, 'Read them and find out how all mankind can fulfil their dreams.' It was when his mother died that I overheard in the back kitchen that my grandmother had tied him to her apron strings and that was why he never married. At that time, I overheard too, that when Dick had been old enough and strong enough he had threatened his old man that if he ever again laid a finger on his mother he would throw him out of the house. Of course, I was shocked to hear this about my grandparents. My grandfather would always give me his seat on the sofa. Later in life, I was to learn how privileged I had been.

My petite grandmother always fussed over me, every time I walked through her front door showering me with fresh fruit, and pennies for every errand. What does stick out like a sore thumb in my childhood memories of my grandparents is that they rarely talked to one another, and when they did, they spat Welsh words at each other, words I did not understand. My grandmother and I used to go to the local cinema together. She always wore high-necked blouses and hats with colossal pins. Our favourite was a child star called Shirley Temple and there both of us would have a lovely cry. It was many years later that I learned that before my grandmother married she had been a cook for Jews in the city of London and that she had had fourteen children of whom only four survived.

Then I was in my teens learning the facts of life in hushed corners away from grown-up ears. When I heard the story of my Grand-mother's life, I thought to myself, 'one day I might go to the city of London and be a cook to Jews, but I'll never get married and have babies'.

My uncle never lived much longer than his half-century. On that next morning shift he was unlucky enough to be walking under-ground when a sheave left its shaft at great speed, hitting him on the head and exposing a part of the brain. My Uncle who had once tried with his huge hands to teach me how to tremolo the strings of a mandolin, died three long years later, a violent, crazed man, not even able to speak his own name.

In the back kitchen, the day of his funeral, the preacher came to sympathize with my father. I remember my father's grey face speaking. 'I'll not weep for the man you buried today, Mr Davies.

He was not my brother – my brother died three years ago in the pit.' And I, still in my green years, no longer able to contain my sorrow, found myself sobbing. *'Duw* Dick, A-men to that.'

Kingfisher of Hope

~

Maggie Pryce Jones

John had always been there. I cannot remember the house without him. As I grew older, we seemed to grow closer. He always had time for me. Even when he worked in the chaff house on top of the colliery, he was never too tired to listen. Mam was always busy with cooking and cleaning, Dad with his friends in 'the party' and his garden, but John always found time for me.

John had come from Mid Wales when the pit was sunk. Many families had come at the same time, my grandparents among them. When Mam and Dad married and moved into the little cottage in Trelewis, John was already installed as the lodger. Mam and he found a bond at once, being able to converse in their native tongue.

He was a strange man, the most methodical person I have ever met. His meals, which he cooked himself, were always on the table at the same hour each day. He was immaculate in his manners and dress.

John was of average height and his appearance seemed to me unchanging even though the years passed by. His balding head was surrounded by a neat edging of snowy white hair; his keen grey eyes looked the world straight in the face from beneath neatly trimmed bushy white brows.

He had no cause to flinch when he met people, for he never borrowed and never owed. I see him now, in his brown suit, a watch across the waistcoat, always a white shirt and brown tie. His black boots shine and reflect his face in their toe-caps; he polishes them every day. Most of all I remember his thick white moustache. I could always tell John's mood by his moustache: when he was angry, it would bristle; if he was pleased, he had a way of whistling through it or would puff it out to make us laugh.

John was devoted to my mother and her children, but he had no time for my father, a feeling which, I sensed at a very early age, was mutual. As I grew older I sympathized with my father. It must have been difficult for him to sit at the table listening to his wife and children conversing in Welsh with the lodger when he had no understanding of the language.

Sadly, his suspicious nature led to his banning the Welsh tongue in our house: he became convinced that we made fun of him, knowing that he would not understand.

I honestly do not think that John Jones had any vices. He kept to himself, never smoked, never drank alcohol. He read his Welsh Bible morning and evening, without fail. He was kind to everyone; he liked animals and children. We often accompanied him on his regular walks and he would tell us stories as we walked. He knew a great deal about the countryside and its animals. From him we learned about the trees, wild flowers and weeds.

The boys, however, soon grew too boisterous to be in John's care, for he expected us to listen to his every word, but I never tired of his company. There was always a minto or a pear-drop in his pocket if our feet faltered on a particularly long walk.

John was responsible for my first visit to our National Museum in Cardiff, one bank holiday. He took my brother and me for a tram-ride around the city, a great treat for us, who never went far from Trelewis. This was the first of many such outings. John was a learned man, a simple, great man who tried to instil in us his love of the simple pleasures of life.

Not long before he died, as if knowing his time was near, John placed a great bolt on the inside of my bedroom door. 'Marged,' he said, 'I hope you will never need to use it; I put it here for your protection, cariad.'

I little knew, then, of the silent prayers of thanks I would offer to my dear old friend in the near future, or of the gratitude I would feel for the strange prophetic powers he had been blessed with.

As far as I know, John had no close family or friends. He was a bachelor to the day he died. I greatly value the Welsh Bible he gave me; it was his most treasured possession. On the fly-leaf is written:

John Jones, Penyffridd, Pontrobbart, Dec. 18th 1877, and inside I found his bookmark, a lovely card written in a girlish hand. I thought of trying to trace his roots, but I decided not to delve into his secret past. I do not think he would have liked me to.

Shadows on the Wall

~

Mair E. McLellan

The street I grew up in was long and narrow. Our side of the street had kitchens which doubled as living rooms and faced into the street, with a parlour behind, and then a small scullery, called by us 'the back kitchen'. The back kitchen opened up onto a longish garden and an outside lavatory. The houses on the opposite side of the street had front parlours. But this was the only difference.

Upstairs there were three bedrooms. The largest faced east, and overlooked our garden. In one of the smaller front bedrooms slept my Uncle Ivor. He had been in my life from before I could remember. He was unmarried, tall, dark and goodlooking, with large, gentle brown eyes. In one eye danced a golden mote. I knew this because I asked him, although it was many years before I found out what a mote was. All I knew was that I loved him dearly.

I did not call my uncle by name. For some reason that went back to when I was first learning to talk, I called him 'Dat' and the name stuck. Obviously, I could not get my tongue around the word uncle, and since my father was Daddy, 'Dat' was a word that made him a bit nearer than 'Uncle'.

That winter, the oil lamp and the flickering fire made shadows on the wall. These frightened me at first, until Dat called me over, and stood me near the wall. My shadow, he told me, was called Daisy. Daisy and I could dance together if we tried. I tried, and to my delight, she did. This removed my fear of the shadows, and my uncle somehow, at sometime, transferred the name to me.

I saw much more of my uncle than I did of my father. My father worked much harder than anyone I ever knew. When he came home from work in the afternoon, he would simply wash his face and hands, cleaning out his eyes with great care, then eat his dinner kept warm for him in the oven, with the day's newspaper propped in front of him so that he could read while he ate. Afterwards, there would be coal to cut, wood to chop up and to be brought in to the back kitchen in readiness for the morning.

Once my father had washed up the dinner things, his own and Dat's, plus our tea things, he would be off. Either to his allotment or up to the club, and he would not be back until about ten o'clock. Anyone seeing us would have thought that it was my mother and her brother who formed the family couple, as they talked together easily and freely. My mother loved to talk and loved company. She described my father as 'unsociable', a description she was later to apply to me.

The illness that had brought me asthma did not go away completely. Sometimes I could run as fast as ever, and there would be no problems. At other times, I would be forced to retreat indoors gasping. Once the 'bout', as my mother called it, was over, she and Dat would urge me to go out and run again. 'You beat it kid,' Dat would say, and off I would go again, running around the block. Usually I escaped a second bout, but the asthma attack plus the second run would leave me very tired. I would be glad to sit down opposite Dat and pick up one of the many books my father brought from the library. He too had joined the library, and how he found time to read the many books be brought in and do all the work he had to do, amazes me now. He must have been blessed with tremendous energy.

This was the era of the Hunger Marches, and although I was too young to understand, it was my uncle – not my father (who was far more politically aware) – who took me to the square behind Pleasant Street, not far from the foundry where he still worked, to see some of the men practising their bazookas.

Dat was a very heavy smoker and he had developed a smoker's cough. My father never smoked and was disapproving, I think, of Dat's weakness. Every now and again, Dat would swear that he was going to give it up, and he would for a few days. Then, instead of sitting by the fireside as usual, he would say that he was going to pop over to the Bridgeman's. After an hour or two, my mother would send me over for him, to tell him that supper was ready. But as Dat never ate supper, this was simply to find out if he was smoking at the Bridgeman's. Inevitably, he was, and the attempt at giving up would be over once again. At least, for a while.

I have often wondered how my parents managed. In comparison with the children around me I fared very well indeed. Partly of course, it had to be my uncle who helped out.

It was Dat who bought me all my clothes. My mother told me this with a certain emphasis, making sure that I was properly grateful. I don't know if I was or not. I loved Dat, and could not have possibly loved him less if he had never bought a stitch of clothing for me. I loved him for his gaiety and charm. The way he had, when fixing his tie on a Saturday night before going to the Dragon's Club, of getting me to stand on a chair and make sure that his tie was straight.

More than once, I asked my mother why he hadn't married, as he was so clearly attractive to the opposite sex, and they to him. He had once been in love with a girl who had worked in the Penny Bazaar, my mother explained, but she had died of TB and he had 'never looked at a woman since'.

It seems to me now that he had sacrificed marriage, first of all for his mother who had been a widow for so long, and then for his much-loved younger sister and her family, me. Perhaps indeed, he was satisfied with his lot. I never saw him as anything other than cheerful.

CHAPTER 4

TREATS

TREATS

High days and holidays. Those special times, bringing respite from everyday routine are always at the forefront of childhood memories precisely because of their out-of the-ordinary nature. The excitement which accompanies such outings and treats remains even after they have long passed, making them particularly memorable.

Distant travel or long holidays were extremely rare for the working classes in the 1920s and 1930s, and unless the families of the valleys were fortunate enough to have relatives in a nearby town, or in West Wales or the west of England (as many did), their experience of holidays was limited to day trips to nearby countryside or coast.

Gabrielle Capus, whose grandmother lived in Swansea, describes (as an observer) the miners and their families on their annual outing to the seaside. Her work also illustrates the contrast between town life and the valley communities.

Many such trips were organised by the chapels, as was Iris Roderick Thomas' Sunday School trip from Merthyr Tydfil to nearby Pontsarn, an outing which typifies the hilarity of many similar valleys' trips.

A cheaper alternative was to take a picnic to the mountainsides above the coal mining towns and villages, so accessible, and so much a part of life for valleys' people, particularly during childhood and adolescence. Maggie Jones' description of the family outing shows how much work was involved for busy mothers of (invariably) excited children and (sometimes) reluctant husbands. Her contribution also emphasises the gendered nature of the outing which becomes an opportunity for women to engage in women's talk away from confined neighbourhoods.

The carnival, as in Menna Gallie's colourful and evocative description, was another opportunity of release from everyday worries, although, as in this case, its underlying purpose was often to raise funds for the working class cause and to provide miners' children with basic necessities. This extract, again from her novel *Strike for a Kingdom*, is set during the 1926 Lock Out. The carnival, organised by the local Strike Committee, shows the community using time creatively to boost morale. The quality of the 'turn-out' was largely dependent upon the women who stitched and sewed to create fabulous costumes using very limited raw materials, as they would for the dramas and operettas mentioned by Heulwen Williams in Chapter 9 which were also highlights of the children's year.

Early Years in the Thirties

~

Gabrielle Capus

Travelling to Swansea by train was exciting, the acrid smell from the smelting works indicating we would soon be there. It was far worse than the train smoke. Pulling up the leather strap on the door window tight shut, we pinched our noses until we had passed. We gazed at the moonscape that purported to be Llandarcy, and when the train drew in at High Street station, it was the end of the line . . .

Few people went away for holidays then and to have a Gran near the sea was a bonus. The Slip was the part of Swansea Bay in the vicinity of the Brangwyn Hall and the Floral Clock. A foot-bridge spanned the Mumbles Road and from it you could see crowds of people clustered along the wall dividing the railway lines from the sands. We always referred to this beach as the Slip and the Gower beaches as The Bays.

On August Bank Holiday, it would be black with trippers. They tumbled from bus and train and packed themselves neck and neck and cheek by jowl into deck-chairs, devouring sticks of rock, ice-cream cornets and trays of tea for the grown-ups. Swing-boats, Punch and Judy and chair-o-planes provided entertainment for the children. Solo acts – breaking free from ropes, sacks and chains, similar to Houdini, for the adults. The Church Army would gather crowds of promenaders to sing and praise the Lord on a Sunday evening.

It was different at The Bays, more space to spread around the rocks. In big family groups from the valley towns they came, with assorted children, prams and dogs, dragging their chairs in Indian file, tramping over the pebbles and sand looking for that quiet place to settle down. Forming large semi-circles, they deposited themselves at different levels, some high, some low, and the men, unwrapped from cap and jacket and white knitted silk scarves, displayed their belts and braces to the wind. They covered their heads with the valley man's sunhat, a pocket handkerchief tied with knotted corners, partially keeping the seaside sun from their pale white faces, but exposing their milk white legs to the air. Sporting umbrellas and parasols, the ladies shaded their faces from the burning sun. The children dug holes and sculptured sand-castles until they were tired and shouted 'Dad, come and bury me,' which he did, turning the shapes into motor boats and racing cars. Their turn then to bury Dad. But now it was time for tea. With hands brushed clean on bathing suits, they would consume what sand-wiches hadn't fallen in the sand and wash it all down with gallons of lemonade made from lemon crystals.

When it was finished, into the sea they rushed, in Peacocks cotton costumes clinging like a second skin to sag and bag as they danced in the waves. The dogs sat in the cast shade of their owners' deck-chairs, with tongues hanging out and panting until urged to chase along the beach, splashing in and out of the water and up and around the paddlers, the ladies with dresses tucked in knickers and the men with trousers turned up to the knees. Rarely did they go in 'all over' as we did.

I remember spending time at Swansea Market where my uncles had a stall. It was a wonderland for me, weaving my way through the Gower ladies sitting with their cockle baskets and laver bread ...

Sometimes, when no one was available to take me to the sands, I would go down to the cellar in my gran's house, where the packing was done. My favourite job was sticking the labels on the tea packets. A large slate was covered with glue, the labels dragged across and placed on the folded end of the packet, before being turned upside down to stick.

Another treat was watching sausages being made. The machine mixed the saltpetre and spices with the sausage meat and pushed it into the thin skins, which were twisted by hand and packed up for market.

The girls in the packing department also worked at the market stalls. There were two stalls, a tea stall where my labelled packets were sold and the mixed goods and bacon stall. Girls left school at fourteen in those days. They were like big sisters and would take me to spend my holiday shilling in Marks & Spencer, where such a fortune might purchase some presents to take home. But Peacocks in the Market provided more for my money, and Woolworths too had a multitude of exciting items. It was also where the boys would gather and my companions seemed to know plenty . . .

Little did I think then that Hitler's bombers would completely wipe out, in a single night, the area of my holiday paradise.

Thanks for the Memories
(Sunday School Trip)

~

Iris Roderick Thomas

The trip to Pontsarn was no further than six miles at the most, but even on so short a journey three-quarters of the children felt sick. Even the toughies didn't look too healthy. The old time buses bore no resemblance in any way to the comfortable, air conditioned luxury coaches of today, and so, learning from past experience, the best way to overcome this swaying and shaking was to create as much noise as possible, hoping that this diversion would prevent the feeling of nausea from raising its ugly head. Although we did not start the journey until eleven or more likely eleven-thirty, we'd all be awake at the crack of dawn and waiting in front of Adulum Chapel by ten o'clock prompt, a whole hour and a half before Sharky Davies's driver arrived – late as usual. This did nothing to dampen our ardour, however, as we joined the stampede for the back row, away from the prying eyes of the Sunday School teachers who were there to supervise.

You'd swear by the excitement and jubilation that we were going to America for a month or more, and it was an education in itself to hear the rendering of 'Ten Green Bottles' and 'The Farmer Wants A Wife'. More hysterical still was to witness the teachers standing up in the front seat in turn, trying to issue last-minute instructions, warnings and open threats to well known renegades. It was an utter waste of time and energy as not one of us could hear a word, the din being so intense. Nevertheless, to demonstrate the Christian love they taught us and to show that there was no hard feeling, we gave each one a separate and hearty cheer for wasting their time and energy, as they sank exhausted and completely deflated into their reserved seats.

Very soon Merthyr, Cefn and Trefechan were left behind and the bridge leading to Pontsarn loomed up directly in front of us. This was a cue to lean out of the bus as far as the open window would allow and shout our names at the top of our voices, a procedure observed every year in order to hear the echoes boomeranging back. Another three hearty cheers for the echo, and the Aberglais could clearly be seen as the driver swung round the sharp bend, throwing the teachers into the aisle among the renegades, who were still fighting it out to be the first boy off the bus.

By now all caution had been thrown to the winds with the result that when the bus stopped in front of the Pontsarn Pavilion, we were like a lot of lunatics. This condition came to an abrupt halt when the first boy off the bus felt a stinging sensation that warmed his face and was followed by the sound of the sea in his earhole. Order was quickly restored, so after lining up to be counted we marched in twos, seating ourselves at the set tables inside the pavilion, opposite a knife, fork and spoon. There we sat with eyes glued on the bevy of twittering waitresses as they waited for the sign to serve ham salad with beetroot and a slice of bread. The command to stand was given and we each studied the wooden floor while Evan Arthur said grace. The salad was attacked with such ferocity that any observer would come to the conclusion that this was the first meal we'd ever eaten and, if staying to see how the swiss roll in Ideal Milk was devoured, would be compelled to admit that never had so much been consumed by so many, in so short a time.

Having swilled the lot down with warm lemonade, it was time to relax on the grassy field until Mr William Morgan was ready and able to organise the games and competitions. Everyone enjoyed the next hour or two and it's fair to say that the teachers let down their hair, entering into the spirit of the thing, while Miss Milward, becoming almost human, entered the sack race. I think she was later reprimanded by the minister for losing her decorum, anyway she disappeared after that and no one saw her until she boarded the bus on the way home.

After the various races like the sack race, wheelbarrow, three-legged, egg and spoon and obstacle races had been challenged and won, the winners lined up in the middle of the field so that all could envy these victorious champions their rosettes and their bags of mixed sweets, kindly donated by Mal the sweetshop. The last game was rounders, at the end of which we were all winners, and given an orange, an apple and a banana. This contribution was from Mr Morgan, the head deacon who sold fruit and vegetables round the streets on his lovely painted cart, drawn by the most docile of horses.

After counting us all again, we marched two by two down to the river, there to eat the fruit as the pangs of hunger started to be felt. Some had brought their swimming suits along but those who had forgotten tucked their clothes into their knickers and paddled in the shallower pools. As usual, someone fell into the river and had to be rushed into the Aberglais for hot drinks and a blanket, but this only helped to make the already enjoyable day even more memorable.

Although the evening was still warm, the sun was beginning to set and the effects of a strenuous day started to catch up with the younger children. Still, no annual trip would be complete without the last half hour being spent on the yearly pilgrimage to the famous Blue Pool, the DIY for those wishing to end it all, and believe me, the popularity of this notorious death trap became manifest, time after time, in the ghastly reports printed in the *Merthyr Express* at regular periods. I confess that this was the only activity I hated on such an enjoyable day, but I hated even more the thought of being called a sissy, so along I went with the others, taking my turn on the narrow stone bridge to view the evil-looking water far below. I shuddered as my eyes took in the high jagged rocks flanking the long drop down to the murky depths beneath, confirming for a certainty that even if the plunge to the pool was miscalculated, the rocks promised sure success.

As the last spectator moved away from the bridge, Miss Rhys blew the whistle to warn that the bus was waiting to take us home and the time had come once more to be counted before boarding the vehicle. All present and accounted for, the signal was given to the driver to start the engine and we were on our way, tired to the point of blissful silence until the bus pulled up outside Adulum Chapel once more. There, our parents were waiting to hear how the day had turned out and conduct us safely home. A final three cheers for the organisers and a feeble 'He's A Jolly Good Fellow' for the driver, rendered by the valiant few still awake, and another Sunday School outing was over until the following June.

Kingfisher of Hope

~

Maggie Pryce Jones

The summers seemed to be always long and always hot when we were children. We lived out of doors. The only time spent indoors, which was not given grudgingly, was when we ate. We picnicked whenever we could. Whole families would pack a simple meal: meat – or fish – paste sandwiches, a few welshcakes and bottles of pop made by shaking sherbet into cold water. Mams, Dads and grandparents who were fit enough, all would come on these spontaneous outings. The great delight to the children was having their fathers to themselves for hours on end and playing all the games we wanted, each of us choosing in turn, until the womenfolk would call us to eat.

Mam always brought an old white sheet for a table-cloth, the food was placed out and we ate a communal meal. There were no quarrels about who got what, for our Dads were there and we were too afraid to fight in their presence, knowing that, if we did, retribution was quick to follow: a clip on the ear or a strict order to go straight home and stay indoors. The former punishment was preferred to the latter.

If the juicy whinberries were ripe, we would fill our empty containers before leaving the mountain, in readiness for the tarts and pies which would be cooked during the next few days.

The younger children would be carried home on their fathers' shoulders. Much to the envy of the older ones, we would be running ahead of the cavalcade, gathering nuts or blackberries from the hedgerows.

Sudden summer storms were a hazard, but even they could not spoil our enjoyment. The rain was warm on our bodies and the sun would soon be back.

The women would be walking far behind, enjoying their hours of freedom, and we children were not allowed to walk with them in case we overheard their gossip. Someone would always call,

'Little pitchers', whenever we drew near and the talking would change to comments on the weather . . .

During the summer, we were assured of at least two outings, one with the Church, and the other with the British Legion. We saved our pennies all the year round for these trips.

The long excursion train filled us with excitement as we rushed to find seats by the windows. Dad shared these outings with great reluctance. The night before the big day, when Mam was busy bathing us all in front of the fire, lifting the heavy kettles of hot water from the hob and pouring them into the zinc bath, he was heard repeatedly complaining, 'Why should I come, Jane? You'll be all right with the other women. Dai next door isn't going, nor Stan Top House; we thought we'd spend the day in the allotments.' Mam remained silent. She knew that the only gardening done while she was away would be talk in the Bont pub, so she carried on with her work, banishing the boys to the parlour while I bathed first. Dad had to follow the boys, knowing that his protest had fallen on deaf ears.

Once at the seaside, the women would place their chairs and bags in a circle near the rocks and the younger children would play safely at their feet. On our way back from the water, our circle was always easy to spy, so we rarely got lost.

The tide usually came in late in the afternoon, so then came our annual shopping spree in the Barry Dock Woolworths. Baskets of rock fruit and purses with 'From Barry Island' stamped on them were bought: a purse for Mam, a packet of cigarettes for Dad and, of course, sweets for John, who would be meeting us at the station on our return.

The rock fruits were our presents to ourselves and it was always several weeks before we could bring ourselves to break the shiny package and eat the sweets.

On our return, Dad would be off to the Bontnewydd pub for the drink he considered he had earned. Mam was left, with our lodger John's help, to wash and change us all for bed, then prepare supper before emptying the bags we had filled with our wet bathing clothes and towels.

Fortunately, John would have tended the fire and there was always a bright fire with the kettles singing on the hob to welcome us home.

I was happy that I would not be having my hair tortured into false ringlets tonight. My hair was straight, but on special occasions Mam would insist on twisting it up with strips of rags or Hannah from next door would crimp it up with her crimping iron, so that I would have ringlets in the morning.

I hated having my hair scorched by the hot iron, even though Mam was always proud of the result. 'You look like a little lady,' she would say as she helped me into my cotton dress. I never felt like a little lady. I was used to playing with the boys and I would have preferred to wear pleated shorts, like Liza and Megan, but Mam could not afford them. I never told Mam; I knew she would have been so disappointed.

I tried to ignore the sly whispers of 'golliwog' from my brothers. My heavily starched dress worried me far more than my bushy hairdo; the petticoat beneath the dress was uncomfortable and hot. I was always the first into the sea, and the last out of it. Mam was happy and that was of first importance to me.

No nights out in the Bont or the Ffaldcaiach for Mam; only the men went there. As Dad said, 'We men work hard, and anyway pubs are not fit places for women!'

Strike for a Kingdom

~

Menna Gallie

When D.J. Williams left his home he stepped into the chaos of dress rehearsal; clowns and gypsies, fairies and beggars, crinoline ladies, ministers, wedding parties, negro minstrels, Red Indians, all wearing Cilhendre faces, looking foolish and feeling ridiculous, the courage of their homes melting like the blacking on their faces and running down in sweat between their legs.

They went down to the field in shy little clusters, trying to hide, waiting for the procession and the crowd to bind them, to dissolve them and submerge their identities. They straggled into the field and formed an untidy queue near the judges' table which had stood small and lonely in the middle of the big field. Confidence began to seep back as they saw their neighbours looking even more foolish than they felt themselves, and, suddenly, the Carnival was on. It was officially opened with a speech given by the oldest member of the Strike Committee. He was sixty-nine and still a collier, his face and hands very scarred and one eye was pulled badly out of shape. Old Eye was no Lloyd George, no orator, but miners have a touching faith in the Seniority Rule.

'Comrades,' he began, 'Comrades bach, we have gathered here today to have a carnival. It is a good idea to have a bit of a spree, like, to cheer us up in these unhappy times. But, comrades, they are good times too because they are showing that we *are comrades*, that we are one behind the other against those up by there who have brought us to this pass. All my life I have been a Trade Union and a Co-op and I am proud to say it. We will have wonderful today again and now if you please we will sing all together 'Are we downhearted? No, Comrade, no!'

There was a cheer for Eye and then, with voices that moved your bowels and made the goose-flesh creep up your arms, the crowd sang the song of the defeated, 'Are we downhearted? Oh, no, no.' Then, intoxicated with their own splendid sounds and led by a tenor who 'has long since drunk himself to death,' they sang softly a local parody of 'When it's Springtime in the Rockies' – 'When it's Springtime in the Rhondda and the men are on the dole.' They followed this, because it was a day for the children too, with

> 'Rock-a-bye baby on the tree top,
> When you grow up you'll work in a shop,
> When you get married your wife will work too,
> Just for the rich to have nothing to do.'

Not bitterly, just singing, because they were in a crowd, holiday colliers.

In a wave of catcalls and comments, the Strike Committee men tried to form the procession up in twos: tutting and fussing and shouting orders to which nobody listened. At last they managed to get the smallest ones, two fairies in white and tinsel, to the front and the rowdy Red Indian jazz band at the back. The smallest fairy was already tired and sticky and trailed her curtain-rod wand in the dust. The mothers of the fairies hurried up to take their hands and give them courage. Next to the fairies were Joe Everynight's twelve children, all dressed in flour sacks, Spiller's Fine Ground. The smallest child's sack trailed to the ground and the sack of the eldest one scarcely covered her bottom. This one wore a card on her back 'The Bread Line'. Their mother twitched them tidy.

Jack Look-Out was a great success at the Carnival. He had thrown off his earlier depression and was a little drunk. He had dressed in a borrowed tweed suit and had pushed the trouser legs into his socks to make thin plus-fours. He carried a cane and wore a tweed cap, snappy, at an angle. Arm in arm with him walked one of his drinking cronies, a bookie's runner, in a makeshift policeman's uniform. The runner's face was painted bright red with post office ink and he wore a white cotton-wool moustache. He did look something like the Police Inspector, the Manager's friend. On their backs their cards read 'Birds of a Feather'.

The fattest man in Cilhendre, Moc Cow-and-Gate, the Royal Baby, was undressed in a small raffia skirt which hung just below his deep, dimpling navel. Under this he paraded a large pair of knickers, directoire style. The rest of him was covered with Zebo, and he glistened in the sun like Sunday shoes. He wore a necklace of four large bones, stolen from some unfortunate dog. He carried a wooden spear with which he made terrifying darts at the other characters. That finished the second fairy, Blodwen, who promptly wet her knickers and had to go home to have them changed.

There were two football teams dressed like young ladies in feather boas and hats and skirts and stockings that always needed hoisting up so that suspenders and underwear could be revealed. The Impossibles and The Improbables. They upset the procession by kicking balls about, trying to undress each other and clanging the saucepans that they carried.

In the end the Committee men gave up trying to tidy them and retired, hurt, to their table. The Red Indians started playing Sospan Fach on their horrible whistles called gazooks. This set feet on edge and off they went . . .

As they passed through the gates of the Welfare Field, Jim Jesus was standing on a kitchen chair, preaching. He preached against carnivals, against football, against the pictures, against being happy and laughing and smoking cigarettes. He kept making gestures with his arms as though he were throwing something far out. He was 'throwing out the life-line, someone is drifting away'. Nobody felt inclined to catch it that afternoon and the procession went on, singing now, as a tribute to Jim, 'Jesus knows all about my troubles'.

Somewhere in the rout dragged a little daunted girl whose faith had been destroyed for ever and ever. Nan had been found in her hiding place under the parlour table, in spite of the plush table-cloth that nearly reached the floor. She had stormed and kicked and shouted and finally had hopefully compromised by announcing that she would only go as a queen. This, she imagined, would be quite beyond her mother's contriving, but her mother was a woman of spirit who felt a moral obligation to the organisers to send her children to the carnival. She snapped 'Right' at Nan. 'You shall go as the Queen of the Flowers. I'll make a pink paper dress and sew it on your best petticoat. You shall have a crown of paper roses and a basket of flowers like a bridesmaid. Lovely it'll be. You wait. Mammy'll make it real pretty.' Nan went away to kick the front door, and heard her big brother say, 'But w'at will you do for a mask?'

CHAPTER 5

SCHOOL

SCHOOL

'The people of the valleys have a high regard for education,' says Maggie Pryce Jones as she describes her memories of the 'scholarship' in this chapter. Certainly the drive for education was strong in the culture of the valleys in the inter-war years, and, as her autobiography shows, mothers invariably made personal sacrifices to secure a better education for their children than they had received themselves. Yet, girls remained disadvantaged in the struggle for education, as subsequent extracts from Maggie Pryce Jones' autobiography and her short story, 'Chrysanthemum is Hard to Spell' illustrates.

From 1918, schooling was compulsory up to the age of fourteen, but thereafter working class children did not generally continue their studies unless they had passed the scholarship and could secure a free place in the local County or Grammar School. Yet even if a free place was won, it was often not taken up because of the considerable incidental costs (clothes, books, travel) involved. Although the opportunity to obtain free places increased during the inter-war years, by 1935 only 223 children per thousand passed into Secondary education in Wales as a whole, and despite a considerable increase in the number of girls, there were many more boys. When there were boys in the family, they would, more often than not, take precedence over their sisters as Maggie Pryce Jones' own case illustrates. Many parents believed that the expense was not justified in the case of girls since they would not need or make use of knowledge gained in their future rôles as wives and mothers. It was thought that a period doing shopwork, sewing or domestic service would provide them with a better, more relevant preparation for life. Lucy Arundell's grandmother's attitude (Chapter 8) was typical of many. These attitudes remained strong despite the fact that an increasing number of girls from working class families were entering higher education, particularly Teacher Training colleges during this period. School organisation and curriculum content continued to reflect the gender division, particularly at elementary level.

School memories of this period often portray stark surroundings, harsh teachers and strict discipline. The reminiscences of Nessie Williams, who went to school in eastern Monmouthshire (second extract), fit into this category, while Heulwen Williams' memories of Lower Rhymney Infants and Junior Schools (also in Monmouthshire at that time) are of a less oppressive atmosphere and regime, albeit a strict one, where it was possible to have fun, and of which happy memories remain. Her experience as a Welsh speaking child entering an (almost) all-English institution (despite the fact that several of the teachers were able to speak Welsh) was something of a culture shock and illustrates the anglicising influence of the education system. Her contribution also raises the point that, for children of chapel-going parents, the Sunday School still had a rôle to play in education, particularly for Welsh speaking children in encouraging the reading of Welsh. The image of the unmarried female teacher is also touched upon here, and is discussed further in Chapter 10. Katie Pritchard's memories of school in Gilfach Goch show how school did not command a central place in the lives of many working class children, but had to be fitted in around the various chores and jobs which they were expected to do, this being a major cause of the common problem of truancy.

We return to the story of Maggie Pryce Jones in the final extract. The strain placed upon children by the expectations of their parents and community, given the pride involved in passing the local grammar school's entrance scholarship and the public nature of the announcement of the results, is clearly illustrated by Maggie's experience.

Memories of Lower Rhymney Infants and Junior Schools

~

Heulwen Williams

I can't remember actually starting school, but as it was right up against our back door in Hill Street, I started very young. Mam says I was three. Miss Howells was my teacher, she lived in 'Cartrefle' in Moriah Street. She came to school past our back door and we children used to run and meet her and push each other to catch her hands and arms.

There was a big rocking horse in the classroom and after we had ridden him we had to pat him and say, 'Thank you, Jack'. Miss Howells had some small dolls and a doll's bed and bedclothes. She used to hold them up and show them to us, but we shouldn't touch them. We were given flat boxes with a little sand in them, and we could draw pictures in the sand with a finger. I loved Miss Howells. She had a very quiet soft voice, a lovely face and a watch pinned to her chest. It was only later I knew she was deaf.

In Miss Morgan's class we sat in long rows on galleries and had boards and chalk. I was very upset one day. After walking out to tell the teacher something, I was hit on the back all the way to my seat. There was a girl called Joyce Andrewatha in the class, we all had to say good-bye to her as she was going to Australia to live. In Miss Williams' class we used to sing 'Gentle Jesus meek and mild, Look upon a little child', and we sang 'Pity *mice* implicitly, Suffer me to come to Thee'. We also said 'Our Father . . . Harold is Thy Name'. I was a Welsh-speaking child at home and had only heard *Ein Tad* in chapel and Sunday School.

Our governess was Miss Polly Jones, and she was very nice and had twinkly eyes. She showed us how to peel an apple with a knife and asked us to spell words. She asked me to spell 'could' which I *could*.

At seven, I went down to the Wellington School where there was a huge corridor (so I thought). The school bell was rung for morning and afternoon, if you were after the bell you had a cane. Mr Mathews was the headmaster, he was big and had a gruff voice. I was very much in awe of him. Miss Evans was our teacher in Standard I. She was from Forge Street and went to our chapel, Moreia. She had to have a stick to walk as she was lame. She had favourites, and the one in favour had to go up to her house at dinner time to fetch her lunch. She used the crook of her stick to pull naughty boys out the front. A young teacher called Miss Davies from Llanofer came to do teaching practice, she was lovely and pretty. We thought we were lucky.

Six months later, I was put up to Standard II to Miss Richards who was very nice, but whom I offended by telling a girl that her voice (Miss Richards') was very crackly. She told teacher and I had a cane. I was having trouble doing my £.s.d., halfpennies and farthings and lost my way somewhat, I'm afraid. In Standard III our teacher was Miss Jones who later married our headmaster. I was still in trouble with sums about trains going so many m.p.h. and water running in and out of bath tubs. In Standard IV I had my curls cut off (shingled) by Uncle William. I took one look at myself in the glass and howled. I thought that the teachers were making fun of me, especially Miss Woods. We learnt area, perimeter and so on, but I was still at sea in *sums*!

Standard VI was Miss Lilian Ethel Jones' class and here I met my Waterloo. She was a member of Moreia and her sisters and brothers were much respected by my father who was a deacon there. She gave us piles of homework, which I insisted on doing by myself, unaided. She said I would never pass the scholarship as I was too untidy. She caned me for doing my Fundamental English in my Common Sense English Book and vice versa.

There was a fight after school up the quarry not far from Garden City where Miss Lilian Ethel lived. Her boyfriend, Morgan, who was taking her dog for a walk, happened to see the children. Next day, all the culprits were caned in front of the class. She used to call Alice Kendrick 'the cabbage carrier' as she *carried out* for her sister who kept a shop, and often missed school. She called Gwladys Roberts '*Lady* Gwladys' as she was 'just so'. Olga Salmon she called by her surname. She was a very large, well built, red faced girl who dared to answer back. One day, Olga opened her desk, which we weren't allowed to do unless told. Teacher shouted, 'Salmon, what are you fishing for?' The answer came like a shot – 'Trout!'.

She screamed at us and caned us willy nilly, but I actually got my sums sorted out. We learnt Sol-ffa with the notes chalked on a piece of black leathery material. We had to learn a poem a week and we learnt many, many Welsh folk songs out of the little Urdd songbook with Ifan ab Owen Edwards on the front. When we learned we had passed the scholarship, we had to help girls who had trouble reading and writing.

I had been caned, as I said, for using the wrong books and protested to Mam during the dinner hour. This upset Mam greatly as I had insisted on going to school with two very inflamed boils in a very tender place where I sat down. Mam decided to write a note to protest at this treatment. I was crying because I didn't want to give the note and Mam had trouble in spelling 'necessary'. 'Is it necessary to cane Heulwen etc.' Well, I had to take the note. Miss Lilian Ethel called me after school and promptly told me I was a 'sugar-baby' – one of her favourite terms! She eventually married Morgan and moved to the country and, I believe, mellowed no end as she got older.

My Childhood in the Valleys

~

Nessie Williams

My first school was old with a hard unyielding playground, and in the winter, when the frost was keen, we made long glassy slides and our bodies were seldom free from bruises, for we fell so often. We chanted multiplication tables and spelt out words until we were dizzy with the sound of them. I can hear now the squeak of the chalk on the blackboard and the dry sound when the check duster rubbed off a cloud of smoke, which tickled the throat of the teacher and made her cough. The mouths of the old black stoves were always open waiting for more coal and when the wind was high they belched their smoke into the classrooms.

A cane hung on the wall like the sword of Damocles. It was often used. It was said that a horse's hair placed on the palm of the hand would tear the cane in two and I longed to prove it, but my courage failed me. Discipline was strict and when we went home, we were made to bow to the headmistress as we walked past her desk, a final act of submission.

There were terracotta-coloured wash-basins, and there was terracotta-coloured soap reeking of carbolic, and roller towels stiff as a starched collar.

The teachers often enforced silence by clicking a small wooden object, which was rather like a skipping rope handle, yellow and shiny. At other times a pin was dropped and we were supposed to hear it.

There were maps on the walls and long map poles and inkwells in the desk which were always dry and a long-spouted inkcan was brought around by the monitor, who poured in the ink.

Overflow classes were held in the chapel vestry. Here wet clothes steamed on the benches, and on the wall in bright colours, Ruth promised life allegiance to Naomi and the father greeted his prodigal son, and Sunday's hymns loitered on the blackboard. There was a mongrel atmosphere in the vestry. There was less discipline, for Sunday school mingled with day school and there was no headmistress.

After having received the prime coating of education, I was sent to another school. Here black-begowned teachers, heavy with learning, strode the corridors like penguins, and another coating was applied, some of it without success. But whereas, hitherto, I had chanted out the spelling of words, I now thrilled to the sound of them. I remember one of the penguins reading Keats:

> Perhaps the self-same song that found a path
> Through the sad heart of Ruth, when sick for home
> She stood in tears amid the alien corn
> The same that oft-times hath
> Charmed magic casements opening on the foam
> Of perilous seas in fairy lands forlorn.

I have heard this read many times since but I have never quite recaptured the mesmerism of that first reading.

The Story of Gilfach

~

Katie Pritchard

Life for schoolchildren was hard in those early years. Advantages in the educational fields were few. Strikes, disasters and low wages deprived them of their leisure hours. Most children worked in the evenings and weekends, delivering groceries, papers and searching for coal on the coal tips. The girls were employed to work at home and at weekends many helped to scrub classrooms and chapels. They were paid two shillings (10p) for a weekend of scrubbing and cleaning. Hardships did not stifle or cloud their sense of humour and originality. Truancy continued, but in Abercerdin, Jack the Road had a certain cure for would-be truants. If he encountered a child playing truant he threatened to lift one of the large gratings on the side of the road and put him down the drain. No truant dared to cross Jack the Road's path.

It was customary in most schools to employ the older boys to perform menial tasks such as chopping firewood, filling and carrying large buckets of coal for the stoves and fires, and running and walking long distances on messages. These laborious duties were never rewarded. The boys decided it was time they were acknowledged for their services. The Headmaster was approached and a request made for the payment of one penny each per week. The appeal was flatly refused. The boys with great spirit decided to *strike* and spent the following day in the lanes and by-ways. It was a refreshing change from chopping wood and filling coal. The experience was exhilarating, and never had familiar haunts appeared so pleasant and enjoyable. With stout hearts they proceeded to school the following morning, well prepared and covered with several pairs of trousers. The master was also prepared. Being far sighted and experienced in such situations he applied punishment with extra effective force. The application for wages was a complete failure. The experience however was remembered with pride, with the boast that they were the first generation of schoolboys to demand wages and to go on strike.

Kingfisher of Hope

~

Maggie Pryce Jones

Mam always insisted that we change into old clothes as soon as we came home from school so that our clothes were always tidy. I think tidy was the most important word in Mam's vocabulary . . .

Mam was very keen for me to go to the grammar school at Hengoed. Her brothers had sons who had passed the Scholarship, and she wanted to be equal to them. Dad encouraged us all, but it was Mam who saw that our homework was done, although she had to ask Dad to check whether it was well done.

She murmured, as if to herself, 'I must stop Mr Griffiths on his way to school tomorrow, Maggie, just to ask how you are getting on'. I dreaded this. Mr Griffiths, my teacher, had to pass our cottage each morning and evening on his way to and from school and Mam would stop him and keep him until she had answers to all of her questions. I am sure that the poor teacher dreaded these meetings as much as I did, but there was no other road for him to take.

The mornings brought the usual answer, 'Maggie is excellent at English, but she has no idea when it comes to Arithmetic.'

Poor Mam was so dejected that each time I decided to work harder at the hated Sums and Mental Arithmetic. I knew how much my passing the Scholarship meant to Mam, who looked up to her brothers although it seemed to me that they cared little about her, for they never visited our humble home. Still, I was quietly determined to surprise Mr Griffiths and give Mam something to be proud of . . .

Scholarship Day was March 1st and as the New Year came in, dread began to rise in me. I wished that I could break my leg, just a little break, so that I would be unable to attend school. I had no confidence in my ability; I dreaded seeing Mam and Dad's disappointment when I told them that I had failed.

The fateful morning saw me set off for school carrying all the good-luck charms we could muster: a piece of coal, a new pin, and best of all, the little pearl crucifix which Dad had carried thoughout the war. I had a new pen and pencil and John gave me a few sweets to chew, but my confidence, delicate as ever, took a nasty blow when Dad said drily as I was leaving, 'All the good-luck charms in the world won't help you if you haven't learned the work, Maggie.' I was glad that this day I had allowed to spoil so many hours for me would soon be in the past.

I chose as my essay subject 'My Home Village'. My pen flew over the paper as I described its quiet beauty. I wrote about my little valley, and of the miracle I hoped would save it from the fierce onslaught of its black enemy. A description of the main street on the first day of the strike ended my composition.

I was happy with my work, especially as I had found the Mental Arithmetic to be within my capabilities. The results would be announced on the last day of the summer term, so I was free to enjoy the weeks ahead. But my world ended, or so I thought, when my friend Liza left the village. I came home from school one afternoon to find the next door cottage empty. Our neighbours had moved out during the early morning, as soon as their lodger had gone to his early shift in the quarry over the hill.

They were the first of many to leave the village. Some, deeply in debt, left during the night, doing a moonlight flit, as Dad said, leaving their debts behind them. They had nothing else to leave – everything of value had been sold long ago and, of course, their houses were rented. I heard that most went to the Midlands where the new car factories were looking for labour and there were plenty of houses to rent. There was nothing to look forward to in the valley: gloom and despondency were everywhere. Even in better times there was only the pit, and no parent really wanted a son to spend most of his life in darkness, with only damaged lungs for a reward.

Better pay and a better standard of living for their families drew many men from the pit. I often wondered why Dad had not taken us away, but John explained that he was always fighting for better conditions for the men and needed an aim to make his life worthwhile.

The summer was lonely for me. Liza had gone, and Megan, now fifteen years old, spent most of her time away, with her Aunt. I walked in the woods watching for my kingfisher. It was safe to walk alone in those days. I often walked up the farm lane to the gnarled old tree which we children called 'The Monkey Tree'. Here I would sit and gaze over the tops of the houses below, looking into my own world of dreams.

The week before school broke up for the long summer holidays, the classes were all assembled in the school hall to hear the results of the Scholarship. The staff stood along the back of the hall, ready to console the losers, who usually ran out in tears. Those of us who had taken the exam sat at the front of the hall with our fellow pupils behind us. I wished that Megan or Liza was with me, but both were far away. My heart sank when the head announced that only three girls and three boys had reached the required standard. I was trying to conjure up Mam's face when I had to tell her that I had failed when I heard *my* name called. I could not believe my ears. I jumped up and ran from the school. The staff, smiling, made no effort to stop me.

Everyone knew that the results would be out today, so as I ran past their houses the men and women called, 'Well done, Maggie!' My excited haste to reach home told them that I had passed.

Mam cried when she heard my news, and held me close, then, drying her eyes, she said, 'Go quick and tell your Dad on top pit; he's waiting to hear the news, good or bad.' She reached for her coat with a laugh and said, 'I'm going to tell your aunts the news.'

Today she was the proudest woman in the village, for the main topic of conversation would be the examination results and she would be given as many congratulations as I would. From today she had something in common with the shopkeepers and the quarry owners' wives as well as her middle class sisters-in-law: they all had children in the County Grammar School.

Dad called the other men around to hear the news and they all came over to fuss over me and offer advice for the future.

The people of the valleys have a high regard for education, as they proved in neighbouring Edwardsville by raising the money to build a grammar school there. Our neighbours helped by buying me pens, pencils and a ruler with which to start at the new school in September. Gran and Grancher Argoed helped too, with items from the shop, but my success brought a lot of worry with it. I needed an expensive uniform and now Dad had no overtime to help pay for it.

Our neighbours were proud that someone from our end of the

village had been successful. There were many children who had the ability to pass the exam, but were held back for financial reasons. Many belonged to large families where it was decided that only the boys could or should be educated. I thanked Heaven that my parents were more liberated in their views.

There were no grants available to help pay for clothes or equipment, but thanks to Mam and Dad's progressive attitude I was given every encouragement to work hard and, if necessary, leave the valley to find a better future. As usual, Mam solved the problem: she took out a club to pay for my new clothes, and one Saturday afternoon we set off for the Emporium in Bargoed, Mam's favourite town.

Although she had to slave for months to pay off the club, I know she thought it worth while. On the first morning of term, all the neighbours were out to see me off and their pride in me pleased Mam enormously. I was one of the best-dressed new girls starting school, and I was always dressed that way, she saw to that. I lacked for nothing.

When I returned home after my first day and told her that my neighbour in class, my new friend, was the daughter of a bank manager, her eyes rounded in excitement, but all she said was, 'Fancy that now, our Maggie!'

CHAPTER 6

POVERTY, STRIKES AND MORE POVERTY

POVERTY, STRIKES
AND MORE POVERTY

'The children are hungry, the men are hungry;
but most hungry of all are the women.'

As explained in the introduction to this volume, the economic circumstances resulting from low wages, unemployment and inadequate strike relief affected the quality of life of the women and children very severely during the long years of the 1920s and 1930s. While the fortunes of the coal industry fluctuated during the 1920s, the Lock Outs of 1921 and 1926 meant that families were not able to recover from their effects before deep, long term poverty set in post 1929.

This chapter draws upon the experiences of two authors, Beatrice Wood and Maggie Pryce Jones. The first extract from Beatrice Wood's autobiography relates to the 1920s and paints a vivid picture of dire poverty and its effect on the life of a child who had no nightdress and who regularly scavenged for scraps outside the fish and chip shop. The dramatic effects on the health of the community of the long stoppage of 1926 are also reflected here with references to epidemics, suicides and back street abortions. The second extract from the same work is set in the 1930s when life becomes focused upon avoiding the Means Test inspector and the future seems very bleak indeed.

Maggie Pryce Jones' family was rather better off materially than Beatrice Wood's, yet the 1935 strike in Taff Merthyr colliery which particularly affected the villages of Trelewis and Bedlinog, drained the family's resources. The issue of strike-breaking or 'scab' labour as it is referred to here, created a very bitter division in the community with women and children playing a prominent part in ostracising the blacklegs. Because Maggie's father was one of the activists, he was unable to obtain work when the strike ended. The selling of furniture illustrates the obvious and immediate effects of the strike, but the underlying consequences are deeper and longer term. Poverty is gnawing at the quality of life and, in particular, affecting the health of Maggie's mother who exemplifies the sacrifices that so many mothers made in order to feed, clothe and educate their children.

Wednesday's Child

~

Beatrice Wood

Saturday night was bath night. We were all put into the tub one after the other, the tub being half of a large beer barrel which we could buy off the pub landlord. There would be two pieces cut out for handles. The water was heated on the fire in a bucket, and if you were lucky enough to be first in the bath you would have lovely hot water – but if you were last then the water could be cold and not too clean after the others. Then when we were bathed and dried, the tub was taken out. It was time for our senna – if we needed it or not. My mother used to say, 'It does you good to have a good cleaning out'.

The trouble was we didn't have enough food inside us to clear out. I used to hate it, and would wait until last so as the jug would be nearly empty. My mother used to try every ploy to get us to drink it, telling us it was cold tea – but I knew different. I had seen the jug on the hob all night brewing with a saucer on top. Then we girls had to be deloused. My mother would put us between her knees in a firm grip and comb our hair while it was still wet, with a tooth comb. If she found a louse, she would put it between her two thumb-nails and squash it with a crack. Then she would scrape the tooth-comb through our hair to get at the nits. We used to be crying. Our hair was long and tangled. Woe betide us if we moved or fidgeted. Then our hair was put into rags to curl for chapel next day . . .

My father was taking me to see his brother in Bargoed. We were going to walk there because we didn't have any money for the bus fare. We had walked a long way and my father had to sit down by the roadside often with a fit of coughing – he had been affected by gas during the Boer War. We were used to him coughing. Then, as he was coughing his lungs up, we saw a milkman with his horse and cart. He saw my father coughing so he asked us if we would like a lift and where we were going. My father told him Bargoed, so the milkman said, 'Well, I am not going far from there. Jump on.' So we gratefully accepted. He lifted me onto the cart and said to my father, 'Good God, man, there's no weight in this little girl at all.' There was a lot of milk churns on the cart where the milk was kept. In one of them was a tin cup with a long handle that the milkman fills up the customers' jugs with. He saw me looking at it, so he filled it up and gave it to me to drink. It was lovely. We never had fresh milk at home – we used condensed milk in tins, and if our tin was empty, and it was Thursday, my mother used to put warm water into it and swill it around to make do until Friday.

We went a long way in the cart, then we got off. My father thanked the milkman and we walked the rest of the way. We got to my uncle's house in time for tea. We had bread and butter and jam, and I had a fairy cake. It was lovely. Then I played with my cousin for a bit until it was time to go home. I was dreading that long walk home, but we didn't have to. My uncle gave my father sixpence for the bus fare, so he decided we would walk to the next stop where it would only cost fivepence. My uncle could afford to give us the fare home because he was working. That was the only way my father could save a penny. My Auntie gave me an apple. I shined it on my sleeve all the way home. My brothers and sisters all wanted the peeling and the stump of my apple. Well, I couldn't give it to them all, so I ate it – peeling, stump and all.

My mother wasn't feeling too well when we got home. Her throat was bad, so she failed to finish sewing some curtains she was making for someone, so she couldn't get paid, and as it was Thursday – the day we used to call starvation day – we had nothing in the house. No food and no money. My father made my mother lie down and took charge of the situation. He asked us children to look around to see if we could find some empty jam jars to take back to the shop where we could get a ha'penny each back off them. My little brother was crying, as he had to give his up. He had tadpoles in it. My other brother had minnows in another one. We threw them down the lavatory, telling my little brother they would find their own way home. But two jars wasn't enough, so we were sent next door to ask if they had any to lend us. They found two for us so, with a ha'penny on four jam jars we had tuppence, and the penny my father saved on the bus fare made threepence. We had a loaf of bread for tuppence-ha'penny. My father found some dripping at the back of the pantry shelf, so we all sat down to bread and dripping. With the ha'penny that was left my father bought a lemon for my mother. He cut it up and poured boiling water over it and gave it to my mother. Then my mother asked for the goose grease to put on a stocking round her neck, but it couldn't be found. She said, 'It's on the pantry shelf at the back'. Then we realized what we had been eating – bread and goose grease, but we survived.

We used to go up to the Market when it was nearly closing time to help the stallholders to pack up and load their vans to go home. I wasn't very big. I was a small nine, so my sisters and brothers used to do the carrying and I would clean the trestle table and sweep up the floor. Sometimes we would pick up cabbage leaves that had fallen off the outside of the cabbages, and damaged apples and oranges that had been thrown out. We used to take them home to my mother to sort out. She was glad of them. We had to be quick when it was closing time in the Market because there were many more children like us waiting to clean up. If we were lucky to catch the biscuit man, he would give us broken biscuits for helping him. The trouble was we didn't often get the chance – the children were all queuing up because they were all hungry like us. If we did catch him, we would share all the biscuits out between us, making sure we all had the same amount of cream ones. It was not unknown for us to get our school rulers and measure them. We used to put some in our pockets for our mother, but by the time we got them home there would be nothing left but crumbs. But the thought was there. Sometimes we found potato sacks. My mother used to boil them and make sack aprons for herself out of them. They were used for all sorts of things, such as towels, dish cloths, floor cloths and rag mats, and many other uses.

As bad as we were, there were people a lot worse off than us. I used to call for a girl and they never owned a cup – they used to drink out of jam jars or half-pint milk bottles. They didn't even own a kettle and couldn't afford one. They boiled their water in a dried-milk tin. The husband had put a wire handle on it. I have also seen people in the depth of despair because their money had run out before the next money was due, so they couldn't buy food. They would go to the butcher's for bones for a dog they didn't have, just to make some kind of stew.

We lived next to a slaughterhouse, and if there were animals left there overnight to be killed next day, we used to hear them during the night – the cows mooing, the sheep bleating and the pigs squealing all night. Was it any wonder I used to nod off in school? I was always having a clip for not paying attention, but I was always so tired.

We used to watch them killing the sheep by putting the tub up-side-down and putting the sheep to lie sideways in it with its head over the side. Then, with a long-bladed knife, they would plunge it into the jugular vein. The poor sheep would utter its last bleat – the blood would flow into the sink below. Then they would hang it up by its hind legs and skin it. Sometimes they would cut out the lights while I was there and swill them under the tap and give them to me to take to my mother while they were still warm. They would go into our broth. I looked up the definition of lights in the Oxford Dictionary. It is as followed: 'The lungs of a sheep or pig; used in food for animals'.

And that is what we had become – animals scrounging, scraping, begging, pleading, all to no avail. Nobody would help us and we had nothing to help ourselves with . . .

Rickets was raging about now because children were not getting enough food for their growing bones. You would see many a child with what you called bandy legs. Also tuberculosis was about. The TB hospital was full with people with consumption. We used to pass the hospital and see beds on the verandas. It was said it was part of the treatment. I would have thought they all would have caught pneumonia: they were put out in all weathers.

Then there was an epidemic of diphtheria. A lot of children died at that time. I lost a lot of my friends during that time; the little boy next door died, and a little boy across the road, a little girl from the next street who was in my class, children were dying all around us. We children used to knock on the door and ask to see them in their coffins. We were never refused. The little children would be in their coffin with perhaps a flower in their hand, or a favourite toy that the parent had put in the coffin.

Anyway, to quell it, the doctors and nurses came around the schools to examine our throats. They took two girls from my class. One of them died. They were put in isolation wards in hospital for six weeks. The poor children had no bodies to fight with; they were nothing but skin and bones . . .

The colliers had come out on strike in 1926. Things were even worse now. Their wives were running up big bills in the grocery shops by getting their food on tick, as it was called. Some shops went bankrupt. My mother was missing my brother's money now, because he was on strike. There was a lot of friction among miners too, because some men went to work during the strike. They were called blacklegs. It was the worst industrial strike in history. By now our house was condemned as unfit to live in, but we couldn't go anywhere else . . .

The men were paid very little strike pay – and some no pay at all. They couldn't claim 'Unemployment' money because it was said that there was work for them to go to. They were forced to go and seek what they called 'poor relief'. Before they would give anything you had to sell anything of value in your house and live off the proceeds. And before they could consider giving you any money you would have to produce the bills to prove how much money you had got for what you had sold in case you were cheating.

Then they wouldn't give you money but a 'relief note', as they called it. It was a note for you to have a certain amount of food. And of course you could only go to the shops that were stipulated on your food relief note. And boy! didn't the shopkeepers flaunt it! Their prices were sky high. Also, there were things on the list that you didn't want. Then you would ask the shopkeeper for something else instead of the same value. The shopkeeper wasn't supposed to change it, but they rarely refused. It got to the ears of the authorities, then the shopkeepers were heavily fined. Then the shopkeepers complained because, they said, it was the ones who had asked for the goods to be exchanged that should be penalized.

There was no work around for the men. Things were getting worse, not better: a terrible time for the men. They were just standing around street corners with nothing to do, day after day standing around aimlessly. The tobacconist was now splitting up a packet of cigarettes so that the men could buy one at a time for a halfpenny each. (A whole packet of cigarettes cost tuppence.) But some men couldn't afford that. I also used to see men picking up nips off the floors. Then they would take the paper off and put the tobacco into a small tin and make their own cigarettes. Some used to go out and collect dock leaves and dry them in the oven, then crush them, and try and make cigarettes out of it because they couldn't afford to buy any . . .

I remember a lot of suicides. My friend's father drowned himself in the Penywern ponds, the same ponds where the unwanted cats and dogs were drowned. I was there when they pulled him out. They were dragging the pond with a long thick rope with three iron prongs on the end of it. They also had a boat on the water. It was a bit of excitement for us children, if it wasn't so tragic. They pulled him out after being there for hours. We watched them lay him out on the bank on his back. His eyes were open. It was a gruesome sight. His eyes were bulging out of his head and he was all swollen up with water . . .

There was a slogan going around now – 'All Paupers Together'. The Salvation Army had opened up for free breakfasts. What a boon to us children. After picking our cokes, we used to go up there before school. We could have as much bread and jam as we could eat and a mug of cocoa. That was the first time I have ever tasted cocoa. It was lovely. Then we would go to school from there. Also, canteens were opening up for weak children. Well, I was classed as weak, so I was usually picked to go. It was one less for my mother to feed. Nobody could afford to buy coal now at ninepence a sack, so the men used to go up to the mountainside, which we used to call the patches. The men would open coal levels. Most of the men on strike were skilled miners, they knew exactly where to find the coal. Most men knew the location and they would help the ones that didn't. A few men would get together and kept to their own patch (hence the name patches) to protect it, especially at night. There was always somebody left on their patch.

Many is the time you would hear scuffles with the police because what they were doing was illegal. They would take old prams, trucks or anything with wheels. They used to dig the coal by day and bring it home by night. Sometimes the police would turn a blind eye, but sometimes they would give chase. Then you could hear the wheels of their cart or truck and the men's hobnailed boots clattering through the streets. And if the police were catching up on them they would have to leave their precious coal behind that they had worked hard all day for. And of course their little carts or trucks would be confiscated. Then you could hear the men's hobnailed boots clattering down the street with the policeman in pursuit. Their footsteps would go further and further and further then suddenly stop. Then you would know that someone had opened their door to let the man in to hide until the all clear.

Kingfisher of Hope

~

Maggie Pryce Jones

It was an ordinary day at school until mid-afternoon, when we were called into the hall. The headmistress instructed us to hurry home. 'And no dawdling'. No reason was given but we knew from the serious tone of her voice that something was very wrong.

Davy and I, with the other children from our row, hurried to the square. We could have gone by the lane, but some instinct sent us the longer way home.

We sensed the tension as soon as we reached the square. Groups of men stood around, talking loudly and excitedly. I could see that they had been to work because, although they had washed, there was still the black rim of coal dust around their eyes that only Vaseline would remove. Their flat caps covered their damp hair and they had thick mufflers around their necks. I looked at these grim-faced strangers and felt afraid. These were not the friendly men that I knew. Dad was there too, and he ordered us all home at once. 'Stay indoors all night,' he called after us.

I ran as fast as my legs would carry me, though even then I was far behind the others, past the paper shop, the grocer's, the old grey stone church which we attended every Sunday. Groups of women clad in the uniform floral wrap-around pinafores stood on all the doorsteps. White-faced they stood, arms folded across their breasts, whispering as we sped by. They were frightened, Davy said.

Mam was polishing the brass when I burst in and Davy was sitting in the corner, sulking. Mam had told him off for leaving me behind. Bryn was already home from the junior school. 'Now, Maggie, you get started on your homework, while I finish my brasses. Extra time tonight for you to study your Arithmetic,' she said.

Mam had never been one to stand and gossip, there was always too much work to be done. When she was worried, she worked harder, and the shine on the furniture and the brass told me that today she was very worried.

It was late when the men from our small row returned home. We heard, in the morning, that heavy boulders had been rolled down the mountain onto the little engine, to prevent coal leaving the colliery. We heard that the police were hunting the culprits. I was afraid, and I felt that Mam was afraid too: we knew that Dad had been out very late the night before. I prayed that he was not guilty of this act. In fact, several younger men were arrested, taken to court and sentenced to several months in Swansea prison. Dad said he thought they were not guilty: it was impossible for the police to know who was guilty because, he had heard, there were over a hundred people present when the boulders were rolled down.

It was strange to see the men leaning on their garden walls as we walked to school next morning. They were on strike now. They could have stayed in bed and enjoyed their enforced holiday, but the habit of early rising is hard to break, so they were up at their usual hour, even though there was no work for them to go to and no one was sure when they would work again.

Young as I was, I felt sorry for them. They were loyal, hard-working men who were given nothing unless they fought for it. I heard Dad telling Mam that the colliery owners could, had they so wished, have settled the matter without a strike. 'They're afraid we'll get too powerful and they'll have to give us a decent living standard', he said. Mam sounded angry when she answered, 'All they care about is their fat profits, never mind that we have to work all hours to keep our children tidy.'

I was made more aware of the trouble by hearing Mam speaking so bitterly. Things must be very wrong, I realized, if our quiet gentle Mother was forced to speak like that. I had never heard her speak about any subject in that manner before. When asked her opinion she would always laugh and say, 'Oh, go on, you know I don't understand things.'

I did not know then that mothers the world over take arms when their children are in need, even the most gentle of them. All I wanted was for there to be enough money coming into the house to save Mam having to go out to work. We were not used to luxury. As Megan once said, 'If we had money for luxuries, we'd save it all and go away from the pits before the men die a slow death, as the black dust turns their lungs to stone.'

A few days later we passed the first tarred house as we walked to school. The front window was smashed and there was tar all over the door and window-sill. Mrs Prentiss was crying bitterly as she tried to clean it up.

We kept quiet until we were well past the house, not knowing what to say, then Davy burst out, 'Serve their own right, the Scabs!' I was so shocked I ran all the way to school, afraid to say to my own brother and friends that I was sorry for the people who had had their homes spoilt. I could only think of their children, but what if Davy hated them too?

When we were alone that evening, I told Mam how I felt. I felt guilty because I thought Dad would be angry with me. Mam sighed and said, 'You are too young, Maggie, to care about loyalty; your heart rules your head. You're right, of course, the children *are* innocent, but it's the innocent who have suffered most since they hung our innocent Lord on the Cross.'

She sat for a while darning John's sock, then she said sadly, 'At least it is only their property that is harmed, cariad. They will have food in their bellies, and their children's bellies too. We may be without, before this row is settled.'

A few days later, Mr Griffiths called me back as I was leaving the classroom, 'Maggie', he said, 'you are a friend of Mary Winters. Will you call and see when she and her brother, Huw, will be back at school? They have been away for a week now.'

I knocked on the door of the terraced house where Mary lived. It, like the window, was spattered with tar. I nearly turned away, afraid of Dad's temper if he knew I had called at such a house, but as I was about to leave, the door was opened a little way.

Mrs Winters' eyes were red from weeping. 'She is innocent too,' I thought as I followed her into the small kitchen.

'It *is* nice of you to call, Maggie,' she said. 'I just can't get these silly children to go to school. Try and change their minds, will you. Children have no part in this trouble, but since we were tarred last Thursday, and people shouted 'Scab' through the letterbox, they are afraid to go out!' She dabbed her eyes as she said, 'People who have sat by us in Chapel for years have turned their backs on us. Silly isn't it now?'

I was glad when Mary and Huw came downstairs and I could give them the message. 'Will you call for us, then, Maggie?' Mary pleaded, and I could not refuse. 'I'm sure Mr Griffiths will let you out of school before the rest of us, if you ask,' I told them.

All the way home I worried about what Dad would say if he found out whose house I had been in. I could see both sides of the argument a little better now.

There was Mam, working hard and worrying about food for us, even before the trouble. Mrs Winters had carpets on the floor, plenty of food and went on holiday every year. Mam had never had a holiday. She asked for so little from life, yet both she and Dad worked all the hours they could. It was not fair, even I could see that, but Mary and Huw could not help it, any more than I could. Mr Winters was an official in the pit, I knew that, but there seemed to be a very big difference between the pay they earned and that of the miners. It couldn't be right, could it?

The strike went on and on. It seemed, to us children, to last for ever. There were no picnics, although the weather was lovely, and it was getting colder and soon we would be unable to have any.

I asked Mam about it one day. 'We're not in the mood for picnics. It's enough to put a dinner on the table, Maggie,' she said. 'Surely you know how little money we have?'

I had not thought much about money until then. I could see that Mam was looking more worried every day now, but Dad was always out to some meeting or other. He always smelled of beer when he came in, and was in a happy mood. I asked John about it and he told me that Dad's friends bought the drink. Most were single men who had no families to look after.

John had less time than ever for Dad these days, they never spoke to each other. I learned a long time afterwards that John had paid our rent all though the strike, and Dad resented being beholden to him. John did not sympathize with the strikers and this made matters worse.

Another worry beset Mam as the strike went on. The coal which we received from the pit when Dad was working was almost gone. The open fire heated our water, Mam cooked on it, and, of course, it heated the kitchen in which we lived, so it was a serious blow.

One evening Dad asked Davey and me to keep watch while he climbed into the coal trucks which were lined up on the rails almost outside the door. He threw the coal out, and while we watched for Twmas, the bobby, he quickly put it into bags and carried it indoors.

I failed miserably as a look-out, because as the last bag was hurried indoors, a glint of brass buttons told us that the pit police-man was coming our way. I hurried after Dad and warned him. I knew that he had been seen.

'Ssh girl', he said. 'Sit down and be quiet.' A minute later there came a loud banging on the door. Mam left her ironing and walked very slowly to answer the knock. She returned almost at once with Twmas on her heels.

The look on his face when he saw Dad sitting in the corner reading the paper was so comical that even John, who was sitting in the opposite corner disapproving of the whole proceedings, was hard put not to smile. I could see his moustache twitching.

'I saw you stealing coal from the wagons outside,' said Twmas, a little uncertainly.

'When?' asked Dad in a surprised voice.

'Just a few minutes ago,' the policeman insisted.

'You can take a look in the shed if you like, but my hands are clean,' said Dad, holding out his hands for inspection.

Twmas looked at the hands free from coal dust, he hesitated, reddened and decided better of it. He knew if he failed to find coal in the shed he would be the laughing-stock of the village in the morning. With a long, hard look at Dad, he left.

'Well, we have enough coal for a while, although I wish we'd paid for it like respectable people,' said Mam, a few minutes after the front door slammed shut.

'The coal is outside my door, and I'll steal before I see my family freeze,' Dad answered. 'It's the owners' fault we're on strike! Here, Jane,' he said, passing her an old pair of heavy woollen stockings which he had used for gloves, and she laughed as he continued, 'Poor old Twmas, no imagination at all!' . . .

Money was very scarce now. When Bryn got pneumonia, the parish could not help with his medicine, so the little bedroom suite, Mam's pride and joy, that she had worked so hard to buy, was sold. It broke my heart to see it carried out of the house, and we had only a little money for it because it was being bought on weekly payments and the shop had to be paid first.

Next, the piano, a pride to the whole family, had to go. Mam cleaned the house for a music teacher in exchange for one hour's lesson a week for me. She and Dad were keen for me to learn to play: it was a great thing to have a pianist in the family, and we were the only family at our end of the village who owned a piano. I can remember the dark sheen of its wood to this day, and the words 'Dale Forte' printed inside its lid.

Bryn got better, that was all that mattered. We hoped that no other illness would attack our family – the plain food we ate contained little of vitamin value and there was a great deal of illness in the village. Our meals were planned to fill us; we were lucky to be eating at all.

An air of triumph blew through the village. The men were gathering again in small groups on the little square. Their faces were free now from any sign of coal dust; only blue scars, the hallmarks of a collier, were visible where dust had entered an open wound. Few men were without at least one blue scar.

It was a bright, spring day as they stood there in the weak sunshine, their shirts open at the neck, their mufflers forgotten. Today they wore their caps on the back of their heads, at a rakish angle; hope made them happy; there were signs that the strike was about to end.

The end came one Thursday evening. Dad, hurrying in from yet another meeting, called out excitedly, 'It's over, Janie, it's over and we won. They're sending the boys home from prison, too, and we're putting 'Welcome Home' banners across the road.' I ran out to join my friends, who were dancing and shouting outside; we were happy because our parents were happy again; we had no real knowledge of what was happening.

The strike was over. They said the men had won, but I wondered how when I saw so many houses from which almost all of the furniture was gone, sold as ours had been sold.

Mam's face, when at last the piano was brought back, is something I shall never forget. She set to polishing its already gleaming surface. I thought it must be the shiniest piano in the world. When it was back in its old place in the parlour, she stood back and smiled. 'At least we have one good piece of furniture, Maggie,' she said. 'Now we must try and fill the other gaps.'

The men returned to work on Monday after welcoming home their butties from prison. Things seemed to be going well, then Dad started staying home instead of returning to work for a 'double' (a double shift). He was always home on a Saturday where previously he had always worked. Since breaking his leg underground he had worked on the surface, first in the quarry and later at the colliery itself. The pay was less there, so he relied on overtime to bring home a living wage. Dad was never a lazy man; he would work all the hours he could.

Now he was never asked to work overtime. It had been a hollow victory after all – many of the activists were being penalized. I remembered the private meetings held in our parlour and wondered what they had been talking about, Dad and his friends. Like the other men in the same position he grew bitter. His temper grew short, now that he had to choose between cigarettes and beer. He could not afford both.

As we sat, one evening, listening to the wireless, Mam busy with her rag mat, Dad said, 'Maggie, one day things will be better for the men in the pits. Another government will change things: better pay and working conditions, proper hospital treatment, free holidays with pay, and no stoppage of wages when you are ill. Just think about it, girl.'

'When, Lew?' Mam asked.

'When we have a government that cares about the likes of us, Jane,' he answered. 'We've made a start. Now we've got a committee of sorts to negotiate between the men and the management. It *will* come, Maggie,' he said. 'If not in my time, in yours.' At the time I thought his dream much too good to be true.

Wednesday's Child

~

Beatrice Wood

The Government brought in a new scheme. It meant that everybody working in the house had to keep their parents. What a blow to men's pride! There was a lot of friction between fathers and sons because the boys resented keeping their parents. We tried to live an honest life, we really tried, but society wouldn't let you. The Government was making honest people dishonest because of their rules.

The Means Test man would come often, asking the same question. So we devised a plan with the help of my mother's friend. We would say my brother was living with them. It didn't matter to them because her husband was working. My mother didn't like doing it, but we had to in order to live – if you could call it living. There was a lot of people doing it. The trouble was, my brother couldn't be seen in our house because he wasn't supposed to be living there.

The Means Test man came when you least expected him. Sometimes he would call just as my brother had come in from work. He would be eating his food, and if there was a knock on the door there would be one mad rush to get the food off the table (because we only had one room) before we opened the door, and my brother would have to hide in the pantry for the Means Test man not to see him, and stay there until he had gone.

The Means Test man came one day when my brother was bathing in front of the fire in the tub. Well, my brother jumped out of the tub wet and naked and went into the pantry to hide. We didn't have time to take the tub out, so my mother, resilient as ever, caught hold of our dog and plunged him into the tub, pretending she was bathing the dog. My brother was freezing in the pantry. When we opened the door to let the Means Test man in, the dog jumped out of the tub and shook himself all over the Means Test man. It took all my powers not to laugh, because it was like a comic strip if it wasn't so serious. We had hysterics once he was gone. Then my brother had to finish off bathing in the water the dog had been in. Just imagine:

before the knock on the door my brother had finished washing his top half, so the water was black with coal dust when my mother put our dog in it, and our dog was black and white, mainly white. He was dirtier coming out of the tub than when he went in. It was so funny.

Those Means Test men were horrible men, and very arrogant. They would sometimes lift up the latch and walk in. So my mother went one better – she kept the door locked. They weren't above looking through your window. I was always told that your home was your castle. But not us – we might as well be living in a field: we had no privacy – this was the dreaded nineteen-thirties. How people suffered.

Our priority was food, not eating it, but how to get it. We were always scheming and dealing and trying to find ways of cooking what little we had to our best advantage. For instance, we used a lot of flour in our food because it was filling. We put it in our broth to thicken it, and in eggs so as they would go further. Sometimes, if we didn't have bread on Thursday my mother would mix flour and water together and add a pinch of salt and cook it on an enamel plate in the oven. Then we would have it with dripping. It tasted all right, not like real bread perhaps, but it was edible. Yes, we made some odd recipes in those days. Dripping was something we had most of, and that was thanks to the slaughterhouse. They would sometimes give us a bit of fat to melt down, and if the butcher would give us a bit of meat (which wasn't often) we would mince it up. It might be only one slice of beef, but with an onion and plenty of bread it would be enough for us all. There was more bread than beef – three times as much – but when they were fried they weren't too bad. We put anything edible into our pot, anything and everything.

At this time men were getting very depressed and frustrated. They could see no future and were getting deeper and deeper into debt. So whatever went wrong – either in the house or outside – they would take it out on their wives and children. You often saw a woman with bruises or a black eye walking about. They would never say how they got it. Sometimes you passed a house where you could hear shouting when they were quarrelling. Often you could hear a crash when something had been thrown. I remember one woman was regularly thrown out of her house, especially at weekends when her husband was in drink. She had three little ones, one in the shawl and two toddlers. They would sometimes walk the streets for hours until she thought her husband was asleep. Then she would creep into the house. They had to go back, there was nowhere else to go. There was no place then for battered wives, more was the pity. A lot of men couldn't take it any more – no money, no food, and no job prospects. So when they got their dole money, they would go to the pub and drink it. You would often see wives outside the dole office on dole day to make sure they got the money off the husbands.

A neighbour of ours had a drunken husband – when he could get money for drink. She had one kipper in the house, and of course the man always came first with the food, so she was keeping it for him. She came up to our house saying she would love to have it herself, but she didn't have anything else to give him. Anyway, she cooked it because he was expected in. But he hadn't come in an hour later. She was keeping it warm on top of a saucepan of boiling water. It was driving her mad. She said if he didn't come in soon she would eat it. He still hadn't come in two hours later. She was sick of topping up the water in the saucepan, as it was boiling away. So she sat down and ate it herself before it got spoiled. When he came in he was as drunk as a lord. He had met a friend who had bet on a horse that day and they had been celebrating. When he came in he said, 'Come on, Maud, where's my dinner?'

'You've just eaten it,' she said, rubbing the skin of the kipper on his mouth. He was too drunk to notice.

'Lick your lips,' she said.

He put out his tongue and licked his lips.

'Oh, yes,' he said, and went to sleep in his chair.

These things sound stupid now to someone who doesn't understand. Just imagine rubbing a kipper skin onto your husband's lips just because you were so hungry yourself that you ate it. It was a case of first come, first served. Too bad if you came when the food was all gone, because no way could you get any more food, so you would have to do without. Yes, I have been without many a time, not only me but many more like me . . .

Many people were thrown onto the streets with their furniture.

Their only crime was not being able to pay their rent. They were once proud upright people, degraded through no fault of their own. Is it any wonder we all clung desperately together? It was a case of 'But for the grace of God, there go I'. We were one for all, and all for one. If any of the bureaucrats were around, such as the Means Test man, we would all know well in advance through the grapevine in case we were doing something we shouldn't be doing. Oh, yes, Big Brother was around then. It didn't take much for those Means Test men to stop your dole or Parish voucher. There were always stories going around of someone having their dole stopped or Parish. Yes, there were many aching hearts heavy laden with poverty. Women were old at fifty. I would sometimes look up at the trees and think, 'If I was a bird I could fly away'.

Many women were seeking illegal abortions because they couldn't afford another mouth to feed. Many young women lost their lives and bled to death. I used to hear people saying what a painful death someone had had because the abortion had gone wrong and turned septic. Yes, they would go anywhere to get rid of the baby they were having. The abortionists were doing a roaring trade in a dirty back room of their house. There was no Pill in those days. They didn't care about the risks to their own lives. Many left three or four children behind. But could you blame them under the circumstances? One woman even asked her doctor to give her something to get rid of it. She already had five children and she was only twenty-eight. The doctor told her, 'It's good for the country'. How insensitive.

My friend's mother was ill. She had been ill for a long time with tuberculosis. She had been in hospital a few times. Anyway, she died. My friend came to ask me if I would go with her to tell her relations. It was so matter of fact, you wouldn't believe it. Her mother had just died, and her father was sending her around to tell people. Death was becoming the accepted thing in our society – sort of here today and gone tomorrow. The smell of death was everywhere. If you didn't die of fever there was always suicide. The only people who were making money were the undertakers.

At one time parents and children used to have to go to the workhouse, degraded and filthy. They would be put into quarantine to be deloused and bathed, but after a few days they would discharge themselves. It was a common occurrence to see the same family in and out of the workhouse three or four times a year. The children didn't want to go from the workhouse because they were kept clean and warm, and were fed, but the parents would insist. So the authorities were trying to take control of the children till they were eighteen. People were so downtrodden that the used to walk with their shoulders up and head down in subservience. We were out of humanity's reach. We were so hopeless that it felt as if you were buried in a tomb.

Kingfisher of Hope

~

Maggie Pryce Jones

John once said that the valleys were no strangers to tragedy and how true that was! The strike was hardly settled when an epidemic of scarlet fever and diphtheria descended on the village. The colliery ambulance was kept busy taking the victims to hospital. Hardly a house was without a sick child, and some families had more than one child suffering, in different hospitals. Mam often visited one or other of the children in the isolation hospital high on the mountain side at Gelligaer. She said it was heartbreaking, having to speak and look at them through the windows, then leave them crying.

Some children died, one of them baby Molly from our small row of cottages. There were collections for the poor families. People had barely got over the strike, and there was little money to pay for the funerals.

Our family was one of the few not affected by the dreadful ill-nesses. Mam was convinced that the teaspoonful of paraffin which she made us swallow night and morning had defeated the germs. I do not know if there were grounds for this claim; I do know that it was a vile preventative and I often wondered if the illnesses could be as bad as the medicine. We suffered no ill effects, which sur-prised me greatly when I learned what paraffin was.

Even in the presence of tragedy, everyone still looked forward to Christmas. If it was a sad time that year for many who had lost a child, it was very hard too for the children who had survived. As Bryn said, there were quite a few empty desks in the classroom to remind them of their lost friends. And there were fresh little graves in the hillside cemetery, to remind us always of that dreadful autumn.

Spring came as usual, bringing with it a hesitant happiness. Old wounds were beginning to heal, although the scabs would never be fully forgiven. On the surface, at least, things were peaceful. Davy was now fifteen years old and, against Dad's wishes, was working down the pit with Mam's brothers. He was there for a short time only, but became so pale and small that I cried for him, trying so hard to be grown up. I knew how he hated being down in that black hole. He would watch Mam pack his 'tommy-box' and fill his 'jack' with water each evening. Both were made of tin, the only metal allowed. He looked as if he was desperate to fall ill – anything to keep him at home. I knew how he was feeling: I had felt much the same about the scholarship exam.

Davy's problem was not as happily settled as mine. One day the colliery ambulance brought him home: he had collapsed at work and looked dreadfully ill. A month later, Mam took him to an old herbalist living in Dowlais in the next valley. I never found out what the old man had said, but Davy did not go down the pit again. He went to stay on the farm at Argoed, where Grannie could keep an eye on him.

If only someone had kept an eye on Mam. I was too busy working hard at schoolwork, which I was not finding easy. Each evening too there was lacrosse or tennis practice. I had no time to notice that things were not as usual. My new friend, Pat, told me that Mam was having another baby. Her Mam had told her. She was right. Mam told me herself soon after. At first I was filled with resentment and shock. I thought Mam was too old to be starting a new family. But she wasn't old, really, she just looked it.

The baby, Ann, arrived in August, when the roses were in full bloom around the arch in the garden. She was a lovely little girl and she throve, but it was many months before Mam recovered sufficiently to walk as far as the front door.

Mam was soon back at work. I felt guilty because her earnings were mostly spent on me. The demands of the new school seemed endless: now there was a special green outfit required for the

Grecian Dancing classes. Mam never let me down and Marion soon made the tunic from the pattern provided and the material Mam bought . . .

Another Christmas came and went, a happy time even though Mam was far from her usual self. The baby had made a difference to us all: we loved her dearly, but she seemed to disrupt our lives. We had to be quiet because she was sleeping in her pram in the corner and sometimes our meals were late because she had to be fed first.

I did not mind: she was an adorable little girl. But I was becoming increasingly resentful that Dad did nothing to help Mam. Surely he could see that she was ill and worried? Bryn was wonderfully helpful in all sorts of ways: 'My little donkey,' Mam would call him lovingly.

Not long afterwards I would wish with all my heart that *I* had earned that accolade.

Calmly and confidently Bryn sat the examination that I had dreaded so much. Much to our delight, he passed with flying colours. Now Mam and Dad were doubly proud, and doubly worried, although Mam said that Bryn would be easier and cheaper to kit out for his new school because its uniform was much the same as he wore for his present one.

My brother and I were able to borrow many of the books we needed for our studying from the Miners' Library in nearby Treharris. The library was paid for by weekly deductions from the colliery workers' pay-packets.

With two children at grammar school, Mam was looking increasingly worried. Pride was not enough to feed and clothe us. She cried a lot and when I asked her why, she would answer, 'I'm tired, that's all.' I never heard her complain and she was not the sort to cry for nothing. A vague dread affected me so much that my dreams were filled with fear. I dreamed one night that my big doll, which slept in the chest of drawers, had turned into Mam, and she was not lying in a drawer but a coffin. I was terrified, but I knew that I could never tell Mam, so I told Grannie Locke.

'Cariad,' she said, 'your Mam is going to be all right. Remember that dreams always reverse themselves.' I was comforted, but thought, all the same, a *birth* is the opposite to a death. It hardly seemed to make sense.

I had decided that I would like to be a journalist, and I worked hard to that end. The first step, I knew, would be a pass in the seven subjects necessary to obtain the Certificate of the Central Welsh Board. Whether I would go to college afterwards was very much in doubt. With no grant or financial help available it seemed an impossible ambition . . .

The boys were out playing, the baby was out with John in her pram. Mam and I had finished making the beds and were sitting quietly in the kitchen. She was silent for a while, then, with a rueful laugh that I cannot describe, she said, 'I have something to tell you. We're having a new baby.' She must have been upset by my shocked silence, for she said, almost pleadingly, 'There's such a gap between you and Ann, Maggie, it will be nice for her to have a playmate of her own age. I hope it will be a sister for her, don't you?'

When I looked at her I could see that she was afraid, but I could not pretend to be glad, I could only remember how long it had taken her to recover from Ann's birth. At that moment I hated my father with all my heart – now I could see how selfish he really was.

When next I saw Grannie Argoed I told her about my fears. She said that Mam was suffering from a difficult form of anaemia and really should have had treatment, but it was very expensive. 'Even we could not help, Maggie,' she said. 'Your Grancher is losing money fast on the shop and the level is the only real income we have ourselves now.'

I knew that she spoke the truth, because she was unstinting in her help at all times. 'You pray for her, Maggie, the good Lord will know what is best for your Mother.'

I was not comforted. I felt the weight on my heart grow heavier and I remembered the times that she had said, during the strike, 'I had my dinner earlier, Lew,' when she was serving the rest of the family. The best for Dad, the next best for the children; for her, I suspected now, nothing.

I sat my exams that year, finding consolation in work. I had also found a special friend, Gareth. He was a senior pupil at Bryn's school, and he kept a seat for me on the school bus.

Gareth was tall and fair, while I was dark and of medium height. He was a popular boy and my friends envied me his attentions, especially when he danced for most of the evening with me at the annual party for the pupils of both schools.

Being the only child of well-off parents, he was likely to go on to university. He had the ability to pass the required exams. I did not tell Mam about Gareth; she was very strict with me about boy-friends, and I well remember how ashamed I was the day she caught me talking at the top of the lane. There was quite a group of us, boys and girls. Mam came by and, taking me by the arm, walked me home. 'Plenty of time for boys later, Maggie,' she said. I was almost fourteen at the time.

In spite of my worries about Mam, that summer was one of the happiest for me. I was able to talk to Gareth, who understood my fears, although I was too shy to mention the coming baby to him. I think he knew from Bryn.

I met Gareth's parents when we were out walking one Sunday afternoon. Mam had met Gareth a week or so earlier, and liked him. When she heard that he intended going to university she was delighted. 'He'll help you to get on, Maggie, not hold you back,' she said . . .

I was in my fifteenth year when Helen was born. Mam was in bed for weeks after her birth. Money was as scarce as it had been during the strike, because now Mam could not work.

Davy was still on the farm. Bryn and I knew there was no money for extras, but Dan and Ann, who was now two years old, still expected their twopence each week, one penny for Ann's jelly sweets and a penny for Dan's ten bobby-dazzlers (ten mixed toffees). Bryn now went where I used to hate to go – up the street to ask for six pennyworth of bacon offcuts.

I think Mr Harries often cut a slice off deliberately, because there was often a whole slice in the parcel. That always went to Dad, as did the egg straight from the hen, that Mrs Watkins, who lived in the cottage on top road, often sent down for Mam.

I had decided that if I passed my C.W.B. I would go to London to find work on a newspaper there. I knew that Mam would not approve of my going to London. She had considered the city to be a place of vice and degradation ever since Ivy Thomas came home on holiday from her 'place' in the city, wearing thin stockings and lipstick. I never told her that Ivy smoked as well – that would have been too much for Mam's sweet, narrow mind.

The only thing I did not like to think about was that I should be leaving Gareth, but I considered that he too would leave to go to university if all went well.

Mam was still very weak. It seemed as if Dr Foster was always in our house these days. He ordered a liver extract for her to take as well as glucose powder. She said the medicine was terrible and though she tried to swallow it, it made her sick, so she was given injections instead. Where Dad was finding the money to pay for expensive medicine I do not know. John's sovereigns, hoarded in his Bible, were almost gone, that I did know. I think the men from the Legion were very good at this time, too, though it did not prevent the much-loved piano from leaving its loving home again. Grannie and Grancher helped in all sorts of ways as usual. Dad was too proud to ask for help from Mam's quite wealthy family: they had always despised him and he was aware of it. He disliked them just as much. What they had never been able to accept was that my parents had a happy life and a loving family.

1

2

1. Beatrice Woods with her mother, older sister and two brothers, wearing the new clothes that had been bought for their father's funeral.

2. A recent photograph of the one down, two up house at Dowlais where Beatrice Woods lived with her family of seven.

3. *Beatrice Woods in her twenties.*

4. *Maggie Pryce Jones with her brother.*

5. *Maggie Pryce Jones' mother with baby Ann, she died two years later aged 39.*

6. *Maggie Pryce Jones aged 18.*

7

8

9

7. *Mair McLellan in 1932.*

8. *Mair McLellan with members of the Young Communists League in Mardy.*

9. *Mair McLellan.*

10. *Mair McLellan's uncle Dat.*

11. *Iris Roderick Thomas at a school concert, aged six.*

12. *Dorothy Craig sitting at the window that looked over the Penydarren Tip, 1935.*

13

14

15

13. *Eunice Hughes Thomas, 1935.*

14. *Eunice's mammy for whom she bought the pearls.*

15. *Barbara Walters aged 8, with her miner father. Babs was about to have an operation for tubercular glands.*

16

17

18

16. *Margaret Lloyd, age 7.*

17. *Enid Mavis Mitchell.*

18. *E. M. Mitchell's mother ran a milk round whilst her father worked at the local pit and kept a busy small holding on a mountain top at Pontypridd.*

19

20

19. *Jerusalem Chapel outing to Porthcawl. Heulwen Williams stands at the back in a white hat, next to her mother. Her sister Nanon in matching hat sits in the front with Ewa Bob, c.1930.*

20. *Winifred Griffiths, second left, with husband and family.*

21

22

21. *Edith Davies aged 25 in 1932.*

22. *Edith Davies teaching in 1934 at Abercynon Senior Mixed School.*

CHAPTER 7

DEATH

DEATH

'The only people who were making money were the undertakers,' wrote Beatrice Wood in her account of the effects of poverty quoted in the last chapter. That death was an ever present reality to both sexes and in all age groups has been borne out by the numerous accounts which we as editors had to choose from. Deaths of fathers, husbands, uncles and neighbours from pit accidents, suicide or the effects of coal dust, the deaths of mothers in childbirth or from puerperal fever, pernicious anaemia or the effects of miscarriage, the deaths of young women from consumption, the premature deaths of schoolfriends, siblings and newborn babies. Almost all the contributors had their personal tragedies, which were all too common before the advent of antibiotics and the National Health Service.

The examples selected present a range of experiences and illustrate how death was encountered early on in life. Children were not sheltered from seeing corpses, and the tradition of laying out the corpse in the front room, keeping vigil and inviting members of the community in to pay their last respects gave groups of little girls a fascinating, albeit a rather morbid pastime, as Lucy Arundell's account of visiting Willie in his coffin in the second extract shows. The memorable short story by E. M. Mitchell tells a common tale, even though infant mortality rates were actually in decline in the period.

The thousands of colliery workers who were the victims of the pits are represented by Gertrude Harris' account of the fatal accident suffered by her father on the day her younger brother was born, and by the death of Lucy Arundell's neighbour, Henry Jones, whose post-mortem examination took place, not unusually, on the kitchen table. The mining company's refusal to award compensation to his widow is another common story.

We return to the life histories of Maggie Jones and Beatrice Wood for the two final extracts of this section. Maggie Jones' poignant description of the loss of her mother encompasses so much of the history of women in the valleys in this period. Her death was to transform her daughter's life, as is revealed in the next chapter. Beatrice Wood's family circumstances also worsened, following her father's premature death.

Fairy Albert

~

E. M. Mitchell

'Where's Mammy, where's Mammy?' said Hilary and Brenda together.

'Sh!' Dad held up his hand. 'Quiet now, Mammy's in bed.'

'In bed?' I said in amazement. 'Mammy always gives us breakfast.'

'She caught her foot in a briar last night and fell,' Dad replied, 'and she has to stay in bed for a few days.'

'I 'xpect it's because Mammy's so fat,' said the practical three-year-old Brenda.

Turning to me Dad said, 'You and the girls will have to stay home from school for a few days – Bill can take a note to teacher to explain. I'll need you, Ann, to help with the girls and Mammy.' Bill, my eldest brother, at ten years old was already outside doing his chores, and at seven I was the eldest of the three girls, so I straightened my shoulders and prepared to take on Mammy's jobs.

I wiped the girls' faces and hands with the flannel and combed their hair as best I could. Dad took Mammy some breakfast and we sat down to eat ours. When he came back Dad smiled and said,

'As you've been so good and quiet I have a secret to tell you.'

'A secret,' I breathed. We loved Dad's secrets; there had been so many over the years. 'Tell! Tell! Tell!'

'Well,' he began, 'last night something very special happened – a fairy came to live with us.' Six saucer eyes stared at him.

'A fairy!' we said in unison. 'Where is it?'

'Ssh, now, he's in the bedroom with Mammy.'

'A boy fairy!' we three girls chorused in disgust.

'We're very lucky to have any fairy,' said Dad. 'They rarely stay in houses, maybe he came because you've been good children.'

'What's his name?' asked Hilary.

'Albert,' Dad replied.

'Albert? That's your name, Dad.'

'Well, could be that's why he came here,' answered Dad.

'Can I see Fairy Albert? Please?' Brenda pleaded.

'You shall all see him,' Dad told us, 'but you must be very quiet as Mammy's resting, and we mustn't make a noise as fairies are frightened of noise.' On tiptoe, and scarcely breathing, we entered the bedroom; a quick glance at Mammy, then over to the little basket, where Dad stood, finger on lips. Together we all took our first look at Fairy Albert, who was barely visible. Wrapped in cotton wool, he had a face as big as a Marie biscuit and that was half-hidden by a cotton wool hood.

Within a week Mammy was up and about and Fairy Albert in his basket on the couch. Dr Jenkins called every day and always shook his head as he gazed at Albert. 'He's still with us then.'

'Of course, he likes living here,' we'd say, and the doctor would smile, patting the nearest head. Weeks went by and still Fairy Albert stayed, but I was worried so I told Dad, 'The girls in my class don't believe in fairies, should I tell them about Fairy Albert?'

'Mm,' said Dad. 'Children who don't believe never see fairies and maybe if you told them about Albert they would want him and you wouldn't like that, would you?'

'No! No!' I protested.

'Why not tell them you've got a new brother who's very small.' I breathed a sigh of relief. Not lies really, he was almost like a brother and very, very small.

'How long do you think Fairy Albert will stay with us, Dad?' I asked.

'If we're lucky, about three months. Dr Jenkins said we're very lucky he's stayed this long. I expect it's because he likes living with us.'

Fairy Albert must have liked living with us very much because at one and a half years old he was still with us, propped up amongst the pillows on the couch. He was still very tiny, with pale blonde hair that matched his pale face, but he had vivid blue eyes.

'His eyes are the same colour as yours, Dad,' noted logical Brenda.

'Yes,' Dad said. 'They're called Albert Blue eyes.'

He was too small to play with our toys, they were heavy for him, but Dad had dyed different-sized corks. The dyes came from beet-root for red, onion skin for yellow and rhubarb leaves for green, all boiled. He also dyed some feathers and stuck them in the corks and

Albert, propped up amongst his pillows, would play with them until he fell asleep, often clutching a cork.

At two years old Fairy Albert was still living in our house, hardly any bigger – but then Dad said fairies didn't grow very quickly – but he had grown four very tiny teeth.

'Why can't he eat boiled eggs like us now he's got teeth?' asked Brenda.

'Ah, his tummy's different, fairy tummy you know, that's why Mammy has to beat his eggs in milk.'

'What's that stuff he has from a jar, Dad?'

'That's calves' foot jelly,' said Dad. We all fell about laughing, we knew what calves' hooves looked like.

'How can you get jelly from them?' we hooted.

'For fairies anything's possible,' Dad explained and yes, this we accepted.

When we came home from school it was straight to the couch and his Albert Blue eyes would light up and he would smile at us.

'Tell him where you've been,' Dad would say.

'We've been to school, Fairy Albert.'

'Tell him what school is,' Dad would persist.

'It's a big, big house, big as the field.' Fairy Albert knew how big the field was, Dad carried him out there on fine days to see the horses, dogs, chickens and Mammy's flower garden.

'There are four steps up to the school,' Brenda told him.

'Show him what four is, Brenda,' Dad would urge and she would collect four corks and count them out for him.

'Do you think our Fairy Albert will ever talk, Dad?' Brenda asked.

'Maybe some day, if we keep talking to him, he may learn our language as well as fairy language.'

And talk he did. One day he shouted 'No!' at Brenda when she picked up one of his corks. She jumped and dropped the cork and we all burst out laughing and Albert chuckled too.

When we were sitting on the couch one day, Hilary asked what the lump was on Albert's back.

'Well, well,' said Dad, 'I'm surprised you asked me that. Where else should a fairy keep his wings? I have told you before that fairies don't stay for ever, soon Albert's wings will grow and he will fly away.'

'Up to heaven,' stated Brenda.

'Maybe, maybe. Haven't we been lucky that he stayed in our house so long?'

'Yes, yes, Dad,' we all agreed. Nevertheless we anxiously looked at his wings-holder, not wanting his wings to grow. Doctor Jenkins still called and would always have that amazed look on his face. 'I thought three months at the most,' he told my mother, 'and now he's nearly three years.'

We arrived home from school as usual and ran to the couch. Three neat cushions stood upright along the back – no pillows, no Fairy Albert. We knew without asking that he had grown his wings, but Dad told us that although we couldn't see him he could see us as he soared amongst the clouds.

'In heaven, of course,' said Brenda.

Living with Grandma

~

Lucy Arundell

I was about twelve or thirteen years of age, I think, when the subject of ghosts came up. Weird stories circulated around the classroom, or were told and retold in playtime. We frightened ourselves half to death. No one had actually seen one of these strange phenomena but always knew of someone who had or knew someone who knew someone else who had and so on. Such stories have a habit of taking more upon themselves than was originally intended, especially after the third or fourth telling.

Imaginations went rioting around. It is a wonder we did not die of fright ourselves. Fearful of the dark nights in case these ghoulish fiends came to our own bedsides, we were yet intrigued by the subject. When Maggie Evans invited us to go and look at her little cousin Willie in his coffin we felt it was a challenge. Led on by fascination of the unknown, or perhaps morbid curiosity, three of us went, Maggie, myself, and another girl called Katie.

Maggie knocked on the front door. It was opened by a lady not known to Maggie who, putting on a suitably grave voice, said, 'Please, we've come to see our Willie.' The lady looked us over in turn, then said, 'Well, I don't know. Who are you? Only relations are supposed to come in.' 'That's all right,' said Maggie. 'I'm his cousin and these are my friends who used to take him for walks,' she lied like a trooper. Evidently impressed, the lady replied, 'Come on in then. Don't make a noise. His mam's upstairs trying to get a rest, poor dab.' 'Poor dab' was an everyday expression as one would say 'poor thing' or 'poor soul'.

We crept softly into the parlour. Beneath the window, supported by two chairs, lay the coffin. Nearby, propped against the wall, stood the lid. The brass plate said simply:

'William Henry Morgan
Born October 4th 1916
Died June 17th 1924'

Fear left me as I looked down at him, a still small figure. How could anyone be afraid? Nearly eight years of age, yet hardly big enough to be a four-year-old. There was not much to be seen of Willie, except for the bluish-white face and tiny hands, such fragile hands, folded across his breast. There was a mysterious smile on his face, almost as if he'd found out something that we did not know. He lay there resplendent in new herringbone tweed Norfolk jacket and matching knickerbockers with a grey cap on his head. Feet and legs were encased in long black woollen stockings and heavy laced-up boots. It was probably the first complete outfit he had had since he had been put into his baby garments at birth. Well, the Co-op was a blessing at these times, especially if you had been able to leave a bit of 'divi' in.* I wondered who had put his clothes on. Had it been his mother and had she cried when she did it? The girls tugged at my elbow, 'Come on, Lucy.'

We went back out into the world of the living, where the sun shone hot and brilliant and there were no dark clouds in the sky. We did not talk much on the way home, just our usual farewell, 'So-

---

* dividend paid to members of the Co-operative Wholesale Society.

long', when we parted. I could not remember having seen Willie during his lifetime, and I hoped that dreams of him would not haunt me now that he had died. I also hoped he would not have minded me going to see him for in my heart I felt that I had intruded.

The Valley of my Childhood

~

Gertrude Harris

My father found work at last in the pits after being out of work in London for some time. With no dole in those days, it was hard going and he managed to get enough money together to come to Wales on the 'football' train as they called it. He got work at last in Tonyrheol and had to learn Welsh to be able to speak to the land-lady with whom he lodged as she could not speak English, he worked there for a time, sending mother what money he could to keep us on until he found a house of some kind to bring us to live.

Dad at last found a little cottage at Hafodyrynys. It was a tiny place and called Cwm Cottage, Sunnyside. It was in a bad state but Dad patched it up somehow and on a late September evening we all arrived.

We had come to Crumlin Low Level Station and Dad came to meet us. I was only five years old but still remember the long walk all up the hill. I had to walk as my brothers, who were nine and twelve, had to carry some of the luggage. Dad carried the sister next to me who was three years, and mother the young baby sister who was three months ...

So here we were right from the East End of London in the heart of the Welsh countryside with no home, only odds and ends that Dad had come by and some he had made, but we were all together and in a beautiful spot and lovely garden. It was on the side of the hill with the road going uphill at the back of it so that you could touch the end of the roof ...

Dad worked at the Navvy as we called it, the Navigation Pit at Crumlin, and later at the Hafodyrynys pit as a sinker and repairer. He was not a collier and had to take what work was offered him, this was often very dangerous work and not very well paid . . .

He was working on Sunday repairing the pit, it was nearly finishing time when he fell from one staging to another and was killed instantly.

It's the same old story, the poor pay and he just had to go when there was work. My mother had asked him not to go as she had just had my youngest brother, he was born early Sunday morning and Dad was killed Sunday night.

I had gone to bed but I was not asleep. My mother had her bed in the front room, or parlour downstairs, while she was being confined. She had been lying waiting for Dad to come home, the person who was looking after her had put her right for the night and Dad was to take over when he came home.

Our house was the fourth house from the end of the row and we could always hear when the men were coming home from the pit as they wore heavy nailed boots, so that we would listen for our man and got to know his step. Dad's pal was sent to tell my mother and when he knocked at the door she was surprised, she had thought it was not Dad's step and when she heard the knock and not the door opened, she had at once got frightened as she realized something had happened to my father.

Luckily we had a young woman looking after us and she slept in the next room to me. I knew there was something wrong so I kept very quiet listening and looking out of the window as our bedroom was on the street.

The young woman very quietly went into my brother's room and woke him up and told him mind not to wake us girls as she did not want us down. All this time I could hear talking in whispers and lots of walking about, and presently there was lots of muffled footsteps and I had to look out of the window, there I saw all the workmen had come to bring home my Dad's body, it was covered in dark blankets on a stretcher carried by the men, with a pit lamp at each corner. I was so frightened and afraid to go downstairs to worry my mother. I seemed so utterly alone just then. I laid awake all night not daring to wake my younger sisters and tell them and afraid to go downstairs to find out the news I already knew.

It got so very quiet. When it was nearly daylight I decided to go and look for myself, so I crept downstairs. The stairs led into the living room and there in the corner was my Dad laid out with blankets covering him, so I crept up to him and took them back to see his face, then I saw he was all bruised on the one side. I was still keeping very quiet and went into my mother's room, as I said she was in the front room. She was very surprised to see me and told me what had happened. I said I knew. I had seen my Dad. By this time we were both crying and comforting each other. There were no funeral parlours in those days, we had our loved ones in the house with us until there were buried and in our case Dad was 'laid out', as it was called, by Mrs Davies who lived near and always did that kind of thing. Mrs Davies brought all her own sheets. I guess she kept these specially. So Dad was laid out in the living room and we had to live in the back kitchen and go through all the time to my mother's room, my mother was not allowed to see my father and my aunts kept watch day and night. Poor mother, what she must have gone through, having the baby in the morning and losing her husband in the evening. My brother was named after my father and sad to say he was killed in much the same way but not in the pit, he fell through an asbestos roof and died six hours after the fall.

Living with Grandma

~

Lucy Arundell

Coal governed, controlled, in fact, ruled life within the valley. If you scuffed at the ground beneath your feet you turned it up in black dust. When strong winds blew, gardens were covered in it. When it rained, black rivulets like tears ran down the mountain breasts. The people lived off it, by it, with it. Men died because of it. A miner happily singing his way to work or joking with his butties could be maimed for life or dead before the shift was over. Usually docile ponies could be startled in the confines of their working space, lash out with their hooves and injure their leaders.

Mr Henry Jones lived across the road, opposite our house. His was a happy home, his wife and his mother shared the work and lavished their love on his only son with never a hint of 'mother-in-law' trouble. Miners were never well paid by any standards, yet they kept their homes together with love and pride. Furniture gleamed from years of devoted polishing, and brasses, ranged along the mantle top, reflected borrowed light from coal fires in the evening. Tables were scrubbed until they could not possibly be made whiter, the weekly wash still came up like the driven snow.

William Henry was ten years old, and always given his full name. Grandma said they made their house their God, and William Henry was spoiled. Time would tell, she said. They were making a rod for their backs. I liked William Henry. He too was an 'only child' and given to doing a lot of reading. He was the proud owner of a full set of children's encyclopaedias. He lent them to me one at a time: in return I lent him my annuals, *Tiger Tim, Pip Squeak and Wilfred*, and *Blackies*. Together we did the puzzles, exchanged riddles and found a lot to laugh about.

Suddenly, tragically, it all ended. Mr Jones was brought home in the ambulance one afternoon. His companions said that he had been kicked by a pony, he was in dreadful pain. They laid him on the couch and the doctor came. There was little that he could do and Mr Jones died later the same day. The matter of compensation arose since the accident had occurred below ground. Two eminent doctors came, employees of the company no doubt. They would make an investigation.

The kitchen table was newly scrubbed and washed with Lysol. Everything that could be taken out of the kitchen was removed and the rest covered with freshly laundered sheets, also impregnated with Lysol, and the floor well scrubbed. There, on the kitchen table – that friendliest of all pieces of furniture, around which things great and small are settled daily, for it is the hub of daily life – the great men performed the *post-mortem* examination that was to establish the cause of death. Mr Jones' kidneys were found to be bruised, but they decided that there was no conclusive evidence that the bruising had been caused by the hooves of a pony. The men who had brought the dead man home had not actually seen what happened. They only knew what Mr Jones had told them when they found him lying beside the track. Compensation was therefore ruled out.

'Scandalous,' said Grandma. Everybody knew what had happened. It was a proper cover-up job. 'Well, that's that,' she said summing up. 'The owners beat you down in the end.' She meant, of course, the pit owners. The Joneses moved away after the funeral so I did not see William Henry again. I missed him, he was my first close friend.

Kingfisher of Hope

~

Maggie Pryce Jones

Helen was just seven weeks old on the day that is etched on my memory for ever. It started out as usual. John and I helped dress and feed the baby while Bryn helped Dan to dress for school. Grannie Locke came round as usual to sit with Mam, then Bryn and I hurried on to catch the bus.

It was Friday, late May, sunny; we were looking forward to the Whitsun break. Gareth had kept my seat as usual. It was such an ordinary kind of day: there was nothing to suggest that our family in Pen-y-groes Heol was about to be robbed of happiness, security – even faith.

I was not apprehensive when I was called out of the Algebra lesson to go to the Headmistress' study. I knew that, for once, I was innocent of breaking the school rules – indeed I was quite pleased, and curious to know why I had been sent for. But when I saw our curate sitting near the desk, I knew at once that something was very wrong. He rose as I entered the room, looked at me for a while, sympathetically, then said. 'Your mother is rather poorly today, Maggie; we thought you could help a little with Helen.' As

I turned to leave the room, the head said, softly, 'Try and be brave, dear, and keep up your studying. Remember, knowledge is never wasted.'

Rhys Emmanuel had borrowed a car to fetch me. He was very quiet for most of the way home, and when we reached the door of our house, he caught my hand before following me in and said, 'If you need friends at any time, Maggie, remember that God is always near.' I still had not realized the seriousness of the situation. Mam was going to get well, of course she was. Bryn and I prayed for her every night, pleading with God to help her.

Dad was home from work. It was only when he told me that the police had sent a message asking Grannie Argoed to come at once that I understood how ill Mam was, I remembered the premonition – my dream, and a terrible fear swept over me.

Reverend Emmanuel came back to pray with us. Grannie arrived just as we had finished – she had travelled on the back of Bill's motor bike and took charge. I was in the kitchen with Ann and Helen, Davy sat in the corner with John, the other boys stood outside on the doorstep.

Grannie called out, 'Come and see your mother, Maggie,' and I rose quickly. They had not allowed me to see Mam before. I went to the parlour, where she was lying in the bed, her eyes closed, her lovely chestnut-coloured hair, gone prematurely gray, cut very short. She looked very ill and very old; her eyes were closed, her breath rasping and laboured. She looked at me, but it was her family she was thinking of, for she said, 'Oh God, what will become of my children?'

'I'll look after them, Mam, till you're better,' I said. I don't know whether she heard me. Grannie led me from the room. Our Mam had left us.

Bryn and Dan were inconsolable; Davy, silent, seemed in a daze. He stayed for the funeral, but Grannie took Helen and Bryn back to the farm. Bryn would come back home for school when it was all over. Never again could he believe in God, in spite of the many times the curate spoke to him. 'I asked him to make Mam better, and he didn't,' he would say. Before her death he had read the lessons in church, and I told him that Mam would never want him to stay away, but he never went to a church service afterwards.

The Reverend and Mrs Emmanuel were rocks to whom I clung for many months. She altered her own dark clothes to fit me and she supplied me with hat and gloves, though they had little enough themselves . . .

I could not cry for Mam, the house was too full of strangers busy deciding our futures, aunts and uncles we had not seen for years. They cried about the babies and decided that we should all be put into care.

'Except Maggie and Davy,' said a stranger who called herself Aunt Maud. 'Davy's looking well now; perhaps he'd like to live with us. He can go back down the pit.'

'And Maggie can go into service,' put in long-lost Aunt Tydfil.

The day was saved for us by our wonderful Grannie Argoed. 'I'm taking the baby,' she said in a loud voice, 'and Maggie is better off here looking after the rest of the family than she would be in service.' Then she added, 'If all of you visit and help her one day a week, she'll do fine.' There was murmuring and shaking of heads, but no one challenged her words, God bless her.

Once the funeral was arranged, Dad took no further interest in the proceedings. He shed his responsibilities the day Mam died and now he was sitting in the gwli,* drinking home-made cider and crying with his friends, Will and Stan. The empty frail on one side and the cider bottles on the other spoke ill for the future.

Wednesday's Child

~

Beatrice Wood

My father was never really well. He would have bouts of illnesses, but he would get better. This time he was having a bad bout, and of course a doctor cost money. It was two shillings and sixpence a call. Well, we couldn't afford it. Anyway, he was very ill this time and

---

* Narrow alleyway between houses.

he went into a coma. The ambulance came and took him to hospital. My Auntie Rachel used to look after us while my mother went to visit my father in hospital. My mother came from hospital this day and Auntie Rachel asked, 'How is he today?' My mother burst into tears and said, 'He's gone'. We were all there and, curious as ever, I asked, 'Where is he gone, then, Mam?' She said, 'Gone to God, love.' I said, 'Is he coming back?' trying to hold back my tears, but my big brother cried, so we all cried.

Times were very hard for us now, my mother a widow with five children all under thirteen. The day my father died there was a lot of coming and going and a few hurried telegrams were being sent out, so we children were scattered amongst the neighbours for them to look after us. I was next door in the grocery shop. The lady there was very kind. She gave me fish and chips for my dinner. I had a whole fish to myself. It cost tuppence. I know because I went for it.

When I looked outside I saw a lot of people outside our house, so while the lady was serving a customer, I went to see what they were doing there. I wondered what they wanted – and they were bringing my father home in a coffin. There were four men carrying the coffin and another two carrying the trestles. I strained my neck to see it. Then my sister came and took me into the house.

The chest of drawers had been moved to make room for the coffin. They put it on two trestles and took the lid off. They gave their condolences to my mother, and left.

The house was full of people. All my aunties and uncles were there, and all the neighbours. My sisters and brothers were looking at my father in his coffin, and crying. My auntie was showing them. She asked them to touch his hand because it was said that if you touch a dead person it would help you to forget them. My auntie asked me if I wanted to see my father in his box, as she called it, but I said I didn't want to – I was afraid. 'Anyway,' she said, 'take a quick look at him'. She took me over and lifted me up to see him. His fingers were all brown, so I said, 'Why are his fingers all brown?' My auntie said, 'It's from his smoking. Touch it.'

But I didn't want to touch it – I was too frightened, so she took hold of my hand and forced it onto my father's dead finger. I was terrified. And from that day onwards I was afraid to pass a house with the blinds drawn down because I knew there would be a dead person in the house. I would either cross the road or go round the long way not to pass the house.

My auntie and uncle came back from the funeral. They had tea. My mother had bought a whole pig's head and made two basins of brawn. She also made mustard to go with it, with the help of her neighbours. So they had sandwiches and tea. My mother also bought a whole pound of jam-and-cream cake. We had borrowed the basins and the cups and saucers because ours were all odd ones.

I was eating my sandwich of brawn, and a tear dropped onto my hand. I wiped it off quickly – I didn't want anyone to see me crying. I was thinking how my father loved brawn, and here we were with two basins full and he wasn't able to eat it.

I was wondering how long they would keep him in this place they called heaven. My auntie must have seen the tears because she took out her hanky and wiped my eyes. I felt as though I wanted to get away – anywhere, upstairs or up our den. I wanted to be alone in my grief. I desperately wanted to cry. My throat was burning. Oh, how I wanted to cry.

After the funeral my mother had to get work. My eldest brother was thirteen, sister eleven, me eight, my brother six, and the baby four. So to make ends meet my mother took a job cleaning from nine in the morning until three in the afternoon. She used to get us children up about seven o'clock. Because we couldn't afford coal now at ninepence a sack, we three eldest used to go up to the engine lines and pick up the cokes that fell out of the engine boilers. They would be red hot. We used to have a game to see which of us could pick up the hottest one. Of course, my brother always won. Then we came home to have our breakfast of bread and jam, providing we could get some empty jam tins from the bakehouse that was a few yards from where we lived. There was one man who was very kind – he would leave more jam in the tin than he ought to have . . .

I was missing my father a lot now. Who was this God who wouldn't reveal himself to me, and was taking everyone I loved away from me? I couldn't accept the fact that he had gone. I used to look in the street at the men to see if I could see him coming home. I used to wonder if they had made a mistake in the hospital. After all, there were a lot of men there – they could have been mistaken. And Tom was a very common name. I was afraid now that something would happen to my mother. I used to lie awake at night listening to hear if she was breathing, and if I thought I couldn't hear her I would call her to ask her the time just to hear her voice. Then I would be reassured and go to sleep.

My mother must have been out of her mind with worry. She was knitting, sewing and cleaning, but still couldn't make ends meet.

My mother wanted a sewing machine. She always wanted one but could never get together the two shillings and sixpence deposit. The machine cost five pounds – a lot of money in those days. It was two and sixpence deposit and sixpence a week. Anyway, she had eleven pounds insurance money after my father died – she used to pay a penny a week on it. So after paying for the funeral expenses – which came to about three pounds – and buying black costumes for us girls with white blouses trimmed with black, and sailor suits for the boys and shoes and stockings for us all, she was left with just about enough for the deposit.

She had her machine off our packman. She used to buy men's second-hand trousers in the market and make two pairs of trousers for the boys out of one pair. Then she used to alter dresses for my sister and me, also bought from the second-hand stall in the market. She also took some sewing in, now that she had the machine.

She thought she would always be able to pay for it every week, but she fell behind with her payments, so it was put into the hands of a bailiff. Now, these men were big overpowering men. Most had been in the Police force, and had retired and taken on the job.

The bailiff's house was in the town. We children used to take the money down in turns. Not one of us wanted to go – we were afraid of him. Anyway, it was my turn this week. I used to hate it. I was very frightened of him – he was so big. His house was about a mile from where we lived. I walked up to the house. The door was huge. I could only just reach the knocker. I knocked it. My heart was now pounding and my knees were shaking with fright. He came to the door and I handed him the card and the sixpence. He looked at me hard and said, 'Where is the other sixpence? Your mother didn't pay last week,' he shouted, and said, 'You tell your mother from me she didn't pay last week and I want that sixpence today – or I will be up there for it.' I was terrified – we hadn't long buried my father and I hadn't got over it. I felt more protective towards my mother now, since she didn't have a man to help her fight her battles. So I was afraid for her. I had visions, as I was walking home, of my mother between two policemen, being dragged off to jail. I started to cry. By the time I got home I was sobbing. I told my mother what he said, and asking at the same time, 'Will he take you to jail, Mam, will he?' 'No, I am not going to jail. Look, I have finished these socks – I will get sixpence for them'. She sent my sister with the socks to the lady she had done them for and got the sixpence, but no way was I going back down with the sixpence. My eldest brother had to go – it was a long walk there and back.

In our school they were giving free boots away for children without fathers and, believe me, there were plenty of children about without fathers, what with tuberculosis and emphysema. Anyway, I wasn't lucky, but two of my brothers were – they had a pair each. My mother always used to put studs in our boots. She would squat on the floor with the last between her legs and fill her mouth with studs and fill our boots with them.

The first Christmas my father wasn't with us, my mother couldn't afford to give us children anything for Christmas. She was worried sick. She didn't tell us children, but my sister had overheard her telling a neighbour that she had been having a rough time since my father died.

A local character who lived in our town, but spent all his days in Dowlais doing odd jobs for tradespeople, knew everyone in our street and also knew our circumstances and understood. He said to my mother, 'You leave it to me and don't worry – they won't be without'. She didn't see him all day, then when he came back that night he handed her a paper bag. Inside was a little teddy bear about six inches high, a toy deck-chair, a whip and top, a small wooden horse about six inches long made out of fretwork, and a round piece of wood with four chicks on it made of wood, with a piece of string hanging from it with a wooden ball attached, so that when you swung the ball on the string around, the chicks would do pecking motions. That, too, was made out of fretwork. He remembered us all – we all had some little thing . . .

As it was the first Christmas we were without my father, my auntie sent us five envelopes with each of our names on, and, believe it or not, they came on Christmas Day, so my mother said. I think she had them in the week and kept them for Christmas Day. There was great excitement as we opened our envelopes. Inside was a handkerchief with a nursery rhyme on it and a silver thruppenny bit. We were over the moon comparing our hankies. Then, to make our Christmas complete, somebody gave us a food parcel. My eldest brother answered the door and didn't ask who it was from. They just handed in the parcel. It might have been from the Salvation Army or the Quakers. We never found out who it was from, but they would never know how grateful we were. There was more excitement now opening the parcel. We all stood around the table to see my mother opening it – and would you believe it? It must have been someone who knew us because there was something for each of us. There were three smoker's outfits for the boys (a smoker's outfit was a little box with liquorice pipes and sweet cigarettes), two cardboard plates with sweet eggs and bacon. We were so excited. Beside that, there was a Christmas pudding, a Christmas cake, a piece of home-smoked ham, some tea, sugar, margarine and a tin of condensed milk. To think my mother had been worried sick at the beginning of the week, and now we were surrounded with goodwill.

I was wishing my father was here to see all this food and share it. He would have loved a slice of ham with mustard. I wanted to cry. My emotions were getting the better of me. I didn't want to show everybody I wanted to cry, so I went up to our den in the graveyard. I wanted to see my father so badly. It was five months since he had died; to me it was eternity. How I missed him. I was still looking at the men in the street to see if he was coming home. I had a little weep to myself. It was funny – I wanted to laugh as well. My stomach was all twisted inside. I was happy, yet sad.

CHAPTER 8

LITTLE MOTHERS, LITTLE SKIVVIES

LITTLE MOTHERS, LITTLE SKIVVIES

From an early age, girls were expected to be 'Little Mothers', caring for siblings and helping with housework and cooking. It was common during the inter-war years for one daughter to be kept at home to help, having very little choice in the planning of her future after leaving elementary school. Duty to the family would override any personal wishes, although choices were extremely limited in any case. Maggie Pryce Jones' experience following her mother's death illustrates the expectations placed upon older daughters to take over a mothering rôle in the event of tragedy, and the great responsibility and personal sacrifice this entailed.

The economic structure of valleys' society and the limited opportunities for secondary education, discussed in the introductory chapter, meant that most young girls who went out to work after leaving school worked either in domestic service or in shops. Lucy Arundell's unhappy experience shows how girls' cheap labour was often misused locally.

Both Beatrice Wood and her sister spent periods in England as domestic servants. Domestic service, viewed as the most suitable occupation for working class girls, being a preparation for home-making, was in crisis at this time due to a dearth of servants. The government's solution to both the middle classes' 'servant problem' and to the problem of unemployment among young women was to encourage girls into service.

Schemes for the training of female domestic servants included the establishment of a number of Home Training Centres in the South Wales valley towns from 1921, for example, in Aberdare, Maesteg, Neath, Pontypridd and Merthyr Tydfil. The successful completion of a short course led to the offer of a post, but this was usually far from home, commonly in London or the Home Counties. 1936-7 was the peak year of juvenile migration, with around 10,000 young people leaving South Wales. Yet, many girls refused jobs in domestic service, much to the annoyance of government agencies. Ginzberg, (see introductory chapter), writing on the basis of his observations of South Wales in the 1930s, speculated that to say 'no' to the government was one of the few pleasures available to young girls who had no power to protest. However, most were unable to refuse, and their experiences were often negative ones.

The trauma of cultural transition, loneliness and harsh discipline of the regimes under which they worked caused many to desert their posts, and Beatrice Woods' story is by no means uncommon. Many girls returned from service because of illness or if their mothers were ill. The strong feelings of familial duty were commented upon in this context at the time, as was the high incidence of TB among Welsh domestic servants in the 1930s, a condition which owed much to the impoverished circumstances of their childhoods during the 1920s. Many juveniles were sent to reconditioning centres to build up their health before being transferred to positions in England, and this included girls as well as boys. The great gulf between the employers and employees is amusingly illustrated by Beatrice's sister's adoption of gentrified manners on her return from service, but underlying the lightheartedness lies a deep social and geographical division which many young girls from South Wales came face to face with during the Depression.

Having left her post in London, Beatrice returned to dodging the Means Test inspector. The 'homework' which she and her mother had secured for themselves had to be concealed for fear of having benefit payments withdrawn. The family's position was such that the risk had to be taken, and the sewing which they took in, for which they were paid a pittance, is yet another example of how the labour of girls and women was exploited.

Kingfisher of Hope

~

Maggie Pryce Jones

Mam was thirty-nine when she died. She was laid to rest beside where her parents lay. Her earthen grave was a mass of flowers, her funeral hymn the music which had accompanied her from her home to her last resting place. 'She would have liked that,' we found comfort in saying, over and over again, in the days that followed.

John was never the same afterwards; he mourned her till the day he died. His place in our house was no longer sure, for Dad wanted a lodger more to his own taste. The thought that he was helping us gave John the courage to stand Dad's taunts, and there were many of them in the days and months which followed.

Grannie had arranged the funeral tea just as Mam would have done for anyone else: nothing was stinted. As usual, the men went for a drink while the women sat gossiping over a cup of tea. They sat in the parlour, these strange women, whispering amongst themselves, a few of them looking around for 'a little memento of poor Jane', whom they had failed to remember when she was alive. Grannie ended speculation abruptly. 'There's still a family here,' she said, 'and what little there is belongs to them.' As soon as the men came back, the visitors left us to sort out our many problems for ourselves.

The days passed in a whirl. I was not used to looking after a house and family, let alone one with a baby not quite two years old. It was one thing helping Mam; being in sole charge was quite different. Dad's only contribution was to give me money each Friday and let me carry on as best I could.

I learned to clean the house, easy enough because I had helped Mam often. I had to kneel and scrub the stone floor, then sand it, which was much harder than it looked. I learned to wash and iron, though my whites were often yellow because I had used too much bleach. Mam had never used bleach, but I could not do without it. Megan's Dad gave me good advice; he and Laura, my other neighbour, were very good to us.

I tried to iron on the scrubbed top of the table, testing the heavy iron's heat with my damp fingertip as I had so often watched Mam do. The scars on my arms bear witness to the fact that I was not a proficient tester of irons. I could not turn the irons over for testing without them turning back onto my arms.

I persevered with the cooking, trying to make the meals that Mam had cooked. One day, as I prepared the potatoes for a hotpot, I realized that I was never going to see her again. Until that moment I had been too busy to think; it had been as if she were on holiday and would be back one day. I wept bitterly with the pain of accepting her death, and felt better for it, but the pain was with me for many months.

Grannie came often from the farm, but Mam's family never again came near. I felt bitter for her sake.

My time was spent learning to keep a house clean and a family fed. The old widower who lived near would often call me in and give me simple recipes to try out. They had to be cheap because Dad was drinking heavily. He gave me hints on how to make housework easier by using paraffin – he used it in many ways, ranging from a gargle to washing up – and John would take Ann for long walks so that I could get my work done.

The examination results came out. I had passed, and Gareth had the credits he needed to go to university. We were both happy. Although my own plans were finished and I felt that I was trapped in the valley for ever, I was delighted for him.

Helen was thriving with Grannie and our aunties at Argoed. Ann was doing well with me; the boys seemed settled, although I often heard them crying in bed. Bryn was determined to leave school at fourteen; he had great ability, but I knew that, like me, he would be unable to go to university. There was no one to battle for us now.

Living with Grandma

~

Lucy Arundell

The card in the shop window said:

> WANTED: Clean honest girl for daily work.
> No cooking.
> APPLY: Mrs R. Thomas, 20 Clarence Street.

I found the house and knocked on the door. My heart thumped and I half hoped that the door would not open. It was the first time in my life that I had done anything so important without asking Grandma first about it. She had never encouraged me to use my own initiative. Mrs Thomas asked me inside. The house was bigger than ours, the furniture was very new and very modern. I was led through to the back of the house, the kitchen. She looked me up and down and asked me some questions. I must have given the right answers for she said, 'You are small for your age, you don't look very strong but you seem rather bright. I'll take you on a month's trial. Come along on Monday morning at a quarter to seven and I'll show you what I want you to do. You will get three meals a day and half-a-crown on Saturdays.'

Grandma seemed rather amused to think that I had got myself a job. I think she was pleased but was not going to say: 'I don't think the money is very good, but I suppose getting your meals there is a consideration. We'll have to see how it goes.' ...

I presented myself for work on the Monday morning and was let in by Mrs Thomas. There was a fire going in the huge old-fashioned range and a kettle singing on the hob. She made a small pot of tea, told me to sit down, and poured out a cup for each of us. She was already seated, wearing a pink satin dressing-gown. I thought that that was rather forward of her. I understood from Grandma that dressing-gowns were not be seen outside of bed-rooms unless one was ill.

My general instructions came quick and sharp: 'I'll give you a key to the front door so that you can let yourself in when you come. Your first job will be to clean the range, light the fire and boil the kettle. Mr Thomas and I will have our tea in bed not later than seven thirty. If the fire is slow you may boil the kettle on the gas ring in the scullery, but only if it is absolutely necessary. I like to keep the gas bill as low as possible.'

I was looking at the great range and wondering how I'd ever get it cleaned and operating by eight o'clock, never mind half past seven. However, my employer had plenty more for me to do. Whilst Mr and Mrs Thomas were enjoying their tea in bed and preparing themselves for a new day, I would be 'doing' the front step and porch, then cleaning out the fireplace in the Lounge – they could not bring themselves to have a parlour or sitting room like everyone else – laying the fire and dusting and tidying the room. This meant brushing the carpet and mopping the surrounds which were polished wood. Have own breakfast in scullery, all meals cooked by Madam. Oh, that was another thing – always address her as 'Madam' and Mr Thomas as 'Sir' when spoken to. Wash up the breakfast things, clean and tidy the scullery, sweep out or swill – according to its needs – the back yard and outside lavatory. Do the upstairs landings, stairs and bathroom. Tidy and dust Madam's bedroom, except on Fridays when it had a good turn out. This applied to all the rooms, each having its own special day. Madam helped with this work. Have own dinner in scullery, half an hour allowed for sit down. Wash up, wash self, put on clean pinny in case Madam requires you to answer the front door. Do errands or any other little thing that Madam can think up for you. Have own tea, lay tea in kitchen for Sir and Madam. Sir comes home at six o'clock. Go home at five thirty, perhaps I should have said stagger home! Being new to such a routine and so much work I never finished the jobs as quickly as Madam would have liked. Often I had to carry some work over into the afternoon, but she did not say much about it. She did once remark, 'You are very slow, but you are thorough.' I took that as more of a compliment than a complaint.

Sir worked in the local Gas offices, Madam's father was some kind of an official up at the pit, and Madam had ideas far above her station in life. Her main ambition was to get rich quick, the quicker the better. She needed this in order to give herself all those little luxuries she felt she should rightfully have. I have not mentioned the 'Middle Room'. It was not part of my job to clean in there. It was Madam's shop. She sold ladies' wear to her friends and acquaintances, and other items of jewellery, fine china and handbags. She did not allow me to touch anything in there because some of the china and porcelain was very beautiful and very expensive. Sometimes when she went out I would creep in to have a look around. It was a veritable Aladdin's cave. A regular stream of customers came to try on garments or purchase a gift from the treasures there. I thought it was a splendid idea, having a little shop like that. When I told Grandma about it, however, she had very different views. 'Backroom trade,' she said. 'Backroom traders. Ought to be stopped.' 'But why? She has a lot of customers.' 'Oh I've no doubt about that,' replied Grandma in disgust, 'but it's cheating and should be reported to the proper authorities.'

I still did not understand her attitude: 'They are taking the bread out of the mouths of good honest businessmen. Hiding away their shops in back rooms so that they don't have to pay rates.' I had not known about that. She went on, 'Honest shopkeepers have to try to make a decent living and pay the shop rates. People like her don't need the money, it's just greed and should be reported.' I thought it best not to bring the subject up again in case Grandma got really inflamed about it and did something positive. She was, of course, thinking about her own sons, and the way they had worked to get established in their own businesses, good honest men.

I kept my job right through the winter and up to the following spring. The good effect that good regular meals should have had was quickly broken away by the amount of hard work and running about I had to do. I began to get very tired and Grandma sometimes had difficulty in rousing me in the mornings. Scared of being late, I would run off without a hot drink, snatching a couple of biscuits to eat on the way. She got cross about it: 'It's worse than slavery. Poor we might be but we don't need this. You had better leave, give in your notice before you make yourself really ill.'

I gave in notice in fear and trembling. Madam just could not believe her ears: 'Leave, leave a good steady job?' She gave me a new hat from her 'spring collection', and tried other ways to coax me to stay on. When it came to Saturday night I said firmly that I would not be coming any more. 'Grandma won't let me,' I excused myself. Madam laughed out loud. 'Won't let you?' she said as if it were a joke. 'Why, what can she do? She can't stop you if you want to come.' Fishing around in my mind for a suitable reply I said, 'Grandma is going to report you for dodging the rates with your shop in the back room.' A look of paralysed shock spread over her face. I just picked my half-crown up from the table and ran before Madam forgot she was a lady.

Wednesday's Child

~

Beatrice Wood

My sister was like my mother – strong-spirited, too strong some-times for my mother when she would defy her. She was more rebellious than I was. Where I would worry if I was five minutes late coming in at night, she would put up with the consequences when she got in. She always knew better than me, and used to look after me a lot. But she would sneak off without me if she could, because I was always trailing behind . . .

When she was fourteen and left school there was no work about apart from service. She saw life different. She realised not everyone used newspaper for a tablecloth, or newspaper for use in the lavatory. She worked in a big house and she wanted to change all our manners. She said one day, 'They use table napkins where I work.' 'So what?' said my brother, and went out to the lavatory and brought in some squares of newspaper from behind the lavatory door. 'Here are table napkins,' he said. We were hysterical.

Then she said, 'They use soup plates to eat their soup.' Well, we couldn't better that. So she went on, 'And they have a cloth tablecloth on their table, not like our newspaper one.'

'Oh, yes,' said my mother, 'but they couldn't read the news while they were eating, like we can, can they?'

Then my sister was trying to change our table manners. My youngest brother used to have the habit of leaving his teaspoon in the cup while he was drinking tea. It used to irritate us all, so my sister told him to take it out of the cup, but he wouldn't.

'Tell him, Mam,' she said.

'Oh, leave him alone,' said my mother, 'he's enjoying it. Be thankful you've got tea to put the spoon in.'

My sister was livid now. 'Pigs,' she said, 'you're all pigs.'

Then my middle brother used to love condensed milk, and he would put his finger into the tin and scrape some out. My sister caught him one day and told my mother about his filthy dirty habits. It was alright when she was doing it before she started to work.

Mealtimes were getting murder now with all these high faluting ideas, as my mother used to say. I put my tea in my saucer to cool it, as I always did. So did she at one time if it was too hot. We used to put it in a saucer and blow on it to cool it. Not only was it not nice, she said, but I was always slurping it as well. If I did that in the house where she worked, I would have to go without food all day. 'Big Deal!' That wouldn't worry me. I had often gone without food.

Then she wanted my mother to wear earrings. My mother! Just imagine – with a sack apron and a scrubbing brush in her hand. Now, there's a combination for you! But who could blame her for wanting to lift herself out of this environment we were in?

She always wanted to be somebody. I think if she had been born in another era she would have made something of herself. She was a go-getter and a trier, and she was like my mother – a good strong spirit. But she, too, was deprived of blossoming. We were kept down in our places. We weren't allowed to reach our full potential. But for all that, she wouldn't be trampled on . . .

I was leaving school now. Fourteen was the leaving age. The Government had a new scheme. They were going to take about thirty girls from different schools for them to become domestic servants because there was no work around for school leavers. They picked three from my class. I was one of the three. We had to go to the Town Hall for an interview with the other girls from the other schools. Our mothers had to come with us. We were seen one by one in this room in the Town Hall where there were about five or six men and women. They were throwing questions at you. It was like the third degree! You would think I was being interviewed to be a brain surgeon, not a skivvy. Anyway, I must have given the right answers because I was picked with two other girls from my class. We were going to get ninepence a day and our dinner while we were training for six months. The training school was about a mile from where I lived. We used to walk there and back. We didn't mind walking down there, but it was all uphill coming back.

We used to be ten girls in cookery, ten doing housework and ten would be learning to lay tables and how to answer the door and the phone – thirty girls in all. Then the following week we would change over . . .

We did our six months in the domestic school. Now we had to go away to work. I wasn't yet fifteen, and I was a real home bird. I never wanted to go away. My mother was upset. She didn't want me to go, either, but if I didn't go they wouldn't give me any money, such as dole or Parish, because they would say that there was a job for me to go to. So I had to go. They were sending me to London, so far away. The furthest I had ever been in my life was once to Barry Island and once to Abergavenny. We had no control over our lives. Even our bodies didn't seem to belong to us. It wasn't what we wanted, it was what they wanted. I was bewildered and frightened.

My mother came to the station to see me off. She was crying, so I started to cry. As the train was pulling out of the station my mother was shouting, 'If you don't like it, you come home. We will manage somehow.' I sat down on the train seat and I started to think of all the things I had heard about London. Of how young girls were being kidnapped and taken abroad, never to be heard of again. They called it the white slave traffic. And the Mafia, the murders that occurred there every day, the gangsters and the prostitutes.

What kind of place was I going to? I got panicky. If the train wasn't going so fast I would get out. A tear dropped on to my brown paper parcel that my clothes were wrapped up in. I quickly brushed it away before anyone saw it. I was so unhappy.

There were two men and one woman in the same carriage. I was glad there was a woman there. I looked at the man in the corner seat. His eyes were dark – a sure sign that he was sinister. Well, they always were in my red letter book. Anyway, I looked under my eyes with my head down. That man in the corner kept looking at me. I wondered if he was thinking to himself, 'When the train stops there's another victim for me'. I couldn't keep still, I kept fidgeting on my seat. My brown paper parcel fell to the floor. The man sitting opposite me bent down to pick it up. Our heads nearly collided. I thanked him. I didn't want to get too friendly because even he was now looking sinister. I wondered if he was the Mafia. Then the woman – she could be his accomplice. Here I was surrounded by a kidnapper, the Mafia, a murderer and a woman accomplice, and I was very frightened.

I thought about home, and of my mother getting the news of my death. 'Young girl killed on a train by a gangster, and all her belongings in a brown paper bag stolen . . .'

I was very glad to get out of that train, but I was bewildered. The station was full of people rushing everywhere, and the engine was letting off steam. It was like a foreign country. The people were all talking funny. I couldn't understand them. Then someone touched me on my arm. I jumped and gave a little scream. It was the man that was supposed to meet me. He had seen the badge on my coat. I felt like a slave girl in a slave market being sold. It didn't seem real – me in London being sold. Anyway, the man said, 'I am Mr Clark, the chauffeur. I've come to collect you'. He took me to the waiting car. He wanted to carry my brown paper parcel, but I wasn't leaving go of that. We got to the car, the first ever ride in my life . . .

The car stopped outside a batch of very large houses, three storeys high, and looking very grey and drab. We got out of the car and I was handed over to one of the maids of the house to show me my quarters. She was a Scots lady, and I couldn't understand a word she was saying. She must have told me to take my coat off because she was tugging at it. She must have thought I was dumb. I had a lump in my chest and my throat was hurting. I wanted to cry. I took my coat off. Another girl came to show me where to put it. I went into the room she indicated and put my coat on a nail on the wall. My few belongings were in the brown paper parcel. I could hear the maids arguing amongst themselves about me not using their lockers. They needn't have worried! I had nothing of value worth putting in their lockers. There was a shelf behind the bed on the wall that they said was mine. That would be big enough for my belongings. I looked around the room. The floor was red cold tiles – there were no mats. The beds were bunk beds. The walls were dark green – no pictures on the walls. A cold, drab room. We were not allowed to put the light on during the day, they told me.

I went to bed that night and cried my eyes out. I missed my brick. The bed was cold. How I would have loved my hot brick to keep me warm.

I got up in the morning at six o'clock. I was dead tired – I hadn't slept half the night. I was shown what rooms I had to do. I had four fires to light. I was a bag of nerves. I didn't know where anything was, and they weren't falling over themselves to show me, so I watched where they were getting their things. So by trial and error I had my fires lit.

My white apron was filthy. I was told off for not putting a green one on. Well, how was I to know? Nobody told me and I wasn't psychic. Then it was time for breakfast. I was to clean a whole floor. There were eight rooms, four each side of the landing. I was told not to be too long because I was to help with the breakfast trays and also help to clean the vegetables for dinner.

Then, once dinner was over, I had to help to wash all the pots and pans in a huge sink. I could only just reach it. Then I was told to scrape the grease off the floor and help to scrub it. Then there was the silver to clean. They told me that the silver was cleaned only once every two weeks. I had come the week it had to be cleaned.

We used to work from six o'clock in the morning until about eight o'clock at night. I used to go straight to bed most nights – I used to be tired out. Of course, we had half an hour for breakfast, half an hour for lunch (as they used to call dinner time) and an hour for tea, which they used to call dinner time. It was all so confusing.

I desperately wanted to go home to my three-roomed condemned house, where I felt cocooned, safe and warm. I felt so alone and unhappy, and I began to suspect everyone again. I saw a notice – 'The Underground'. Oh! how I wished I could go down there and just jump on a train for home. I would put up with the fleas, black pats and bugs, yes, even the Means Test man.

I was in London for three months when I had a letter off my mother to come home, she wanted me home. Was I glad? So I went home. I would never ever go away again, not ever.

When I got home my mother told me she used to lie awake at

nights thinking and worrying about me. She was very glad to see me home. And believe me, so was I. I wondered how many more mothers were lying awake at night worrying about their lovely young boys who had to go away to look for work. I had to go to the Parish. I couldn't claim any dole money because I had given up my job. After six weeks they gave me six shillings a week, saying, 'If and when I started work, I would have to pay them back.' . . .

The Quakers brought in a new thing. We had never heard of it before. It was called homework. A firm would send the stuff to the Quakers and they would give it out and give you a date when they wanted it back, and you were expected to finish it by that date.

The work was thirty-six yards of green braid. The braid was always green, and ribbons cut into an inch and a half long of different colours. Then you would pin your braid to the table or wherever you were working and make a daisy out of the ribbon in alternative colours, and sew it on to the braid, which meant you had to make two hundred and sixty daisies for every thirty-six yards of braid, and we got paid one shilling and thruppence for it. At one time it was ninepence until they gave us a rise.

We worked very hard on them. The yards never seemed to end sometimes – especially the last few yards. Sometimes we would have about twelve yards to do at twelve o'clock at night. We would be up until the early hours of the morning because if you didn't finish it to time, they wouldn't give you any more homework.

The Means Test man was still around. We should have told him that we were getting one and thruppence, but we didn't. If he knew, he would stop one and thruppence of our money. And besides, that was the only way we could get our own back on them.

He knew about the homework because someone was caught doing it, so he was always on the lookout for it. The trouble was, the ribbons were so small and kept on falling onto the floor, and we only had the one room downstairs. So every time we heard a knock on the door there was a mad scramble to pick them up in case it was the Means Test man. So my mother kept her door locked, so he had to knock. The people who had a front room were all right because all they had to do was shut the door. We used to do rosettes as well with a clamp on the table, but if the Means Test man came around we couldn't get the clamp off quickly enough, so we kept a piece of cloth to throw over it.

I used to have to go out while he was there because every time he put his book down I would give a little gasp in case he accidentally pulled off the cloth. So my mother made me go out until he had gone. Sometimes my mother and I would work on the braid together, one at each end and meet in the middle. The place would be cluttered up with ribbons and cotton. We had to sew them in alternative colours. I still remember the order they had to be sewn on. It was pink, sky, coral, lemon and mauve. Sometimes, if you were talking, you would lose your concentration and put the wrong colour on. I have seen me doing about a yard of the wrong colour and having to undo it all.

CHAPTER 9

LOVE
AND MARRIAGE

LOVE AND MARRIAGE

From the early excitement of attraction and courtship through the experiences of young wives to the time-hardened relationship of Grandma and Grandpa Arundell, this chapter deals with common themes and experiences mainly through portraits of individual women.

The snapshot of Bopa Kate in the first extract provides two contrasting images and brings into sharp focus the transformation of a slim young woman to a matronly, care-worn figure not so many years later. The early ageing of the women of the valleys was one feature repeatedly commented upon by observers in South Wales during the depression years.

Beatrice Wood's lighthearted memories of teenage boyfriends in the second extract demonstrates the extent of a mother's control over her daughters and the worries and hopes which accompanied adolescent courtship, while 'Bopa Pol' in the fourth extract (another portrait drawn from the vantage point of childhood) reveals an underlying sadness, the consequence of the concealment of a pre-marital pregnancy. Despite the strained circumstances, the memories are happy ones, and the mutually supportive relationship between two married sisters helps make the story's lasting impression a positive, yet poignant one.

In the experience of Rhona, the central character in Florence Allen's unpublished autobiographical novel 'Black Velvet', set during and soon after 1926, (third and fifth extract), marriage into a mining family in another valley is a culture shock which is soon accompanied by a loss of personal freedom as she struggles to live up to the expectations her husband's family has of young brides. Her marriage suffers as a consequence, especially after the death of her mother-in-law, Martha. Here again, the relationships between women are drawn out, as well as those with the opposite sex.

The continuation of the story of the family of Mair Eluned McLellan, provides a rare insight into the motives of a mother who is contemplating self-induced abortion, and threatening suicide after finding herself pregnant again. As noted in the introductory chapter, it is difficult to estimate the extent of terminations of pregnancy in the period, but economic hardship certainly made the contemplation of abortion more likely, and may have had an effect on the higher incidence of known terminations. Depression caused by unemployment and poverty led to suicides becoming more common during this period too, although fewer women than men took their own lives.

The final extract is an amusing portrait of a marital relationship which has long turned sour – if ever it had been sweet. Despite Grandpa's flight, there remains no doubt that Grandma is by far the stronger half of the partnership. Even her husband's desertion of her fails to elucidate any show of emotion or sympathy. As a result, her young grand-daughter's life becomes even less pleasant than before.

Thanks for the Memories
(Bopa Kate)

~

Iris Roderick Thomas

The term Bopa may be unknown to the stranger or the foreigner in our midst, and somewhat perplexing, yet every Welsh child had one at least, and mine was Bopa Kate. She was Mamma's only sister, and entered on the Register of Births as Catherine Mary Jones, but known to the family as Kate.

Each time the family album was sacredly opened to help pass the final hours of a boring evening, trying to entertain an equally boring guest, I'd wait in feverish anticipation for a particular page. For more than an hour, as I shifted my feet from one rung of the chair to the other, I smirked secretly, as I repeated parrot fashion how that snap was taken in Barry, and one in the Mumbles. On I'd go until turning to this special photograph, I'd do a quick count down from ten to zero and wait for the usual reaction. As if prodded by a needle, the up to then disinterested expression on the gentleman's face would give way to unconcealed excitement, and gasps of astonishment, as a vivacious, bobbed hair young woman met his gaze. She wore a high necked blouse, fastened from the lace collar to the seventeen inch waist by at least thirty pearl buttons. From this wasp waist to her slender ankles she was moulded into a pencil slim skirt, one could not but help wonder how she managed to walk at all. The whole concept created the impression of an egg-timer, but it was the long inviting split from above the knee to the skirt hem, brazenly exposing a well-developed calf, which caused all the excitement. To further the fancy of wild abandonment that radiated from this exquisite creature, nothing less than the Devil's weed protruded from an ebony cigarette holder, carelessly suspended between her lips, and held in a precocious pose by a comely young sensual arm. To all intent and purpose, this siren in the form of Catherine Mary Jones seemed to be draped on a wicker fence enshrouded by roses and twisting honeysuckle, an illusion conjured up by the local photographer in his den of iniquity, over the meat and pie shop.

How often after being kissed, squeezed and hugged to a pulp by rotund, happy Bopa Kate did I try to see her as she had been, but it was utterly impossible. The shapeless form bore no resemblance to the sylph-like creature with the wasp waist in that photograph. Even the Devil's weed had been confiscated for ever, by a stern, forbidding husband. If at a loose end, I would wander over to the dresser, unlock the door, thumb through the album until I came to that magical snapshot, then sit and ponder how one could change so completely in such a short period of time, then I'd close the album as it was far beyond my comprehension to fathom it out.

Wednesday's Child

~

Beatrice Wood

My friend and I were both sixteen and of course after the boys, but no way would my mother let me wear make-up. Only sluts wore make-up, she used to say. Anyway I never had any money to buy it. We did once buy a tin of Snowfire cream between us. It cost thruppence. We paid one and a half pence towards it. I couldn't keep it in my house – my mother would kill me – so my friend kept it. We couldn't afford lipstick, so my friend's bedroom paper had all little red roses on it. They were faded now, but you could still get some colour off it – so we used to spit on our finger and rub it on the roses to get a bit of colour for our lips. There were hardly any roses left around the mirror because we had rubbed them off. But I used to have to wipe it off before I went home.

We used to use curling tongs to curl our hair with. You would put them into the fire to get them hot, then you would try them out on a piece of paper.

The trouble was there was no thermostat control on them in those days, and the tongs was often too hot. Many girls went around with singed hair.

There was no setting lotion, either, so we used to mix sugar and water together and set our hair on it. Our hair used to dry stiff with the sugar. Mind you, in the summer we would have all the flies and bees following us around.

Then, if we wanted to colour our hair, we used to boil onion peelings. The water would go brown. We were stinking with onions, but it would colour your hair a bit.

Perms had come out now; they cost five shillings each. I had a job looking after three children, one eight, one six and one four years old. My mother used to have six shillings and sixpence, and I had one and sixpence pocket money. So by paying sixpence a week on a Club card, I was able to have my hair permed once I had reached five shillings. How I well remember having my first perm with all the paraphernalia on your head. You thought your neck was going to break. In the curl you would have an iron clamp, and they were solid iron, and believe me, you had a lot of curls. Then it would be attached to something above you in case it would fall off. The contraptions felt they weighed a ton. It took about three and a half hours, or maybe five hours. And boy! was it worth it. I would have stood another four hours to get the results I had. I was over the moon. My hair had always been straight, and I always wanted curly hair. I used to go around and shake my head just to prove it wouldn't go straight.

I used to go out with a boy, but my mother found out and didn't like him. Mind you, my mother wouldn't like any boy my sister and I went out with. Anyway, she kept me in this night, and my boy-friend was hanging around at the top of our street hoping to see me. My friend, who lived opposite, had told me that my boy-friend had gone off with another friend of mine. I was furious. I wanted to go out but my mother wouldn't let me. Although I was sixteen, I wasn't too old to have a clip. Anyway, my sister came and said she had a pair of fish-net stockings for me. She knew I wanted a pair – they were all the rage. So she said come up with me and then you can have them. So my mother said I could go but I wasn't to be too long – I was to come straight back. Well, really it was an excuse my sister had to get me out because my boy-friend had asked her to try and get me out because he wanted to talk to me . . .

Anyway, we were talking so much I didn't realize the time, so I said we had better go. As we came out of the house I could see my mother coming. I said to my boy-friend from the side of my mouth, 'There's my mother'. He said, 'What did you say?' I didn't have time to repeat it because she came right up to us and raised her hand to give me a clip. I ducked and my boy-friend caught the full blow. I couldn't face him again after that. And he hadn't gone out with my other friend – he just walked her as far as the Post Office just to ask about me.

Another boy I went out with brought me home late. I was supposed to be in at half-past nine. Anyway, it was summertime and our bedroom windows were down to the half because it was very warm. My mother was upstairs when she heard me come in. She shouted down the stairs, 'You are going to the workhouse in the morning washing napkins'.

My mother was always afraid either my sister or I would get into trouble. We were always going to the workhouse washing napkins. She would threaten us, putting her fist up to our face. She didn't seem to worry about the boys though.

Black Velvet

~

Florence Allen

In the Llewellyn home, old Llew rested. He could hear Rhona washing dishes in the scullery. She was a good girl, he thought, never shirking her share of household chores. Different to that flighty young Maggie who would do anything else but wash a dish. He should give her a hand, he decided, but the comfort of his old chair was more to his taste, so filling up the bowl of his old briar pipe, he sank still deeper into his seat.

Rhona took her time with the dishes. There was no particular hurry doing anything these days, she thought. Suddenly she saw herself in Tillery again, getting ready for a dance. How her mother would tease her on who her latest boyfriend was, but then she met Gethin. She hadn't wanted to marry a collier, she knew hardly anything about their lives excepting the coal which they brought up from the pit. The two neighbouring valleys were more different than she had ever realized. The agricultural life of her valley and the industrial one of Gethin's, they seemed like different worlds. Was she sorry she'd left Tillery? she pondered. She'd married the man of her choice and she was happy enough, if only the terrible strike would end.

She was so lost in her thoughts that she didn't hear Gethin enter the room, and jumped when she felt his arms around her, hugging her close. Now all felt well with her world again and resolutely she turned and showered Gethin's face with kisses. 'Good Lord,' he muttered with a grin, 'Kiss me, love, yes, but don't make a meal of it.' Rhona laughed, the colour rising in her cheeks. 'I was thinking of Tillery,' she murmured, hiding her face in his shoulder.

'Wanting to go back?' he asked, but only half jokingly as he remembered Llew's recent words: 'Better watch it, my lad, the girl is getting homesick. You're spending too much time on street corners with the strikers. Remember you've only been married for three months, Rhona is still a bride.'

He had felt huffed at the old man's words at the time. He found the strike meetings interesting and Rhona was happy enough, there was plenty of company in the Llewellyn house and where was the money to take her out, to Tillery or anywhere? But the thought niggled now, perhaps the old man was right, maybe he wasn't being fair to Rhona.

When his grandfather slipped some coins into his hand, he knew what was expected. 'Use it for petrol, lad, take the girl out, make a fuss of her.'

'But it's your baccy money,' Gethin mumbled, shamed by the old man's generosity.

'Don't you worry about me,' his grandfather retorted. 'You're young, enjoy yourselves,' and contentedly Llew sank back in his chair.

****

183

On the mountain top, Gethin looked at Rhona's flushed face whipped by the ride to a beautiful pink, then clasping her half-frozen hands, he rubbed them softly to bring back life to them.

'Are *these* your Black Hills, your mountains?' Her voice spoke her disappointment.

'The only mountains we have,' he said softly. 'We call them black hills because all this is rich coal country, rich like black velvet.' He lifted her from the machine and gently led her to the grass verge where he found a niche to shelter them from the keen wind. Then pulling her down beside him, he sheltered her with his arms.

'Your not sorry you married me, Rhona?' She swiftly turned to look at his troubled face, 'I mean, this place isn't Tillery.'

'No . . . no,' Rhona broke in, 'I'm happy with your parents, Dai and Martha are so kind, but we're never alone, not really alone. I want my own home, Gethin, because,' she closed her eyes, 'we're going to have a baby.'

The silence of the mountain was suddenly between them and Rhona gazed around uneasily. Gethin was stunned, her words taking time to sink in. *A baby*. He'd not given a thought to fatherhood. They were too young to be saddled with a child, without a home, without money.

Rhona turned and stared at him. She hadn't expected him to go into raptures at her news, but he could at least say something, anything. She hadn't wanted a baby, at least not so soon, but the look on his face made her heart sink, and slowly she sank still lower into his arms and the cloak of doom which shrouded her.

Gethin stirred, his secret thoughts ending abruptly as he saw Rhona's hurt face; she was too young, too inexperienced in life in the mining valleys to understand his fears or the difficult times that lay ahead. He squeezed her hand tightly and spoke quietly. 'Kids are good to have. All my married pals have children. We'll be no different to them.'

Rhona pulled her hand away and sat upright, her face contorted with conflicting emotions. Her thoughts were chaotic. She had expected him to make a fuss of her, like they did in the story books. The baby wasn't wanted. A sob shook her slight frame. Remorsefully, Gethin clutched her closer, kissing her wet cheeks. But Rhona made no response to his love-making, she was as cold as the green grass they rested on.

Bopa Pol

~

Heulwen Williams

Bopa was Mam's sister and her best friend. She was a small, very strong little woman with an easy walk and a loud, lively voice. Bopa Pol and Ewa Bob's house in Garden City was a second home to us children. Every Friday night we would go over to be bathed in the iron bath in the scullery. In our house we had to bath in a zinc bath in front of the fire as my father did every day after coming home from Ogilvy, black and covered in coal dust. Bopa would give us our *scrwbad*, a fierce scrubbing down, rubbing our heads very hard with the soap, saying, 'I don't care a bit, I don't feel a thing,' while my sister Nanon and I would shout, 'Bopa, Bopa, you're hurting us!' After the bath Bôp would make us a basin full of chips with a huge plate of Morgans' brown bread, cut very thinly. Oh, that was heaven, to be nice and warm and full up in front of the big fire. Then we would have to dress warmly to go back home to Mam, ready for bed, tired and happy. Ewa Bob would carry Nanon on his large, strong shoulders.

There was always something going on in our house with Mam and Bopa. Papering one of the bedrooms, for example. Nanon and I would have to cut off the edges of rolls and rolls of wallpaper. The place would be a terrible sight, with paper and paste everywhere, but it was worth all the hard work to see the room by evening, scrubbed and polished with clean, fresh-smelling walls. Another time, they would make *diod fain* (nettle pop), boiling the nettles first, then straining them and allowing the water and yeast to stand for a while in an earthenware pot, before bottling and corking it. It went 'pop!' when you uncorked it and we loved drinking it. Often all the mats would be up and they would be washing blankets or curtains with the zinc bath propped on two chairs and water heating in a bucket on the coal fire. This was very heavy work.

I remember very well Mam and Bopa talking in the kitchen, and Nanon and I, all ears trying to listen, when plans were being made to raise money for the chapel. This usually meant a trip on Charlie Hills' bus to Tredegar to buy cheap remnants in the market. Oh, it was fun, especially in winter when the 'naphtha' flames were alight there. It was so exciting for us.

Money was very scarce and sometimes there would be nothing left at the end of the week, except perhaps a few coppers for the bus fare to Tredegar. Bopa, full of fun, would say, 'We can have an eyeful for nothing!' But although she had very little money to spare, I remember Nanon and I being in bed with measles and Bopa Pol bringing us presents, a pretty little weighing scales with grapes to weigh. She would come with Mam to buy new clothes for us in the Co-op or the Emporium, although Mam made most of our clothes.

There was a great sadness in Bopa Pol's life. We were strong, healthy children, but Glyn, Bopa's son was lame. He was born with a deformity and spent months in London undergoing treatment on his leg, which was scarred with stitches from top to bottom. He was a handsome boy with very fair hair. He had a lovely soprano voice and would sing solos in chapel. It was lovely to hear the three of them singing at home, Ewa a baritone, Bopa Pol a contralto and Glyn the soprano.

As children, we were extremely excited to be able to dress up and take part in the concerts which were held in Jerusalem chapel. Ewa Bob always had prominent parts in the operettas. I remember 'May's Marriage' with Ewa as the Baron of Goldstein. Of course, Mam was the dressmaker and made a dark red suit with ruffles of lace around the neck and the edges of the sleeves and trousers. Being a tall, straight man he looked noble too. Bopa also took part in operettas and I can remember her as the Fairy Godmother dressed in a white costume, carrying a wand in a performance of 'Cinderella' in the hall near Rhymney station.

Ewa Bob suffered an accident underground and lost a finger. When he was in pain he would walk up and down the passage and Nanon and I would walk close behind him until we made him laugh and laugh. He was on the dole for years and years, like many others at that time. He was the caretaker of Jerusalem and would go down to light the stove there. I have a very clear, heartbreaking memory of Bopa crying with her head in her hands on the kitchen table in our house. Someone had sent an anonymous letter reporting Ewa to the authorities because he was getting a half crown a week for lighting the stove, against the rules. So money was very, very scarce and Bopa would go out to wash clothes for the family to try and earn a few shillings to help get by, then burn peelings on the fire and riddle the ashes for cokes to burn.

Glyn's health deteriorated. His epileptic fits became increasingly worse. It was very heavy work caring for him. Bopa became ill and was confined to bed for over a year. Mam and Nanon looked after her with Ewa. When she died in 1941 I was in college in Swansea. I tried to come home in time for the funeral, but the cortège passed by while I was still on the bus in Havard's Row. I grieved for a long time after dear Bopa, and it was especially hard for Mam because they were very close sisters, sharing every worry and joy.

After Bopa's death, we went to visit Glyn regularly in the work-house in Tredegar, a terribly sad place, and it was there that he died soon afterwards. Ewa survived for many years and went to live with his sister. When they were clearing the house in Garden City, Mam found a marriage certificate in the dressing-table drawer and it was then that she knew when Bopa Pol and Ewa Bob had got married. Bopa had hidden the fact that she was expecting a baby from Mamgu and the family on the farm. During her pregnancy she had worked like a man, milking and lifting heavy weights. When Glyn was born, Mam cried to hear Mamgu say, 'It would have been better if the poor little thing had not been born'. The beginning of their life together was therefore sad and worrying, but, to us, theirs was a very dear family and home where we spent many happy childhood hours.

Black Velvet

~

Florence Allen

Rhona sat, quietly knitting, intent on a jumper for Johnny, the son born to her six months after Martha's death. Llew sat, as always, puffing away stolidly on his old pipe, that now seemed as ancient as himself.

It was three years since Martha's death and there had been many changes in the Llewellyn household. Maggie was now seventeen, and old for her years in more ways than one. Rhona had long given up on her protection of the girl who in many ways seemed older than herself. Rhona, now twenty-one, had altered too. As promised she had taken over the responsibility of the household and as all agreed, she had done well, but it had taken its toll and the prettiness of youth had deserted her. She now looked a shadow of that old self. The gay laugh and gentle charm seemed a thing of the past.

Three years. It seemed a lifetime. Three years of scrubbing floors and the continual heavy wash-tub washing that had to be seen to practically every day, sometimes all day. Yes, she thought miserably, times had been hard and there seemed little chance of lightening the burden.

Llew looked at Rhona's set face and his thoughts were no happier than hers. Her rounded cheeks of three years ago had worn to a fine thinness which saddened him, and Gethin, who thought that he worked hard enough down the pit, would not lift a finger in the house. Yet he made certain that he'd find his way to the Oxford Inn in Frogmorton Street as soon as the evening meal was over and done with. What was the real attraction over there? He brooded on. Gethin said, often enough, that he was helping the widow woman out behind the bar. Out of the goodness of his heart, no doubt, but from what he heard the flamboyant widow could have any of the men to help her out, and in more ways than one.

With the evening meal over, Gethin made no hesitation in getting ready for his trip to the Oxford Inn. Rhona steeled herself but when she spoke her voice was weak and plaintive. 'Are you bound to go to the Inn tonight, Gethin?' He looked sheepishly in her direction. 'Having taken over the main bar, love, I don't like leaving Mrs Jenkins down.'

Dai looked up from his newspaper. 'Why not take Rhona out for the evening, Gethin lad. It will make a change for both of you.' Gethin's answer, to all their surprise, came almost as a challenge. 'Why not? I'll take you to the Inn but you'll have to sit in the lounge. Women aren't allowed in the main bar. I could do what I have to do and keep my eye on you at the same time.'

'No, I . . . I'd prefer the cinema. Maggie says there's a good show on at the Regal.'

'Good, I'll pay for the pair of you.' He brought some money from his pocket. 'There you are, love, and something left over for sweets.' Rhona moved to her chair, picking up the knitting from where she had thrown it. 'It doesn't matter, I've knitting to do,' she muttered. Gethin shifted uncomfortably and then picked up his coins. 'Have it your way. I've promised the poor woman to help her out and I intend doing it.' . . .

Mary Anne was of great comfort to Rhona. The girl had no friends in Cymafon outside the family and Mary Anne had become a mother figure to her. Tonight, when the older woman made a show of affection, she could not prevent the tears from flowing down her cheeks. 'Now then, my dear,' – Mary Anne had a pretty shrewd idea of their cause – 'sit down there. Cry all you want and I'll make a nice cup of tea. Then you can tell me what troubles you.'

'It's Gethin,' Rhona sobbed. 'I'm frightened. I'm losing him, I know I am.'

Mary Anne calmed the girl's shaking shoulders. 'Now drink that up, love, it will do you good. You're frightening yourself for nothing.' She was afraid to look directly at Rhona, in case she read the pity in her eyes.

'But he can't get down that pub fast enough. He spends all his evenings down there. What am I to do?' Rhona looked pleadingly up to Mary Anne's face.

Mary Anne loved Gethin, he was like a son to her and she could see both sides of the situation but Rhona was almost wailing now. 'It's my fault, it must be. We're just not the same any more. And I've tried so . . . so hard.'

Mary Anne knew she had to speak her mind. 'The answer does lie within yourself, love. You're too earnest in your efforts to keep up the home atmosphere, to match up to Martha. You've let yourself drift, become too overworked. You're sacrificing your youth, your personality.'

'But how did Martha cope?' Rhona looked broken.

'She was older, dear, and they were her family.' But Mary Anne's voice faltered as she remembered Martha's careworn face, etched with lines before its time.

'But Gethin, what of Gethin?' Rhona said huskily. 'He's changed too.'

'I know, but he's young and looking for some light in his life. As you must in yours. He loves you but you've become like his mother, immersed in house-cleaning, cooking, washing clothes. It's not you. He doesn't want you that way, so he's attempting to escape from it, and you must too, Rhona.

'Now, I'm going to suggest that you go to the Oxford Inn this very evening for a night out. There's a nice little lounge there. Nip whatever gossip there is in the bud. I'll come with you, if you like?'

Rhona smiled and put her arms around Mary Anne's thin shoulders. 'You're the sweetest darling,' she kissed her on the cheek, 'but no, I'll ask Dai to come with me, he's asked a few times.'

'Good for you,' Mary Anne said softly, 'now go wash your hair and I'll curl it for you.'

Shadows on the Wall

~

Mair E. McLellan

That Christmas was perhaps the last happy one at number 25. Already, although I could not know it, the shadows had begun to close in around us. Meanwhile, my parents had never seemed happier, even my father's normally serious face was all smiles. He joked, calling me 'Contrary Mary' and 'Coppernob', but I knew that it was Muriel's arrival that had changed him.

I had turned nine in the month just before Christmas, and I had begun to have chest colds again, although none of them were serious. It was the following spring before I saw the change in my mother, and indeed, noticed the change in the atmosphere between my parents. My baby sister Muriel had been put to sit in one of the armchairs where I was minding her. My mother went in to the chest of drawers to get something out, and she had to squeeze past my father who was sitting at the table, book in hand. He said something and laughed. I looked up from my own book in time to catch an expression on my mother's face that I had never seen before. I could not describe it, but the picture stayed in my mind. It was so unlike my mother's natural expression. I had never seen my mother look angry or upset about anything. I knew that she disliked my father's reading so much (as she did my own) and what she termed my father's 'sulking' and his silences. To a large extent Dat's presence made these moods or this behaviour easier to bear, but this was different. She looked as if she hated my father.

I did not have long to wait. This time my mother broke the news to me directly, talking to me as if I had already outgrown my childhood. She was pregnant again, 'At my age,' she said bitterly. 'What will people think!'

In my eyes she looked no different; not a day older than she had a year before. I said, wildly, looking around for some means of comforting her, 'It'll be company for Mu, Mam.'

'It's your father's fault,' she went on, unheeding. 'He promised to 'be careful'. He's known all along. Middle age spread indeed!'

I was puzzled. How could my father know and my mother not? Sex I could understand, and had guessed at, contraception was beyond me at nine years of age.

'I'm going to ask Dr Morgan to give me something to get rid of it,' she said, and she got up to put on her coat. 'Oh Mam, please don't,' I begged her, not knowing why I felt so strongly about it. 'Perhaps you'll have a boy this time . . . '

'Whatever it is it'll be one more mouth to feed, and Dat can't clothe all of you. I don't want another baby, Mair. I'm too old to have another one.' She began to cry and I longed to go to her, to try and comfort her, but just as she showed me no outward signs of affection, I could not show her any, except by listening.

She went up to the doctor's and came back with a small bottle of pink pills which she showed me triumphantly. They made me feel cold inside. She was willing to kill the baby in her tummy. It was dreadful. I later realized that it was highly improbable that kind Dr Morgan would give her anything strong enough to cause a miscarriage, but I did not know this at the time. I waited for the following morning with apprehension. Meanwhile, the silence in the kitchen was filled with a tension I had never felt before. My father ate his dinner in complete silence. Nothing new in that, but his face was like a thundercloud. Dat was affected too, I could tell.

Muriel, who was still being breast-fed at least part of the time, was the only member of the family to be oblivious to the atmosphere.

The morning came and went. The tablets had done nothing. My mother began to cry again, and again I could do nothing. Aunty Lou came down, and I heard my mother talking to her. Aunty Lou, too, did not seem to think it any great matter but perhaps, having no children of her own, she simply felt a little envious of my mother. 'Perhaps you're on the change, Ethel,' she said, 'so you would catch quick.'

The menopause too was beyond me, and I went out into the spring sunshine with Paddy at my heels.

The atmosphere continued to be oppressive. My mother took to going out more, over to see Annie Beese, or up to her sister's. My father continued to do all the usual things, cutting wood and breaking up coal, along with gardening, both in our back garden and the allotment, and serving on the committee of the Labour Club. He also still did the blackleading on a Sunday morning before cooking breakfast for us all. He rarely spoke now and his appetite for books was undiminished. This was something I could share with him. He still made a lot of fuss over Muriel. It's possible that she was now the one bright spot of his life.

One day Aunty Lou came down in a mood of suppressed excitement which meant that she had news to tell. What she told us shocked me. Mildred Davies's father had hanged himself. Aunty Lou suggested that he had been depressed because he had been unable to find work.

While she was talking, I glanced at my mother and saw a curious expression on her face. She looked thoughtful. After Aunty Lou had left, she said, 'That's one way out I suppose,' and fell silent.

Her words disturbed me. But she wouldn't, she couldn't? She wasn't happy, nor was she very well. She was losing weight (except for the bump in her tummy) and her face looked older. It had none of the glow it had worn when she was expecting my sister, or after Muriel had been born . . .

It was coming up to the time for the Flower Service again, and I began to ask for a new frock. My mother was unsympathetic. 'There's Muriel to consider now. You've got a best frock.'

'It's too short,' I protested. 'I've grown out of it.' It was true. My long, skinny white legs stretched out from beneath it. I said as much.

'Don't go then,' my mother snapped.

'But I like going,' I said, which was true. I liked carrying a bunch of my father's flowers – always the best, better than anyone else's, up to the altar. And I enjoyed singing the hymns, which were different from ordinary Sundays.

'Ask Dat then,' said my mother. Dat was now buying clothes for Muriel, I knew this. He had even told me so himself. 'It's her turn now kid.' But he went on putting a shilling a week in the Co-op savings book which he had started for me the day I was born.

Meanwhile, my mother talked to me of suicide. 'Putting an end to it,' as she said. She did not mention this to my father or Dat, but only to me, and knowing how depressed she was, I took it seriously.

Dat came to my rescue over the frock as he did over so many things. I should choose myself, as I had chosen my shoes. My mother shrugged. 'Take Muriel with you, get her out of the house for a bit.'

'It's a long walk for a toddler Eth.'

'Then carry her Ivor!'

My uncle looked at me and I looked at him, and we took Muriel along with us. I should have been happy, but I was not. Part of me was very afraid. If my father had been at home, or if we had not had Muriel with us, I would not have worried. My mother would not hang herself if Muriel was there. We walked quickly. As usual I had to half-run in order to keep up with Dat, and Muriel was either being dragged between us, or carried in Dat's arms.

The woman in the Co-op looked at me doubtfully. 'Shouldn't you take up a few dresses for her mother to pick?' she asked.

'There's no need, she knows what she wants,' Dat sounded almost rude, as if he had subconsciously picked up my anxiety. It wasn't in the least like him, he was always at his most charming with women and girls. In silence, the woman brought out some dresses and laid them on the counter. For a second I forgot my secret fear. I knew at once which frock I wanted. It had a blue background and was covered in pink rose-buds and tiny green leaves. I tried it on and it fitted like a dream. Dat handed over his Co-op book and the money, and we walked home rather more slowly. For some reason, I was a little less afraid, although this didn't last. As we neared the house, I wanted to run.

I was the first to the door, throwing it open and calling, 'Mam, Mam!' There was no answer. Suddenly terrified, I left the brown paper parcel which contained my beautiful new frock on the table and rushed out to the Lav. I pushed open the door. It was empty. I came back in, and called upstairs, 'Mam? Mam?' There was a brief pause and then my mother came down. She had a faint smile on her face.

'Why didn't you answer?' I demanded.

'Where did you think I was?' she asked, and laughed.

It was the laugh which did it. She had known about my fear. She had set out quite deliberately to frighten me. I felt a kind of cold anger towards her. I don't think that I loved her less, but she had lost my respect.

My mother did not talk about suicide again, and she seemed to settle into a kind of apathy. I was called on to do much more.

Derek was born a week after my tenth birthday. It had been a drab enough birthday. My mother suffered constant backache, but would not see the doctor or the midwife. To her dismay, Mrs Davies could not attend her at this confinement. Mrs Davies had been forced to retire because she was 'not properly qualified'. Instead, it would have to be Mrs Prosser from two streets away. I had been in there a few times, as Mrs Prosser doubled as a shopkeeper. My mother was determined to put off having her out for as long as possible. Finally, on the afternoon of the second of December, a Friday, my mother gave in and went to bed. My father was working afternoons, so that Dat was home first. His dinner had been cooked, and was waiting in the oven for him, but as usual, he decided to wash first.

It was while he was in the process of washing, having brought the large enamel bowl through and positioned it on a chair as close to the blazing fire as he could, that my mother began to cry out. I saw him wince at the sound, and he moved sharply, almost overturning the bowl. 'See if she wants the nurse, kid.'

I dashed upstairs. My mother was lying on the bed, her legs apart, and from between them I could glimpse a black head of hair. I wanted to stay, to see the baby emerge fully, but my mother looked up at me, her face wet with sweat. 'Fetch Mrs Prosser, Mair.'

Mrs Prosser passed me on her bike. She had little to do save clean up my mother and my baby brother. Derek had not waited to be born. Like me, perhaps even more than me, he had rushed headlong into the world.

He was very small. Too small to be weighed. Mrs Prosser held out very little hope of him surviving. My father was pessimistic as ever. 'Even if he does, I'll be an old man before he's twenty-one.'

The following morning the streets were thick with snow. It had snowed heavily during the night, and it had piled up in drifts as high as the window-sills. It had snowed soon after Muriel had been born too, but nothing like this. The nurse would not be able to come through this. I fretted, in fear that he would die after all. My mother seemed to take it so much for granted.

Even when the snow had cleared enough for Mrs Prosser to make her rounds a little later on that week, my mother went on believing that Derek would not survive. But he showed no signs of dying, and I, at least, began to hope.

Soon after my mother was up and about, a doctor came to the house, the visit having been arranged by Nurse Prosser. My mother was bathing the small, doll-like baby who still had his thatch of black hair at this time. My mother lifted him up to show to the doctor. 'I don't suppose he'll live,' she said with a quiet sadness.

'Nonsense, Mrs Croome. He's got big bones, he'll live to be a fine-looking son for you.' I ceased to worry!

After this some of the tensions in the home evaporated, and I believe that my mother took a certain pride in the fact that she now had a son.

Muriel no longer cried a lot. The cross-sounding baby had turned into a happy toddler. In some ways it was hard on her, now that Derek was born. As if to make up to him for having done her best to try and lose him, my mother doted on him. If Muriel made an attempt at climbing on my mother's knee while she was breast-feeding Derek, she was told to get down, sometimes impatiently. But there was no doubt about it that she was my father's favourite, just as I was Dat's, and in time Derek became my mother's.

Living with Grandma

~

Lucy Arundell

Grandma possessed a very stubborn streak which could make life rather uncomfortable. Many people came up against it; it often concerned me personally.

One of my grown-up cousins, Georgina, taught music and singing. I had had a few lessons at the piano when I was six years old but the teacher went away from the town and I practised on my own after that. I could play simple tunes and hymns. Georgina thought I was quite good, and, knowing our poor circumstances, offered to teach me free of charge if I would take the lessons at her convenience. I went on Saturday afternoons while other girls were playing in the park or paying their penny to see the latest American film at the local cinema. Georgina decided that I should go in for exams. I had been doing test pieces and she thought that I stood a good chance of getting through. Grandma said: 'No! If Lucy is as good as you say she is, then that will do. She can carry on from there and practise at home.' That was the end of lessons for me in spite of my tears and Georgina's pleas. I passed the exams for Higher Grade Schools; again there was a firm 'No! I'm not having you turned into one of those flighty young hussies getting airs and graces!'

Teacher was arranging a concert at school for the end of term. I had been practising with the other girls, learning a Welsh jig. We were told that we would need a nice white dress, white socks and black shoes so that we all looked the same. Grandma said, 'There's no money in this house for fripperies. It's nothing but a lot of extravagance.' I did not like to tell anyone that we had no money. If I had, I daresay someone would have lent me the necessary attire. Instead, I pretended to turn awkward and said I did not want to be in the concert. Miss Williams was very upset, as well she might be. There was little time to find and train a substitute. I refused to give any other explanation and wept secretly in bed.

During the long hot summer holiday Grandma decided it was time we now concentrated on the garden. Grandpa was already busy in his piece and well ahead with his plans. He promised a regular supply of fresh vegetables and salads next summer. The uncles came often, usually in the evenings, and took over the heavy digging and clearing of overgrown bramble shoots which invaded and intruded into the precious growing land. There was quite a lot that Grandpa could do in spite of his age: he fertilised, weeded and hoed, sang softly to himself as he planted and was happy. Indeed he seemed to take on a new lease of life. He spent almost the whole of the day out in his territory and very soon the place took on that cared-for look which is the delight of good gardeners everywhere. The promise of fresh food in abundance came true, and Grandpa wrought some miracle with the withering fruit bushes which later yielded gooseberries and blackcurrants for jams and pies galore.

Grandma and I toiled and sweated under the hot summer sun and into the glorious autumn. We brought order and beauty to our little garden . . .

Grandpa's sciatica eventually got the better of him and he could no longer get up and down the stairs to see his beloved garden. He remained shut up there in his room. Grandma refused to look after him, she said he was 'paying for his sins'. I took his meagre meals up to him on a tray and hot water for him to wash. I did my best to keep the room clean and tidy for him and when Grandma went out, I would sit and talk to him. One day I found him in tears, his pain was much worse and he had no help. 'I can't live like this any more,' he said. 'It's more than a human can stand. Will you do an errand for me?' 'Yes, Grandpa.' 'Will you get a message up to your Uncle Henry, ask him to come and see me?'

I gave the message to Esther at school and she in turn passed it on to her father. Uncle Henry came the same night. He spent a long time shut up in Grandpa's room. Grandma was very annoyed because she could not hear what they were talking about. Uncle's visit was a complete surprise to her. The outcome was evident the following day when Uncle and Aunt came with a hired car and took Grandpa away to live with them. They gave him a bed and the comfort which he had been denied for so long. I went to see him once. There he was propped up in bed with papers to read and his favourite bulls eyes to suck. I never saw him again. Grandma found out that I had gone and my legs smarted from the weals left by her cane. Grandma's wrath was something to be reckoned with.

CHAPTER 10

OUT TO WORK

OUT TO WORK

The characters portrayed in this chapter represent those women whose working lives were spent outside the home. As noted earlier, most women in the valleys married and left paid work in their early twenties. Pre-marital work was transient and restricted to domestic service, office or shopwork, and although, as many of the extracts have shown, many women continued to take in paid work or do part time jobs such as cleaning or laundrying after marriage, married women did not ordinarily work outside the home. Indeed, despite the legislation of 1919, they were actively barred from the professions and women wishing to pursue a career would have to remain single. Opportunities were limited for single women too. In a period when men returning from service took precedence over the women who had replaced them during the war, those who fought to retain their jobs, or for equal pay with men were regarded as 'hussies'. Yet although single women were in a minority in the valleys, their contribution was a significant one, and although the jobs described in this chapter are not typical of the work of most single women, they serve to demonstrate that not all women were 'mams'.

Ivy, in the first extract, is an exceptional figure. By the inter-war period the number of women working on the surface of coal mines had become very small indeed, although in some areas, for example, in the Tredegar area, women surface workers remained until well into the 1920s. Ivy's physical strength and involvement in 'men's jobs' made her into a local legend.

From the early 1920's, the majority of local education authorities introduced regulations requiring women teachers to resign their posts on marriage. The marriage bar led to many secret and lengthy courtships, as well as contributing to an unsympathetic image of spinster teachers, discussed by Edith S. Davies in the second extract.

Bessie Ann Rees is the archetypal capable (though untrained) midwife who has an intimate knowledge of the community and its people. The traditional midwife who played such a crucial rôle in women's lives at the most critical and memorable times, was a figure of authority who also retained a special place in the affections of local families.

Mabel, the market stall businesswoman, is also portrayed as an authoritarian figure. The market remained a focal point of South Wales towns for shopping and meeting up with aquaintances in this period, and Mabel's business acumen is obviously of great advantage to her as she struggles to make a living on the strength of her own skills.

The Story of Gilfach
(Miss Ivy James)

~

Katie Pritchard

During the first World War women were engaged in place of labourers to empty trucks on top of the tip. The women played a vital rôle in the war effort. Their duty was to empty trucks with all possible speed so that they could be refilled with coal. The rubbish and stones were brought from underground in trams and emptied into trucks.

Some of the girls employed were only fifteen years of age. Their day commenced at seven a.m. If coal could be sifted out of the rubble, the girls would start work at four a.m. in order to fill bags of coal which they sold for a shilling a bag. Life was hard and conditions of work were very grim. The tips were high and bleak. There was no shelter from the cold biting winds or the driving rain.

In addition to heart-breaking conditions of work, the women suffered from the weight of heavy clothing, necessary to keep out the cold. Any garment was worn, including old sacks. These were thrown over shoulders and tied around the middle to act as aprons. At the end of a winter's day, these were covered with ice and snow.

For their meals, the women retired to a hut on the tip, where a fire was lit. If rations permitted, they fried bacon or an egg on a large polished shovel. When clearing rubble the girls searched for fossils at the request of Mr David Davies, Agent. They delighted in cleaning them carefully before presenting them to the collector.

Their work was not entirely confined to the tips. During the war, large allotments were opened and after the ground was turned by the men, the girls planted potatoes. One year, two fields of potatoes were planted, and when raised were carried on their backs to various houses.

When the war ended, women ceased to be paid for working on the tips. However, many continued to unload the trucks in order to earn their living by selling any coal they could find among the rubble. This occupation was very precarious. Sometimes the trucks contained very little coal. When collected and arranged into bags, they had to be carried on their backs to every part of the valley where an order could be secured.

One of the women who continued in this strenuous occupation, until men were employed as surface men, was Miss Ivy James. Ivy was a familiar figure in the valley, with her hair cropped short like a man, a dark Tam on her head, a long navy blue coat tied around the middle and strong hob-nailed boots, covered in coal dust.

She would be seen daily working on the tip or walking around the valley with a sack of coal on her back and a bag of sticks under her arm.

Money earned on the tip was insufficient to maintain her and her widowed mother. After labouring until her back would almost break, she would, after a wash and a meal, proceed to the Ogmore Hotel to help with the cleaning. At weekends she acted as 'Chucker Out' at the Six Bells Hotel.

Ivy was a woman of remarkable strength and could lift a drunken customer who refused to leave, and throw him through the door. For this remarkable feat, she was called 'Champion Ivy'. When nearing 'Stop Tap' at the Six Bells the inhabitants of Maesteg Row amused themselves on Saturday nights watching Ivy throwing unruly customers into the road.

At Christmas time, Ivy dressed as Father Christmas and on Christmas Eve visited houses where there were children. Mothers who had difficulty in getting the children to bed were overjoyed when they heard Ivy's deep voice calling from the passage 'Are the children in bed?'

'No! They are going now!'

'Right! I'll come back later!'

Every child immediately retired to bed to dream of the benevolence of Father Christmas and the joys of the following morning.

Today, Ivy is confined to her corner, paying the price for her long working day, and the cold freezing winds of winter on the dreary black slag heaps. She enjoys relating her experiences as a 'Labourer' and 'Coal Merchant' and still laughs at her exploits as Gilfach's Champion 'Chucker Out'.

Thou Shalt Not Wed

~

Edith S. Davies

Miss Myfanwy Jones, of High Street, taught First Class throughout her whole teaching career, which must have spanned three generations of New Road children. Standard One was taught by another Miss Jones who was also the headmistress. These two ladies shared the same classroom.

Some years later this particular teacher got married and had to relinquish her job, since married women were not allowed to teach. She married a miner, and the astonished comments at home were reiterated over and over again, 'Fancy a headmistress throwing herself away upon a miner. She must have been mad.'

At Trerobart School, Ynysybwl, boys and girls were educated separately. Trerobart Girls' School was staffed by women teachers who were all spinsters since married women were not employable in accordance with the law. Any woman who married had automatically to resign her post. Very few women could afford to do this and so throughout my elementary and grammar school education I was taught solely by spinsters.

There was a high wall separating the boys' and girls' departments at Trerobart, upon which no boy was allowed to climb. Sometimes a few disobedient boys would defy the rules. In a state bordering on hysteria, we girls, eager 'cleckerboxes', would rush in to tell the teacher, 'Miss, there are boys on the wall and they are looking at us!' A brief note would be sent round to Mr Harris, and shortly afterwards the boys would disappear from the wall and be caned for the misdemeanour.

This hostile attitude towards the male sex was unwittingly emphasised by Miss Catherine E. Bedford, the first distinguished headmistress of the Girls' Intermediate School, Treforest. A beautiful and brilliant woman, her morning assemblies were unforgettable. I have never been able to shake off the ideal of womanhood which she instilled in us.

She walks, the lady of my delight,
A shepherdess of sheep,
Her flocks are thoughts,
She keeps them white,
She keeps them from the steep,
She feeds them on the fragrant heights,
And folds them in for sleep.

The result was that when we studied in Biology the reproduction of the rabbit, I in no way related it to human beings! I really was 'sweet sixteen and never been kissed'. Little wonder that I grew up with the notion that there was something noxious about boys and men and that they were, like lepers, to be avoided at all costs. Later, my own problems with the state of matrimony were almost unsurmountable.

My maternal grandmother used to relate, amidst much family laughter, how on an occasion when one of her daughters had been excessively punished for some misdemeanour or other, she had written to the teacher in question a letter of rebuke couched in the following terms:

Madam,
Although I understand the need for correction of naughty pupils in the classroom, I am very angry at the extent of the punishment you meted out to my eight year old daughter for talking in class. This made her ill and afraid to return to school. I attribute the severe punishment to the fact that, being a dried up old spinster, you lack the milk of human kindness.
Yours,
Edith Morgan.

At first I was horrified at this unjust and abusive criticism and yet, upon reflection, there was a grain of truth in this furious protestation.

Looking back on my schooldays, there are very few moments I can recall when learning was fun and something to be enjoyed. There was little laughter in the classrooms of long ago. There was a tendency for these excellent maiden ladies to take their work and themselves too seriously. 'Life is real, life is earnest,' was the chief lesson I learned. I did not question it then but, in retrospect, I now ask, 'Should not life be joyous as well as earnest?'

It is difficult to conceive today of anyone putting up with such tyrants. The schools of the feminine 'Little Hitlers' were known throughout the valleys for their high standard of achievement – but these high standards were achieved by the hardest work under the harshest discipline.

Though all too infrequent, there were also brief moments of relaxation. I recall a last afternoon before breaking up for Christmas. Cupboards had been tidied and all books locked away. The monitoress handed round a small booklet published by Beecham's containing arithmetic tables. This was a Christmas present from the teacher and we were all delighted. As the monitoress went to return some spare copies to the teacher, she stumbled, fell and then sat up, revealing a flushed and rosy face. Instantly the teacher placed the empty waste bin on her head and the result was so comic that teacher and pupils laughed together and out loud.

Dear shades of spinster teachers of the past, a little more laughter and innocent fun in those classrooms might have made you all objects of our love as well as gratitude.

Thanks For The Memories
(Bessie Ann Rees)

~

Iris Roderick Thomas

Bessie Ann Rees was one of the old-school of capable women who were called to help in every kind of emergency, such as laying out loved ones when they passed away, or tending the little ones when they were struck down with mysterious ailments that no one else could cure, and there wasn't any need for a midwife if Bessie Ann was living anywhere near. There are many people like her and thank the Lord for them.

Mamma was so delicate that when she became pregnant Dr Ernie Ward sighed at the news, but kept his thoughts to himself, not wishing to upset her. On the other hand Bessie Ann took charge immediately, keeping a watchful eye, and sitting with her most days of the five months when she was confined to bed. Dr Ward visited regularly, but he didn't hold out much hope for either of our chances . . .

Bessie Ann Rees was the strength that Mamma lacked, and as she busied about with rolled up sleeves and a calm, cool poise, it was difficult to imagine anything going wrong, although Mamma had been in slow labour for three days. During this ordeal, Bessie Ann had left her own family to get on with things for themselves, whilst she sponged her patient with tepid water to reduce her high temperature, on one of the hottest July days ever recorded in Wales.

All that time, words of encouragement were being given to keep Mamma's spirits up and that it wouldn't be long now. Early afternoon came and it was obvious that Mamma was becoming weaker and very distressed, so Ernie Ward was sent for post haste. Unfortunately, he had been called out to an emergency without leaving a message as to where he could be reached. Without a sign of panic, just like the sensible person she was, Bessie Ann, taking Auntie Sarah in tow, got on with the delivery, instructing the patient and assistant what to do when she gave the word. At four-thirty she gave the final command, and there I made my debut into the world bottom first, as healthy as any four-and-a-half pounder could be, small but all there, with cute little ears and a lovely round head, like all breeches.

Dr Ward was utterly flabbergasted on arrival, to find it had happened without his expert technique, but relieved to see me in a basket beside the bed and Mamma sleeping peacefully with exhaustion. So overcome was he, that he did something quite unheard of during his years as a G.P., he sat with two women and drank a cup of tea . . .

Months previously, my parents had decided on a name for me. Strangely enough they never thought of my turning out to be a boy, so they settled for Iris. Both my parents were so grateful for the time and care given freely from Bessie Ann that they asked her to choose a second name for me. She, not being able to think of one off hand, consulted her husband. He had also shown concern for Mamma, and had been more than kind to allow his wife to spend the time that rightly belonged to her own family, with a neighbour. In less than a second he'd come up with a name. 'Call her Muriel,' he said, so it came to pass that Iris Muriel Roderick was named. Each year afterwards, on July 17th, Mr Rees would bring a bunch of iris to our door, and say the same words that never varied, 'Give these to the kid from Rees.'

Yesterday, when looking through old snapshots, I came across one of Mamma, Bessie Ann, young Eddie and myself on the sands at Barry. Mamma was wearing a baggy blouse with beads decorating the front, Eddie was in short trousers held up by braces and rolled-down wool socks, I was building a sand-castle with my dress tucked into the elastic top of my bloomers, and Bessie Ann Rees was sitting in the old type of deck-chair, fully clothed in a buttoned-up suit, buckled shoes and a high crown velvet hat, which in turn had a long hat pin across the front. She was very short and stout, with loads of black hair dressed in the fashion of the day in a bun, but so thick was her hair that the hat appeared to be stuck on the top, while she seemed to fill the deck-chair to its maximum capacity. I closed my eyes, reliving those fun-crammed days, when bikinis hadn't been invented and tanning creams were only used by film stars.

Thanks For The Memories
(Mrs Mabel Hoskins)

~

Iris Roderick Thomas

The biscuit stall was kept by Mrs Mabel Hoskins, a middle aged square-faced lady, with short grey hair parted at the side and held back from her face with a long hair-clip. She had two square brown eyes, a short flat square nose, below which was a square mouth which, when open, as it usually was, exposed two rows of lemon tombstones. She was an impressive individual, jovial to a fault, and blessed with the gift of the gab. Always quick to remind her regulars that the customer was always right, this was altogether a figment of her imagination, as no way could you win a battle against this mighty fortress.

Mabel had the great misfortune not to be Merthyr born and bred, which could be detected straight away from her accent, but having lived for over thirty five years in our town, she considered herself one of us. She and her husband had been born at Headquarters and she still had a broad Cardiff accent, but despite this handicap they were proud to call Merthyr home.

Her biscuit stall was the accolade of all biscuit stalls, sectioned off into equal squares, each holding a deep concealed biscuit box and filled to overflowing with mouth-watering dainties. Every variety was on show, Osborne, Marie, Digestive, creams, ginger-snaps, biscuits with iced tops and others covered with coconut and jam, long, short, fat and thin coloured wafers all competing to catch your eye. Yes, Mabel Hoskins had both of her square eyes to business. It was apparent to the greenest novice that an expert was at work, even attending to such trivial details as the lace paper doilies and ornamental baskets of artificial biscuits, not to speak of the dozens of multi-coloured tins arranged in a pyramid to form an eye-catching background. Hanging from the cord handles on the side-timbers were tiny biscuit tins filled with miniature replicas of your favourite biscuits.

A dropped shelf along the stallfront held square biscuit tins with glass display lids, so the delicious contents could be clearly seen by passers-by. This row of glass-topped tins was Mabel's ultimate weapon, from which the strongest willed could never escape. The square brown eyes would slyly watch anyone about to by-pass the stall, she'd wait patiently until their glances came to rest on a glass lid, then she'd smile a square smile, knowing full well that they were hopelessly trapped like a fly in the spider's web. Also included in the service was a running commentary whilst the purchases were weighed on the brass scale, its two pans suspended on a brass chain and brass weights added ounce by ounce, until the correct weight was achieved, then Mabel would put in an extra biscuit or two for good measure.

As you can plainly see, Mabel Hoskins valued her customers, and was clever enough to think up devious ways of keeping them for herself alone. Was there a better way than pleasing the apple of their eyes, their precious offspring? Each child of a regular customer would be handed a bag containing midget Osborne biscuits dotted with coloured sweets in the shape of stars, so even if customers had sufficient stores to last to the end of the week, let them try getting their children past the stall, with the basket of free Osbornes in full view.

There weren't many women as enterprising as Mabel, this fact becoming apparent when the stall was taken over by new owners, Mabel having reached the glorious age of eighty. No, the stall didn't flourish for very long afterwards, even the shiny glass lids became dingy and uninteresting whilst the regulars took their custom elsewhere.

CHAPTER 11

WOMEN
AND POLITICS

WOMEN AND POLITICS

This section has provided the opportunity to celebrate the part women played in political life, an aspect of their history which is often overlooked due to the strongly male dominated nature of political life in coalfield society. Not surprisingly, given the strength of the Labour Party during the inter-war years, these are the writings of Labour women, although it should be noted that in the chapter which follows it is the Communist Party which attracts Mair Eluned McLellan as she searches for political answers to the questions raised by her experiences.

The autobiography of Elizabeth Andrews (formerly Women's Organiser for the Labour Party in Wales), which has long been out of print, is a document which the editors felt should be made more accessible to present day readers. The edited extracts selected for inclusion cover her background and early involvement with politics and the setting up of the Labour Party's Women's Sections, the campaign for pit-head baths, the part played by women in organising the relief effort during the 1926 Lock Out and women's work in the field of maternity and child welfare and nursery education.

Dr Marion Phillips, Chief Women's Organiser for the Labour Party, drew mainly upon the experience of South Wales in writing her account of women's involvement in the 1926 relief effort, a record which was probably prompted by Arthur Horner. Both she and Winifred Griffiths show how women in the valleys were mobilized to respond to the urgent needs of the crisis year of 1926, yet, like Elizabeth Andrews, their work and careers also demonstrate that the need to fight the effects of poverty and to create opportunities for education and work for women required a long term struggle in several fields of activity. The extracts illustrate the point made in the introductory chapter that it was the *women* of South Wales who kept the issues of maternal and child health and welfare at the forefront of political campaigning during these years. The chapter also provides some insight into women's motives for becoming politically active and touches upon the relationship between socialism and feminism in their lives.

Today, the pioneers of women's politics in South Wales are virtually unknown. For example, Winifred Griffiths' work in local Labour politics and in civic service has been eclipsed by her husband's (James Griffiths) career as M.P. and Cabinet Minister. Her contribution, like that of Elizabeth Andrews, Councillor Rose Davies of Aberdare (mentioned by Mrs Andrews) and others, deserves wider recognition. This chapter does no more than raise awareness of the need for further research and recording of the recollections of the women involved.

A Woman's Work is Never Done

~

Elizabeth Andrews

I was born on December 15th, 1882, at Hirwaun, Breconshire, near Aberdare, one of a family of eleven children – four boys and seven girls. I was the third child. One baby sister died when a few weeks old, and one brother died as a teenager; the other nine reached maturity and all married.

My father, Samuel Smith, was a miner. When his father was killed on the railway, grandmother was left with five young children. How well I remember her in her black lace cap and shawl and lilac print apron! She looked so neat and dignified. She loved her small garden and I learnt much from her about flowers as a child.

My mother, Charlotte, was one of five sisters left motherless, so the girls had to go out to domestic service at an early age for little more than their keep. Long hours, hard work and poor conditions were their lot. Two of her sisters married iron workers and migrated to America, where ironworks and steelworks were developing and held out great promise. Many families left South Wales for America in those early days.

My father died at the age of fifty-seven from silicosis, known in those days as 'miners' asthma' and I have lost two brothers since then from the same disease . . .

I marvel at the way our parents managed to rear decent families in the latter part of the last century, and the beginning of this century, especially during periods of strikes. I remember one strike lasting six months, the only income being a small strike pay from the Miners' Federation. But the women stood loyally by their menfolk in their struggle for higher pay, shorter hours and better conditions. The Masters tried to starve them into submission.

The miners were then paid fortnightly and the first call on the pay in my home was rent, sick fund and Miners' Federation. This gave my parents some sense of security against sickness and strikes, and great sacrifices had to be made to keep up the payments. Many sickness clubs were formed in those days in the mining areas and insurance companies thrived. There was a real dread of being buried by the Poor Law in a pauper's grave.

I remember a favourite refrain to a recitation on 'the Pauper's Grave' heard at our penny readings and concerts:

> 'Rattle his bones over the stones
> He is only a Pauper that no one owns'.

It had a great effect on the audience.

In 1884 my parents moved from Hirwaun to Mardy, Rhondda. My father was one of the rescued from the Mardy explosion in 1885. After this they moved back to Hirwaun. We children loved to hear Mother and Father relate their experiences of this explosion and the way my father and his mates escaped. To make it more vivid to us, Father would draw a plan of the pit in chalk on the kitchen floor. This made a lasting impression on our young minds. The courage, faith and comradeship that exist amongst miners, especially in peril, are worthy to be told . . .

There was no provision for accidents at the pit top, no decent wage and very little concern about the safety and health of the men. Explosions were common and many precious lives were lost. It was only when explosions took place that public sympathy was aroused for the miner and his family.

James Griffiths, M.P., when he was Miners' Agent, summed up the position very aptly when he said that the public:

> 'Weeps for them when there is an explosion,
> Curses them when there is a strike,
> And forgets them the rest of the time.'

I became very interested in politics when very young for Father was a Radical. He could read only Welsh and I used to read all the news to him . . .

In the early days the only outside work for girls in our village was the Brickworks or the Colliery Screens. I was terrified that I would be sent to either of them. But when I was seventeen I was sent to learn dressmaking for twelve months. In 1908 I decided I would try and get into a larger business. I applied for three posts, two in Manchester, the other in Ystrad Rhondda. I had a favourable reply from the three but I chose Ystrad because it was nearer home. It was a flourishing business; it had large workrooms and a number of apprentices. I received £40 a year, living in, and clothes at cost price. But we had to work sixty-eight hours a week, and shops were open until midnight on Saturday night in those days.

It was in the Rhondda that I became keenly interested in politics and public work for the Church and Sunday School. It was here I met my husband Thomas T. Andrews. He had worked in the mines for several years, but had given it up for Insurance. He was a great reader and keenly interested in the Independent Labour Party, being one of five that formed the first branch of the I.L.P. in the Rhondda. I attended political meetings with him before our marriage and often found that I was the only woman present.

I joined the Co-operative Movement after marriage and became interested in developing Women's Guilds in the Rhondda. When the first Guild was formed at Ton Pentre in 1914, I was appointed first Secretary. I also joined the Suffrage Movement (non-militant).

Rhondda in those days was not very safe for Socialists or Suffragettes. I remember on one occasion two prominent Suffragettes came to address the I.L.P.

The meeting was held in a café on the main street. The local Young Liberals' League crowded outside shouting slogans and throwing rotten fruit and stones. They smashed the window, the meeting had to be closed, and the Suffragettes had to make an escape down a ladder to the riverside and walk to catch a train at the next station to avoid the mob! . . .

Because of the part the women played in the First World War, and as a result of continued agitation, the Government made some concession in 1918 and granted women over thirty the vote. But there were certain qualifications – they had to be married, or if single, had to occupy two rooms and own their own furniture.

These qualifications denied many women their rights as citizens. The women were very indignant and the demand for Adult Suffrage continued. Finally in 1928, the Act was passed giving votes to men and women at twenty-one years of age.

The Vote broke down age-long barriers to women in all professions. It opened the door for women to enter Parliament, local and national councils, law, medicine, industry, religion and all social work. Old customs were overthrown. No longer could the men persuade us that women were their intellectual inferiors. We were told when agitating for the Vote – often very patronisingly by men – that woman's place was to fit the child for the world. We retorted that if it was woman's place to fit the child for the world, it was also her place to fit the world for the child, and before we could do either, we must take an interest in politics. To organise the new woman voter into the Labour Party, a women's department was set up and women organisers appointed. I was the fourth and started my work in March 1919 . . .

I and my other colleagues launched out on this work with a deep conviction and missionary zeal, preaching this new gospel of Socialism and prepared to meet all opposition and difficulties. All our work had to be done from our own homes. I soon learnt typing and duplicating, which was essential.

In the early days, women were very new in politics, and were afraid of being called Suffragettes. Much educational work had to be done in simple language, and made interesting.

Realising this, I decided to interest them by charts, and the first one I drafted was 'Mother in the Home' surrounded by all the laws that affected her in every aspect of daily life.

This chart became very popular and I realized that visual aid was to play an important part in my propaganda work. Our Socialist propaganda had to have a sense of reality. We were not only a political Party, but a great Movement, concerned about human personalities and their well-being.

Effective propaganda work on Labour's policy was done by means of attractive tableaux and pageantry at our special rallies and 'Women's Months'. One outstanding procession was in Swansea. Sir Alfred Mond, its M.P., was Minister of Health and his plea for economy by cutting down on milk for babies and housing had aroused the women of the country. Our West Wales Advisory Committee organised a procession through the town with meetings in the Park. The band we had engaged failed us, so we had a silent procession carrying banners with slogans like these:

'LABOUR WOMEN SAY MOND MUST GO'
'STINT THE MILK AND STARVE THE CHILD'

It was interesting to see the public reading these banners as we passed by. At the next Election Mond did go and we won this seat for Labour for the first time!

One Woman's Story

~

Winifred Griffiths

About three weeks after Jim and I were married the glorious news broke on the world that the war was at an end and an armistice would be signed. The colliers had a day off work and Jim and I went to Llandeilo Fair. What a load seemed suddenly to be lifted from all our hearts, and with what hope we all said 'never again'! Now there was to be an election for a new government to tide over the transition from war to peace and from an economy geared to the service of the armed forces to one geared to peace-time requirements.

It was my first taste of an election campaign and I sampled all the various jobs. It was the very first election in Britain in which women were allowed to vote. Even so I failed to qualify as I was under thirty years of age. However this disqualification did not deter me from trying to persuade others more fortunate to vote for the Labour candidate, especially as he advocated votes for women on the same basis as men. I was happy to do any of the other work but when my husband pressed me to go and speak at meetings, I felt very apprehensive. After some hesitation I came to the conclusion that I must have the courage of my convictions and do my best – even if I risked making a fool of myself. As luck would have it the first meeting to which I was assigned was in a small mining village a few miles away. It was held in a chapel vestry and my little speech about women's rights, and how unfair it was that we had not got equal voting rights with men, got a rather cold reception. The all male audience obviously had some doubts about even the women over thirty being allowed to vote. They did not seem at all enthusiastic about demanding any more freedom for their women folk . . .

Our candidate Dr Williams polled 14,409 votes as against the 1,176 he had polled in the by-election of 1910. We were overjoyed at the result and confident that next time we would win the seat. In the meantime propaganda must continue. The Trades and Labour Council organised meetings, sometimes outdoors on the Square, sometimes indoors in the shabby Ivorites Hall. Besides local speakers my husband was able occasionally to get speakers from further afield. One interesting visitor was Sylvia Pankhurst, the only one of the Pankhurst family who was a Socialist as well as a Suffragette. She suffered badly in health as a result of the forcible feeding she had endured when on hunger strike in prison. The only way we could put her up was for her to share a room and large bed with a little girl, an orphaned niece of Mrs Jenkins, our landlady.

In our small working-class homes we almost always had to 'double up' and share in this way, and we thought nothing of it. However when Sylvia arrived and heard of our arrangements for her, she objected strongly and said she must have a room to herself. At first I was inclined to be resentful of what I thought was an example of middle class snobbery, until Jim soothed me by saying that 'poor thing, her nerves are so bad that perhaps she can only sleep if she is alone.' In the event we all went off to the meeting, from where a comrade was sent out to scout around for a suitable room. Sylvia's speech was about a visit to Soviet Russia from which she had only just returned. We had, as Socialists, hailed with delight the Russian Revolution of 1917. We had regarded it as the beginning of the triumph of our ideas. But already in 1919 the golden vision was a little tarnished. Stories came out of Russia which gave rise to doubts, but still we hoped. Sylvia had been full of confidence in the revolution and had gone out to make contact with its leaders. But alas, she had returned disillusioned and sad . . . but hope springs eternal – we could not so easily discard our faith in the great Russian Revolution and its implications for the workers of the world.

A Woman's Work is Never Done

~

Elizabeth Andrews

The first Women's Section was formed at Ton Pentre, Rhondda, in 1918 with the help of the local Trades Council. I was appointed Secretary. There were twelve women present. At that time the South Wales Miners' Federation was agitating for shorter hours and higher wages. When discussing this matter, the women felt that the time was long overdue to get something done to lighten the burden of the miner's wife.

I wrote a letter to the Miners' conference saying we wholeheartedly supported their demands and while doing so, thought the time had come when shorter hours for miners' wives should have some consideration. We also made a request that the question of pit baths should be a part of their campaign. This letter was read to the conference and interest was aroused, as well as some opposition. The Press gave this matter much publicity and I had many lively discussions with some of the miners' leaders . . .

In South Wales, the Ocean Colliery Company, with the personal interest of the two Misses Davies of Llandinam, gave the movement an impetus, and the first pit baths were built at Treharris. In 1919, I arranged for the Ton Pentre Section and the Co-operative Guild to visit these baths. Many other parties from the coalfield sponsored by the miners' lodges followed, and thus the campaign went on.

The Royal Commission on the Mining Industry – generally known from its chairman as the Sankey Commission – was set up in 1918. Dr Marion Phillips suggested that women from the mining areas should give evidence on housing and pit baths. I was asked by the South Wales Miners' Federation to represent South Wales. Mrs Hart came from Wigan, and Mrs Brown from Scotland. We three gave evidence.

When we arrived in London we were besieged by the Press at the hotel, and during the time we were giving evidence we were photographed and a minute description given of our dresses.

Many of the personal remarks amused us greatly. They expected us to be overawed at being in the King's Robing Room in the House of Lords where the Commission was held. They also expressed surprise at our calmness when giving evidence.

I dealt with the overcrowding in the mining areas of South Wales and the strain on the miner's wife, from lifting of tubs and heavy boilers. This accounted for the high maternal mortality. The drying of pit clothes in an overcrowded kitchen played havoc with the health of young children. The infant mortality rate in the Rhondda was 105 per 1,000.

The proposals put forward in the Sankey Commission Report included better housing, pit-head baths and holidays with pay. All these were shelved for many years and the position in the coalfield grew steadily worse. From 1921 to 1932, 250,000 people left South Wales to look for work elsewhere. The aftermath of the 1914-18 War had a disastrous effect on the coal industry in this country. Mass unemployment and the family Means Test drove many young members of the families away from home. Those who remained, unable to find jobs, expressed themselves by mass demonstrations, protest meetings and deputations . . .

The Miners' Lock Out following the General Strike of 1926 will ever be remembered in the mining valleys of Wales. Our Women's Organisations were faced with a tremendous responsibility in mitigating the distress caused by this terrible industrial struggle, in which they stood loyally by their menfolk in the fight for better conditions.

Our Advisory Council worked with the Relief Committee of the Standing Joint Committee of Industrial Women's Organisations, of which Dr Marion Phillips was Secretary, Mrs Ayrton Gould, Chairman, and Lady Slesser, Treasurer. Under the guidance of these three great women, we set up in Wales in a very short time a wonderful network of organisations to look after expectant and nursing mothers, children, and sick people.

Parcels of food, medical supplies, and clothing were given to those in need. Sewing Committees were set up and for these we bought material from money received as discount and dividend on purchases. The private traders as well as our Co-operative Societies were very generous. We made maternity outfits, baby garments, and children's clothes, as well as adult clothing. We cut up old clothing from parcels sent to us, and made thousands of garments in this way. Boot repairing centres were established; our men worked voluntarily and thousands of our people were kept shod as a result. We received in Wales nearly £21,000 from the Relief Committee's Central Fund, which became known as the 'Slesser Fund'.

Besides hundreds of parcels and sacks of clothing, we received boxes of condensed milk, cocoa, and baby food, and also large cases of footwear from the Boot and Shoe Operatives' Trade Union. Parcels came from Denmark, Norway, Sweden, Germany, Canada, Australia, and other countries. In London, Dr Marion Phillips organised an adoption scheme so that friends could look after a miner's child for the period of the Lock Out. Over 800 children came from Wales, selected from the largest families in greatest need. We arranged with the railway company to take parties of forty to fifty children to London each week. A few were adopted in Birmingham and Swindon.

Our Sewing Committees saw to it that each child was clothed decently so as not to be an object of pity on arrival. The hostesses met them at Paddington and took them to their homes.

At first parents were not very willing to let the children go, but once the first party wrote home to say what lovely homes they had, we could hardly cope with the demand. One little girl from a very poor home gave a description of her lovely bedroom overlooking a flower garden. She said it made her think that she was in Heaven. The railway company made generous concessions in fares and provided a special coach on the London train for these parties. Mrs Beatrice Green, of Abertillery, well known for her ability as speaker, addressed meetings in London to raise funds for the Committee. One incident made a lasting impression on her mind. It was an open-air meeting in a thickly-populated district. In the audience was a little ragged boy. He came near, tugged at her frock and said: 'I ain't got a penny miss, but I will sing for you.' He sang a popular song with such feeling that it carried away the meeting and the money thrown into the circle made a record collection. Mrs Joanna James, Tonypandy, and Mrs Herman, Pentre, also addressed meetings in London. The three were miners' wives and good speakers.

The Welsh children, when returning after the settlement of the Lock Out, were so loaded with presents for themselves and families, that we had to reserve two compartments for gifts only. Some of them had forgotten the name of their home towns and it took me all my time to sort them out. Lasting friendships were formed between the children, their parents and their hosts, who were by now 'Aunts and Uncles' to them all. Many a motherless child found a permanent home.

Women and the Miners' Lock Out

~

Dr Marion Phillips

Many of the youngsters when they arrived home and were met by their mothers at the stations had so improved that they did not recognize them. We have one letter which says: 'She looked like a little princess when she came back.'

Though occasionally, the children were difficult, for the most part they were friendly, fearless and grateful, and settled down into their new life in the most charming way. It was often pathetic to find that little girls of nine and ten were already accomplished housewives, throwing a pitiful light on the conditions of their homes, where the mothers have so to struggle against overwork that with the trials of poverty and large families, even little children must be pressed into the work.

Some of the children had never before been in a train. Large numbers had never been in a big town. It took them out of narrow circumstances into a wider life and this was still more the case with our last adoption scheme which bore fruit just before Christmas. In November, a Committee for the Relief of British Miners' Wives and Children was formed in Norway and they asked us to send them some children to whom they would give a three months' holiday in their country. We thought it was not wise to send small children so far away and therefore proposed that this offer should be made for young pit lads who had suffered so greatly during the Lock Out and for whom very little had been done . . .

> *'In the wretched little houses clustered round the silent pit-head, children are being born in homes which have been stripped of every saleable luxury. The mothers had been ill-nourished and living in continuous anxiety and face childbirth without any of the care and comfort which they need.' Appeal issued May, 1926.*

As the Lock Out proceeded, it became clear that some provision was urgently needed for the mothers and young babies.

After a study of the Census figures, we estimated that 400 babies were born every week in the coal-fields. We underestimated. The number was nearer 1,200. Everywhere there was distress at these times and we had to deal with it as quickly as possible. The story of misery and want which the Committee was able to put together from reports from various areas was heartrending, and the pitiful requests for help which poured in every day made it difficult for them to decide what was the most urgent job to be done. The following are a few extracts from letters:

> *'One woman came here to seek a nightdress and chemise to be laid up in. She had been in labour all night and walked up to my house before eight o'clock in the morning for the things. It took us all our time to get her home again. She had absolutely nothing for herself and child.'*

> *'I went to visit a mother who had only just been confined a few hours. The baby had been born in the same room in which they all had to live and eat. Six other small children and no one to look after the woman. Midwife had gone, only her husband.'*

> *'We are desperately in need of baby food. Babies are sickening, losing weight and some have had fits because they can't get usual food and now bread and water sops is their diet. This is an S.O.S. for babies'.*

Our local Secretaries were almost distracted by the many cases of illness and suffering in the mothers and lack of suitable food for the babies which it was totally impossible for them to relieve. Some of the mothers were unable to nurse their babies on account of exhaustion due to lack of nourishment, while others continued to feed them long after they should have been weaned because they could not buy suitable food, and we constantly had news of premature and still births owing to the mothers' weak condition.

> '*I have one baby two years old who has been ill and to provide him with nourishment my husband and myself have gone without. It is against my wish that I ask you to help me, but – I worry over my coming plight, for everything seems so black that I sometimes wonder if life is worth living.*'

> '*This is my fifth baby and I am hours awake at night without a wink of sleep waiting for another day so that my mind can be occupied with my housework und kiddies, as I dare hardly think about this little one. I have nothing for it and cannot get anything. I cannot turn to my own people as they are just pit folks in a sorry plight. I hope you will understand what this means to me, for it is not our fault we are as we are to-day . . . The poverty among the miners is pitiful, and we cannot make ends meet when they are working, so how can we do so now?*'

The majority of the voluntary workers were themselves miners' wives, often as badly off as those they helped. In some districts, however, the Secretary of the Council was not herself involved in the Lock Out, and the same was so of some of her workers. They threw themselves into the struggle with no less enthusiasm and in many cases the husbands of the secretaries, and even the children, took a good share of the work upon their shoulders. Many of them found their houses turned into clothes stores and could never sit down to a meal without being called several times to the door, but they bore it all with wonderful patience.

As the winter came of course the need was still greater, and letters came to us of children who cried at night with the cold, and women who had no bedding when the time of their confinement came. We made special appeals for clothing and blankets of all sorts. In many districts sewing parties were started, both in the mining areas and outside them . . .

Amongst our papers are many reports of women who had cut up their underclothing for their children, and had none themselves. Occasionally a woman was found wearing her husband's coat, and in one case, between them, they had one pair of boots. We redoubled our appeals for more clothes and they were answered. It was said that the clothes that we received towards the end of the Lock Out were better than at the beginning. At first people had sent those they had finished with, and later on they sent whatever they could spare that they were actually using. At Christmas time a special appeal was made for Christmas puddings, cakes, and similar dainties, and we sent out 256 packages as well as 24 batches of toys.

But the problem of boots dwarfed all these. Altogether we purchased for children and women about 34,000 pairs, and in a few cases we made grants to local areas where they could get suitable purchases from local traders. We also bought £750 worth of clogs. It was pointed out to us that if we could repair the boots, we would be able to keep a great many more children dry-shod, and in September we started a boot-repairing scheme through our Women's Committees. By these means more than 40,000 pairs of boots were repaired. Before we started this work, the Society of Friends had been running a similar scheme in the Rhondda and Pontypridd, and some of our grants went to their admirably organized centres where money had become very scarce. A good many Miners' Lodges and Relief Committees had also been doing similar work . . .

The work was undoubtedly a great joy to the colliers, who felt that they were able thereby to do something substantial to help. The children's bootless-ness was particularly serious at this time because unless they could go to school they could not get school meals, and we had reports of parents carrying their children there so that they should not lose this advantage. In one centre a man on a motor-bike took the children's boots in the morning and left them with carpet slippers, returning at night with the repairs done. The teachers always co-operated, and I think in a great many cases were very generous with their gifts.

Here are some of the stories that came to us . . . A four-year-old child came up from South Wales to be adopted in London, wearing such appalling boots that her feet were badly blistered and it would be some time before she could put any on . . . A mother writing a letter of thanks for the help given to her when her baby was born put in a special appeal that the Labour women bringing round the food to her should have some new boots. 'It's so sad to see them with their feet wet.' The truth was that most of these women were miners' wives themselves, had worn out their shoes after tramping the rough roads and had no money to buy new ones . . .

The socialist women in Europe have nearly all sent some contribution. The Norwegians sent us magnificent supplies of clothes and cases of Cod Liver Oil. From the Swedish women we had many gifts of clothes, most of them made specially for our people.

The American Committee collected a good deal of money for us in the early months. The United Ladies' Garment Workers and the Jewish Forward were especially generous donors, and the total sum received in dollars was about £10,000.

During the later months of the year we received the sum of £13,000 from the Russian Trade Union fund. In August, they invited the Miners' Federation to send a delegation to visit their country and help in maintaining and increasing the interest of their workers in contributing. They asked that miners' wives should be included.

The women spent six weeks touring Russia. They addressed a wonderful series of meetings and saw every important industrial area from Leningrad to Tiflio and Buku. They returned not only with a good knowledge of Russia but having done splendid service for the women and children in the coalfields. This was the first occasion on which a delegation of working-class housewives had made an official visit of this sort . . .

The toll of the mines is not only to be counted in the brave and tragic stories of pit disasters. Women and children suffered and some of them died in the struggle of 1926. The Women's Committee ask all who helped then to realize that their work will not be over until the miner's toil and danger is lessened and his family assured of a decent standard of life.

A Woman's Work is Never Done

~

Elizabeth Andrews

The campaign on maternity and child welfare is a story on its own, and has to be told so that women of to-day can appreciate the work that was done in the early days for the care of mother and child . . .

There was a feeling prevalent that it was not very respectable for speakers to discuss maternal mortality and maternal morbidity in public meetings. I met with this attitude myself as Guild speaker, but I soon found that our menfolk were very sympathetic. It was a sad home when the mother died or was maimed in health. Many a sad story I heard from mothers in those early days who were suffering as a result of neglect during childbirth. I could speak with some feeling on this matter for ten of our family were born before 1900 under the 'handy woman' regime.

Between 1891 and 1900 there was an average of 140,000 infant deaths each year. From 1910 to 1922 the death rate of mothers in the Rhondda was the third highest for the country due to lack of housing and hospitals where serious and abnormal cases could be dealt with. The incidence of deaths from sepsis, more commonly known as 'bed fever', was very high. The miner's wife in those days ran greater risks at childbirth than her man in the pit . . .

Our Labour Women's organisations seized every opportunity to get these facts across, and to arouse local authorities to make full use of their powers.

The 1918 Maternity Act made it compulsory on local authorities to set up Maternity and Child Welfare Clinics, but as with all reforms, much work had to be done to convince mothers of their value. Many ghosts had to be laid – false modesty, ignorance, and the old-fashioned idea that mothers knew all about motherhood by instinct, and needed no advice.

The Rhondda Council was ready to adopt any new proposals

from the Government on Maternity and Child Welfare, and so led the way. The 1918 Act suggested that the Council should co-opt two women representing women's organisations on Maternity and Child Welfare Committees. There were no women councillors in those days. We campaigned in all the counties of Wales urging local authorities to do this and get on with this important work.

We were very surprised at the attitude of many County Medical Officers of Health when we made this request. Our letters were quite courteous and business like, but one County M.O.H. referred to them as *'wild hysterical effusions'* and falling back on a scriptural phraseology, said the Council must be charitable to such people *'as they know not what they are talking about'*. In another county we were called a *'lot of interfering busybodies'* . . .

We went forth with our requests to local authorities for a municipal service of Midwives, Health Visitors, Maternity and Child Welfare Clinics, Home Helps and special food for expectant and nursing mothers, and in the rural areas for travelling Maternity Clinics and telephone kiosks in every village to give access to nurse and doctor . . .

We have been spared to see the results of the campaign in the reduction of maternal and infantile mortality and greater care of expectant and nursing mothers in Wales. Precious lives have been saved, mothers are healthier and babies are bonnier, but there is still much work to be done . . .

The Maternity and Child Welfare Act of 1918 provided for the health of babies up to two, and at five the school authorities stepped in, but the damage was done to the child's health between these ages. Nursery schools were needed to fill this gap.

In 1931 our Advisory Council carried on an intensive campaign on nursery schools. We met several Labour groups on Councils to press them to work for one nursery school to be established in each education area. We women felt if this could be done, it would be far more effective to convince them of this need than passing resolutions. We also got them to agree to include nursery schools in their Election addresses.

In 1919 the agitation for Mothers' Pensions received a great impetus from a visit paid to this country by Judge Henry Neil of Chicago, the father of Mothers' Pensions in America. He addressed meetings in many parts of this country, explaining what the United States had done for the widows and orphans.

I was privileged to entertain the Judge at home. He told me he was going to devote all his time touring and lecturing on Mothers' Pensions so that it became a 'universal act of justice' to the widows and orphans. Widows had no alternative in those days but Poor Law relief or the Workhouse. There was a severe means test if the widow gained a few shillings by taking in washing. If she had a piece of furniture that she could sell, her allowance was reduced. Many men, women and children of these brave mothers remember those days of great sacrifice.

Then there was the campaign for children's allowances which we called 'The Endowment of Motherhood'. It took Labour women some time to get the Party to accept this as policy. Trade Unionists feared that it would affect wages and wage negotiations. But it was accepted in the end and the country today enjoys the result of these strenuous efforts of our pioneers.

One Woman's Story

~

Winifred Griffiths

Some time in 1927 I became a member of the local Women's section of the Labour Party. The members were nearly all miners' wives or mothers. Some were very intelligent and took a real interest in policy, while others came to the meetings for companionship and because they were for 'Labour' – our party, right or wrong! Before long I was voted into the Chair and remained Chairman over the years. We had very occasional visits from the Welsh Women's Organiser, Mrs Andrews. She was a dear soul, but the whole of Wales was her parish, so we could not expect to see her often. We were largely thrown on our own resources and had to make do with local speakers, Councillors and the like, and of course we did our fair share of organising money raising events, and social functions for the Party. When the first pit-head bath was opened at Cwmparc Colliery in the Rhondda valley, we organised a trip for our members to see for themselves how it worked. Even so some of them were not won over to the idea, being afraid that their men's clothes would not be dried properly, and that they would get pneumonia coming home after a shower! But the younger ones hailed the idea with delight as a means of banishing at last the dirt of the pit from their homes.

Towards the end of 1927 I agreed to be nominated by the Women's Section as a candidate for the Rural District Council Election which would take place in the spring of 1928. Almost as soon as it had been confirmed that I should stand as a candidate for the Yniscedwyn Ward, in which I lived, I discovered that I was pregnant. In the early months of pregnancy I always felt sick and out of sorts, so I was terribly tempted to withdraw my candidature. However, my husband urged me on and somehow I got through the campaign with its canvassing of the voters, and I also stood my ground all day at the polling booth on the day of the election. The seat I contested had been occupied by the same 'Independent' member for many years, and I hardly expected to dislodge him. The count, which took place immediately after the closing of the polling booth, revealed that I was in by a majority of eight votes. Congratulations were showered on me, but I was almost too tired to care, and was only too anxious to escape to home and sleep. Next day, just as I was starting on some badly needed house cleaning, there appeared on the doorstep a strong contingent of Labour Women from the Ward to congratulate me . . .

I was also one of a deputation to the Ministry of Health in London to seek permission to build more houses. I was able to point out the especial hardship caused by housing shortage in a mining area, where the collier still returned home with all his dirt. I remember citing the case of a miner and his wife who had two small children, a toddler and a baby. They lived in two rooms, a bedroom and a living-room with only a parlour grate. This one parlour grate had to suffice, not only for cooking and heating water, drying children's and baby's clothes, but also to heat water for the miner's bath and to dry his pit clothes. An almost impossible task for the poor young wife. I am glad to say the Ministry officials were sympathetic to my special pleading and we obtained consent to build more houses.

I have written of my early conversion to socialism. If confirmation of my faith was needed I had it in full during my years in the South Wales Coalfield. Those years of depression served to underline the inadequacy of the capitalist system to provide justice and a good life for the vast majority of our people. With his colleagues, my husband was desperately trying to rebuild the membership of the Miners' Federation so that it could be more effective in fighting for better conditions. It was uphill work and controversy often raged as to whether industrial or political action was more effective. The sensible answer seemed to be to use both. In the course of time I had an opportunity to help a little on the political side.

An occasional visitor to our home, when he came to Wales on propaganda tours, was J. Walton Newbold, whom we first met at the Labour College, where he gave a course of lectures. His name came to be more widely known in later years when he entered the House of Commons as a Communist member

He told us of his appointment as editor of the monthly paper called 'The Social Democrat' which was the organ of the Social Democratic Federation. We heard his plans for the paper and among other things of his intention to start a Women's Page. It was not to be of the usual kind but was to have a definite political content. Then he asked if I would write the page! I hardly knew how to answer. I had always wanted to write, but I had no training. He insisted I could do it, and, hearing that I was making arrangements to accompany Jim to the Trades Union Congress, to be held in Belfast that year, he suggested that my first effort should be a description of the Congress . . .

On our return home I duly wrote a report for the 'Social Democrat'. I continued writing for the paper for about two years, only giving up at the birth of my fourth baby. My plan was to write two articles a month, one of topical interest, and one of a series. The first series I called – greatly daring – 'The Life of Women through the Ages' . . . I had been much influenced by the South African woman writer Olive Schreiner. I shared her dislike of forms of society where women were either slaves or playthings of men. Our Western world seemed to be moving towards greater equality of the sexes. In our own country women had, at long last, achieved equal voting rights with men. Increasing numbers of women were getting a wider education and more were being trained for the professions. Though the changes had not yet permeated down through society to the benefit of many working class women, the time would surely come. In my concluding article of the series I wrote: 'Women are out to change the point of view that would consign them to be the drudges of the world or alternatively parasites and playthings of men.' After the completion of these twelve articles I did two shorter series, one called 'A day in a woman worker's life' based on my own experiences as a domestic servant, shop assistant, waitress and miner's wife. The other was called 'Three years as a Councillor' again based on my own experience. Keeping up with all my other duties, domestic and public, left me with little time for preparing the articles, and often I had to steal two or three quiet hours from sleep, in order to get them into the post on time. Even so it was a task that afforded me a great deal of satisfaction . . .

Early in 1936, Dr J.H. Williams, the M.P. for Llanelly died and at once letters began to reach Jim from friends in the constituency saying how much they hoped he would accept nomination for the by-election. I must confess that as we talked it over I argued for turning it down and staying with the Federation . . .

Also I had made a niche for myself in the life of our little community and I hated the thought of uprooting. I soon realised, however, that this was something Jim had always wanted, and I knew he had the ability to make good in a wider sphere. If he was nominated he was fairly certain to become the candidate, and the seat was a safe one which he could not fail to hold for Labour.

And so in mingled pride and sadness ended our intimate connection with the upper part of the Swansea Valley, and we returned to Burry Port to face whatever the new life might have in store . . .

We moved in the summer of 1936 and by that time I was reconciled to the change. I argued with myself that I had often felt cut off from the mainstream of life, up among the hills in Ystradgynlais, with a growing family to care for. I confidently expected that as a Member of Parliament's wife, life for me would widen out with new opportunities. Moreover the salary of £400 plus a small grant from the Miners' Federation seemed to promise opulence . . .

Our son, Harold, came home one day with a request from the headmaster for any shoes the family might have outgrown, as there were a number of children who had no shoes to wear to school. I immediately set to work on plans for a Boot Fund. The heads of the local schools were only too pleased that I had taken the initiative and together we were able to secure that all children in need had a sound pair of shoes that winter. Through the Boot Fund and in other ways, I got to know our poorer neighbours and was able to help them a little through the generosity of friends who sent clothes and Christmas parcels. These small activities together with the care of the children, the house and the garden, kept me busy, but the widening of life and its opportunities did not happen, and I sometimes got depressed and despondent. I am sure this must happen to the wives of many Members of Parliament when the husband is away in London through the week, and occupied by constituency and propaganda work at the weekend . . .

If I was a dictator I would call a standstill to any increase in the personal incomes of people above a certain level until such time as all below that level were brought into line, and I would halt the construction of luxury flats and hotels and of prestige building of all kinds, until the homeless and slum dwellers were decently housed. My next priority would be the rebuilding or modernising of out-of-date hospitals and schools.

I wish we could wage war on poverty and bad housing with the same urgency and single-mindedness we brought to bear on defeating the enemy in wartime . . .

At times I think back to the years before the first World War, when I was still in my teens, and the idea of 'From each according to his ability, and to each according to his need' excited my imagination and made me a Socialist. The idea became a guiding light by which I hoped to shape my life. Since then I have tried to do so with varying success, but the realisation of the dream of a society governed by those two simple precepts seems no nearer . . .

This to me is a depressing thought, as is the thought that Labour may be in danger of becoming merely a Party and losing the idealism that made it a Movement.

After a long lifetime on the sidelines of politics I am convinced that politics are not enough to bring about our dream. The minds and hearts of people must be won over.

Someone once coined a phrase about 'hitching one's wagon to a star'. Hope has always been related to looking upwards – to the mountains or the stars . . . I believe firmly in evolution and look upon it as a hopeful creed. For, imperfect creatures though we are, we can yet reach out towards perfection. 'What I aspired to be and was not, comforts me.'

CHAPTER 12

WAR AND NEW HORIZONS

WAR AND NEW HORIZONS

Today the scene described (1930s) has greatly changed. The waging of war has filled the valleys with work and wages. Boys swagger on the streets with pockets full of money. Omnibuses crowded with women and girls rumble to and fro between the scattered mining villages and the concentrated munition factories . . . The tide of migration has turned . . . The explosive power of new experience has dimmed the memories of the nineteen-thirties. The sufferings of enforced idleness have given place to the horrors of bombing and burning.

But there will be a morrow to this war . . . and when that dawn breaks, . . . it is to be hoped that we shall have profited by this book

(Thomas Jones, foreword to Ginzberg,
A World Without Work, 1942)

In this, the final chapter, the three women whose personal stories have featured throughout this volume are brought together. The coming of the Second World War brought upheaval and change to their lives, but, in contrast to many young women from the valleys, they did not leave their home area, and chose to marry locally either during, or soon after the war. The appeal of marriage and the hope of a stable family life was strong following the uncertainties of wartime, and the government and media reinforced attractive images of domesticity and motherhood. But it was during the war too that both Maggie Pryce Jones and Mair Eluned McLellan became more politically aware and began to identify with the Labour and Communist parties respectively.

The years which followed 1945, brought the industrial and political changes which the people of the valleys had been working and hoping for during the inter-war years. How different their lives would have been had the reforms come sooner. Maggie Pryce Jones, for example, laments that the National Health Service did not exist at the time of her mother's illness. By the same token, it is unlikely that Mair Eluned McLellan would have been denied schooling because of her asthma had she been born after the war. Yet despite her lack of formal education she, like Beatrice Wood, realised her ambition to write. Maggie Pryce Jones later became a civil servant, in addition to raising a family.

This final chapter is one of comparatively unproblematic 'happy endings'. Let us enjoy it, but at the same time be aware that autobiography is a special kind of history.

Kingfisher of Hope

~

Maggie Pryce Jones

There was talk of war. It seemed to me that it had gone away, but really it had not, it was just that I had had too many things on my mind to listen to the old Murphy radio. I took heed one day when the haulier who brought our coal stopped to chat to my neighbour. I heard him say, 'It will be different this time, Tom, we'll all be in it, not just the soldiers, boy!' Tom agreed and I was afraid . . .

Gareth was often in the house, but never when Dad was at home – I was too afraid of him meeting Dad because he had become nasty and rude to anyone who called to see me. I was very depressed. I had instinctively promised Mam that I would look after the family, and I would do so as best I could, but Gareth was going away and would surely forget me. He was the only person that I could talk to. He understood; I could share my thoughts with him. He made me feel that I was worth his worrying; no one else cared as he did.

One sunny Sunday I was sitting in the cool gwli, shelling peas for our dinner, when Bryn and Davy called me into the house. A special broadcast, they said. They were excited at the prospect of war, not really understanding what it would mean.

Dad had been right after all, we were at war. The news did not sink in yet, I was too busy caring for the family. After all, the war was a long way from our valley. But I learned soon enough that no place was far from this war. Soon all the young folk who were old enough to join the forces were gone, not waiting for their calling-up papers. I felt trapped. I wanted, desperately, to join the services myself. Then, a shattering blow, Gareth told me that he had volunteered for the Royal Air Force. 'I'd rather go now than wait to be called up, Maggie. University's out till the end of the war,' he said.

I felt sick. 'I'll write regularly, I promise.' He caught my arm. 'Please, Maggie, I must go. Don't be like my mother; she won't talk to me at all.' A few weeks later I saw him off to a secret destination where he was going to train as a pilot. His parents asked me to keep in touch, but I did not do so.

Next to go was Davy, who also joined the Air Force. We saw him and other young men from the village off at the tiny Halt. Everyone except Dad, who called him 'a silly young fool' and stayed at home, was proud of him. Now I lived in a queer kind of limbo, too young to join in the talk of the older women, although I had exactly the same work and worries as they had, yet too old for the young people left in the village, because I no longer had anything in common with them, even though we were the same age.

Dad was still drinking heavily and was out most evenings. I always tried to be in bed before he got back, but he would bellow up the stairs until I came down to hear the recital of his day's activities. John was failing in health. I prayed that he would not die for many years, for I dreaded the thought of being in the house without him or Davy. Dad was becoming more violent in his drink, mainly, I thought, because his conscience was troubling him.

John shook his head when I told him this. 'I don't think so cariad,' he answered. 'If I could believe that, I would be a happy man. I'm afraid for you, Maggie.'

I laughed and kissed him. 'Don't worry about me, John, I'm all right: God will look after me,' I said.

He smiled. 'You're right, of course He will. I should have known that.' Then he turned to his Bible.

The village settled into a routine as the war dragged on. We were always afraid that the pits would be bombed, but they never were in spite of Lord Haw Haw's threats. We would crouch fearfully in the *cwtch* under the stairs whenever we heard the unmistakable drone of German planes in the night sky. Dad's continual assertion that the collieries were German-owned and never would be bombed did nothing to allay our fears.

As the months went by, so many men wanted to leave the pits to join the services that the government declared mining a reserved occupation, on a par with the armed forces, and men with a conscientious objection to fighting were allowed to work in the pits instead. They were called Bevin Boys after the man who instigated the idea, Ernest Bevin. Many of these men married local girls and stayed in the valley; others took their wives back to their own areas when the war ended.

Children from towns and cities were evacuated to the valleys.

They came in search of safety and many of them fell in love with the quiet place, growing up and later settling here. Quite a few of these children never saw their homes or parents again, but the bombs hardly touched our valley. We often thought how lucky we were when devastation was raining down on our cities and towns.

I had heard from Gareth only twice since he had gone away, but I was not worried, as many families had not heard from their loved ones at all. They were on the move and regulations forbade them to give any information about their movements. All their letters were censored to delete any such information. I was confident that Gareth would never forget me. Had he not given me a bunch of lovely velvet violets on our last walk? 'Real flowers die, Maggie,' he had said. 'These will live and remind you of me until I come home.' Then I heard from Bryn that my Gareth had been home on leave. 'The boys were talking, Mag,' he said. 'Gareth's a fighter-pilot now, he's off to Canada. Went back in a great hurry,' they said.

Intense despair swept over me. It was as if I had been told that my love was dead, just as Mam was dead. Then, I had had Gareth to talk to, I kept thinking. There was no one I could talk to now, no one in the world to understand. I was heart-broken, but could not shed a tear.

I longed to get away, to the forces, to London, anywhere, but I could not leave Ann and the boys. I was seventeen years old, trapped in this valley with no light in my tunnel of misery, none at all. I was worried about John, too. The doctor said his heart was weak. He would sit in his corner, taking no interest in anything around him. My heart ached to see him so white and frail.

One morning, when I offered him his bread and milk, he waved it away and looked at me dully. I called Laura from next door, and she sent me for the doctor. John was in the infirmary at Merthyr by dinner time. That evening a policeman called and said that his condition had worsened. Bryn and I hurried to see him, but he was in a deep sleep from which he never woke. He looked so peaceful in the narrow bed covered by the red hospital blanket. I was glad that his end had been peaceful, not tormented like Mam's . . .

For the first time I felt that God had deserted me. I did not see how I could go on. But where there is a small child, such notions have no time to take root, and the following morning I asked Dad what he was going to do about the rent.

He cried and promised to stop drinking, but offered no real solution. Bryn was now working on top pit, but he could only help a little as he had a girlfriend and spent most of his time at her home. Dad had driven him away with his nastiness and drinking. So I saw the landlady and asked for time to pay our arrears. Fortunately she was agreeable, but now it was imperative that I find work as quickly as possible. Dad forgot his promise and carried on drinking, more heavily than before.

At this time a canteen was opened at the colliery to supply the men with sandwiches to supplement the small food-ration. Clothes were rationed too, and we all had ration-books for sweets and basic foods, and clothing coupons for clothes. Many better-off people found it hard to manage, but I managed nicely. In fact our clothing coupons were often passed on because we could not afford to buy new clothes.

There was a Works Committee on top pit now, responsible for running the canteen. When I asked a member of the committee if I could be employed there, he was delighted to accept me, labour being hard to find at the price they could afford. Most women were earning high wages in the munitions factory . . .

Every morning the colliery officials, 'firemen' as they were called, came to the canteen and stayed long after the other men had left. They were all middle-aged men, and for some reason I was able to speak to them far more freely than I could to the younger ones and I did not feel so shy.

These men were patient and tolerant of my presence in their company. They held lengthy discussions on every topic under the sun, from war news, to my particular love, opera. I listened to their talk about the merits of political parties and politicians. My interest was strongly roused when, one morning, the conversation came round to Winston Churchill.

I had had no real personal interest in politics until then. I had thought vaguely that all members of parliament were the same. When I heard of the troops being sent to Tonypandy in the Rhondda Valley, however, I was anxious to know more. I began listening to talks on the wireless and borrowing books about the history of the Merthyr valley. I read about the ironmasters of Cyfarthfa and their harsh treatment of their workers. Without realising it, I was already moving towards the party I would support all my life, doing so with anger inside me as I read of the hunger and hardships endured in my own valley. All my spare time, now, was spent reading, anything from Dickens to Dumas and Austen, the latter a light relief. The more I read, the more confident I became, and soon I was joining in the discussions with Harold, Bob, Dan and the other firemen. I was still as busy as ever, but I did not mind as much now: I felt that I was working towards a future of my own when the family were old enough to leave home.

Dad was quiet these days. In his own strange way I think he was proud of my new-found ability to hold my own in conversation with men such as these colliery officials. Though in private he professed to despise men such as these, secretly he envied them: they were a close-knit group, made closer by the dangers they shared beneath ground. As the news from the war front continued good, everyone's spirits were lifted by the hope that soon the war would be ended. I believed that Gareth must have found another girl to love. His parents only nodded coldly when we met while shopping. I thought bitterly that they would be glad anyway, they always wanted a Chapel girl as their daughter-in-law. I knew that I was being prejudiced, but I did not care: I was hurt by their coldness.

I accepted an invitation to the pictures from Ronnie, a young surface worker. I was not particularly interested, but the other women in the canteen persuaded me that I should go. 'It will do you good. I know his family and they're respectable people,' Margaret said. She was such a nice person herself that I agreed to accept the invitation.

Dad was now a haulier on the surface of the colliery and he knew Ronnie and his father, who both worked near him. When he found out that I was seeing Ronnie, he went out of his way to be rude to them both.

Ronnie had been taking girls out since he first began working. On our second meeting, he took me home to meet his parents. I realized, as soon as I met his mother, that I had been taken to his home quickly to ease her worries about the sort of girl her only child was consorting with. I must have passed the test because, less than six months after our first meeting, it was his parents, not Ronnie himself, who suggested that we became engaged on the day of their own Silver Wedding.

I was unsure of my feelings. I certainly did not feel the love I had felt for Gareth, but I was happy in his company and I knew that life would not be the same without him, so I agreed to the engagement on condition that we wait at least two years before marrying . . .

I worried about Dan and Ann, but as marriage was a long way off I settled down to my new-found happiness. My worries about living with a man and sleeping in the same bed were pushed to the back of my mind. I knew that I did not want children; I was afraid, after seeing Mam die, about leaving a family behind.

I had, of course, no idea of what marriage entailed. Mam had not told me, and there was no one else to ask. Birth control was a topic I had never heard of until Jen and I were talking one day and the subject came up. Neither of us knew much about the matter, which was not, in any case, particularly important to us, so we forgot about it. It was up to the husbands.

One day Bryn came home from work and said, out of the blue, 'I met Ronnie, Mag. I know how much you liked Gareth. I liked him too, but Ronnie is a nice chap. Don't let Dad spoil it for you again.' I wondered, briefly, what Dad could have had to do with it, but put it down as a figure of speech . . .

Ronnie was pushing me to set a date for our wedding; he thought that Dad was getting more violent and he worried about me. I, for my part, hated the thought of leaving Dan and Ann alone with Dad. It would be several months before Dan was old enough to enlist, as he intended, in the Air Force, and as Ronnie and Dad were completely incompatible, the problem seemed to have no solution. I was afraid too, that Dan would lose his temper and retaliate one evening for all the beatings he had been given in the past. All these worries, combined with my fear of marriage, drove me one day to break off my engagement.

I missed Ronnie so much in the days which followed, however, that I was happy to take my ring back when he asked me to re-consider. Now he was determined that we set the date, so I settled on August 17th, seven months away, confident that by then my worries would have been solved.

Dad's reaction to my news surprised me. He asked me to sit down and listen carefully to what he was going to say. I was expecting him to beg me to stay at home, so when he began by asking me not to hate him, I was mystified. When, however, I heard his story, I was so angry I could have hit him in the face. Gareth had come back for me as he had promised, bringing an engagement ring with him, – and Dad had told him that I was already engaged, to an American airman from the base near Cardiff. As if through a fog, I heard him continue, 'He left an address for you to contact him, but I burned it.' I could not take it in. I heard Dad begging me not to hate him, but hate him I did, how I loathed and hated him. How could he have been so cruel – and why tell me now? Was he trying to stop me marrying Ronnie? I called the dog to heel and left the house. As I left, I heard him call out, 'I didn't know how we could manage without you, Maggie,' but I did not want to listen.

I walked up the mountain, along the path that Gareth and I had so often followed, the dog, Jock, at my side looking up anxiously as tears poured down my face. It seemed so long ago that I had sat there with Gareth, yet nothing had changed. There was still a little whitewashed cottage, Maes-y-gollen, nestling in the midst of the tall, dark woods across the valley; the river still flowed along the valley floor; the air was still sweet, the birdsong as clear as ever in the silence of the mountain top.

I thought about my lost love, glad to know the truth at last: he had not deserted me, after all. I felt sick when I remembered the thoughts I had harboured against his parents, – how they must have hated me for hurting their son. 'He's probably married by now; after all it's been years,' I thought. 'And Ronnie's here. He's good and kind, he loves me and . . . and I love him, though not in the same way.'

My mind calm, my anger under control, I made my way home, remembering, as I did so, Bryn's words, 'Don't let Dad spoil it for you again, Maggie.' My brother must have known the story all along, but I felt no animosity towards him: he had felt the weight of Dad's fist too often.

Back home, I took the velvet violets from their place in my drawer, placed them between the pages of John's Bible, then put it away in a safe cupboard. The past was over, and with it my dread of marriage. I was free to plan my future with Ronnie.

Wednesday's Child

~

Beatrice Wood

My brother met a girl while he was stationed in Stoke-on-Trent. She was in service there, and they were going to get married, so who better to be his best man than his best friend, whose name was Jimmy. Well, the young man came down to stay with us the night before the wedding. He slept on our couch downstairs. After the wedding they went back and they were posted to Catterick.

Then my brother was posted to Italy. They were trying to capture Mount Cassino. We heard that it was a suicide mission. Thousands died, my brother among them. He was just twenty-seven. He was driving an army truck when it was blown up.

My mother went nearly out of her mind. She would just sit and stare into blank space. She was beside herself with grief. And to make matters worse, they had buried him in Italy. She never really got over it.

Jimmy, my brother's friend, went back to his unit, and there was a letter waiting for him, releasing him from the army to work in industry. It seems that they needed planes more than soldiers at the time.

He wrote to my mother asking her if she minded if he came down for a week as he would like to see us all again. My mother said yes. Then the teasing began. 'Oh, it's a sprat to catch a mackerel,' and punning remarks like that. My mother, being the person that she was, could see a match here. She liked Jimmy very much. I came home from work at dinner time as I always did, and my mother said, 'Take that boy out somewhere – he is on holiday and hasn't got anyone to go out with.' I was making faces behind his back at my mother, who wasn't taking any notice of me, so what could I do? I had to say yes. I took him to the pictures, and by the time I had come out I was smitten. He was so attentive and pleasant. I thought he was wonderful. I don't know what he thought of me. My mother liked him, and that is saying something, because she never liked any boy I had been out with before.

Anyway, he was going home to Barry (where he was from) the following day, and he asked me if I would like to go with him for a few days. I said, 'You must be joking. No way would my mother let me go away for a few days with a boy.' He said, 'I have already asked your mother and she said it was all right.' Now, this is not the mother I knew! She must have liked Jimmy a lot for her to say yes.

We went to Barry and I met his parents and his sister and brother. Then after tea we went for a walk, and while we were out he asked me if I would get engaged, and out of the blue I said yes.

Now, getting engaged is not as easy as it seems. You don't know how much money the boy has got. We met in Cardiff to buy the ring the following weekend. But I didn't know the jewellery shops were closed for half-day on Saturday. I was so disappointed, I was in tears. You see, I had told all the girls in work that I was getting engaged, and they would all want to see the ring. Well, we came back to Merthyr as the jewellery shops were open. Was I glad! There were three in town. Anyway, it was very embarrassing. I didn't know how much money Jimmy had . . .

We went into the two shops. I couldn't see what I wanted, and besides, I was very shy, so I wouldn't speak up and tell them I wanted a ring with a square stone. Anyway, we came to the third and last shop, and the smallest. I didn't think I could have anything in there. I had a lump in my throat. And we didn't have a lot of time because the shop would be closing. We had wasted a lot of time in Cardiff. We went into the shop and were shown the usual tray of rings with the sales patter. I wanted a ring so badly I picked one out of the tray and tried it on. I even asked the price of it. I was determined I was going to work on Monday with a ring – round or square.

'That one, madam, is three pounds ten shillings.' Now to me three pounds was a lot of money. So, thank goodness, Jimmy said at last, 'You want a better one than that.' But I still didn't know how much money he had. So the shopkeeper picked one out and I asked, 'How much is that?' 'Seven pounds,' he said. I couldn't let Jimmy pay seven pounds, so just to get out of the shop, I managed to say, 'Well, really, I wanted a square one,' hoping I could get out of the shop before the tears would flow out. I had had enough, and I was so disappointed. But undaunted, the jeweller went off and brought another tray, and there was just the ring I wanted. But I didn't like to pick it up because I didn't know how much it was. Jimmy said, 'Look, there's a square one. Is that what you wanted?' The jeweller took it out and asked me to try it on. It was a perfect fit and looked so nice. The jeweller could sense a sale here, so he said, 'That is just you, madam! It's just perfect!' He turned to Jimmy and said, 'Don't you think so, sir?'

Jimmy just nodded his head. I think he was getting a bit fed up with a hard-to-please fiancée. But it wasn't that I was hard to please – I just didn't know the money situation. I was hoping Jimmy would ask 'How much?' – but he left it to me. I thought of all the girls in work, how they would envy me, but before I could ask how much the jeweller said, 'That one is ten pounds, madam.' I put it back. Ten pounds! Ten pounds in those days was at least three weeks' wages.

Jimmy got his money out and paid the ten pounds and still had money to spare. It was a beautiful ring. I had never owned a ring before.

When I got home I was showing it to my mother and stepfather. My stepfather said, 'Ten pounds! He must be mad!' When my mother heard the price she went straight away and told all her neighbours about my ten pounds ring. The house was full of people pulling my hand this way and that. My mother was beaming with pride to think of a daughter of hers having a ten pound ring. I am sure she gave Jimmy an extra potato for his dinner that day, she was so pleased . . .

I had only known Jimmy four months when we were engaged, and married four months later. The following year I had a lovely baby girl.

Shadows on the Wall

~

Mair E. McLellan

Despite the asthma, I took a great interest, not only in the war, but in politics. My early feeling that the French Revolution had been a good thing was strengthened by the books and papers I read. My father had both *Das Kapital* and *Mein Kampf* on his bookshelf. He also had books on Astronomy and Physics which made riveting reading, although I found *Das Kapital* dull.

There was a woman evacuee, evacuated along with her little boy, and she had taken to calling on my father every Friday night. She brought us the *Soviet Weekly* and also the Friday edition of the *Daily Worker*. Although I found the *Soviet Weekly* interesting at first and liked the idea that there were no poor there but equal opportunities for all, I rapidly found it too simplistic. The *Daily Worker* was a different kettle of fish. It helped me form my idea of the country I would like to see being built after the war was over. I was not the only one. After the battle of Stalingrad, when the Germans had been defeated, several small flags with the hammer and sickle could be seen, some from bedroom windows and even a few stuck in shop windows.

One evening, Rona took me to the pictures as her treat. We went to the Park and Dare hall in Treorchy. Rona did not mind going 'first house' so that I could be home and in bed before my asthma started. She and I very often went to the cinema together. This particular night they were showing 'Song of Russia'. I don't know if it was a good film or a bad one. But the music held me enthralled. I gave myself up to it, trying to ignore Rona's whispers, I just shut my eyes and listened to the music. I had at last discovered classical music . . .

My mother had somehow managed to buy me a new coat that Easter. She bought it of course, as she had to buy most things, by paying small amounts of money weekly. The coat, as with all the children's things, was bought from Edwards, The Flannel Shop. I liked the colour of the coat, which was turquoise, but I did not like the style. It had the padded shoulders of the forties look, and although I had stopped having my hair cut once a month by my father and sometimes tried to curl the edges with 'dinkie' steel curlers, I still looked like a little girl. Puberty seemed as far away as ever. I did not like myself in the coat, although my mother insisted that it suited me.

By now I was forced to wear blue tinted spectacles, the final blow to any hopes I may have had of growing up to be 'pretty'. My eyes had finally turned rebellious after all the nights of reading.

I don't know if Rona was becoming slightly broody or not, as one day she borrowed a friend's baby to walk him in his pram. She got me to join her and then go on back to the house. He was a pretty little boy of about nine months or so and, for some reason, seemed to have taken a fancy to me, although I was never the kind to drool over babies simply because they were babies. Now, I took over the pram and began to wish that I was not only old enough to get married but that I was much prettier, and more likely to attract a boy-friend. Then, suddenly, I felt a trickle down my leg. It was not pee, I knew that. I could hardly wait to get back home and go out to the lavatory to check.

I thought of all the little pink pills 'for pale people' and the iron jelloids my mother had bought for me in the past, worried about my delayed puberty. I was filled with hope. I thought too, of how my mother had commented on Betty Mathias who had now come home to live with her father. 'She's got a nice figure, low down too,' she had said approvingly. I had not told her of my budding breasts, or the thick fuzz of red pubic hair I had grown almost overnight.

The visit to the lavatory confirmed my hopes. I was having a period, at long, long last. I had reached puberty. I felt delirious with happiness. I had longed for this moment so much. I was no longer a little girl. My mother was pleased as well, relieved perhaps, but when she cut a piece off an old flannelette sheet for me to 'use as a diaper' I was less than pleased. It was rough and by the following morning, I was sore underneath.

'It's what I've always used,' my mother said in surprise, 'you can wash it out after a few days.' I told her I wanted sanitary towels, grateful for the fact that Rona had told me about them. It was Rona who had to persuade my mother into giving me the money to buy them. I felt myself blush slightly, as I asked Mr Jenkins the Chemist for a 'packet of sanitary towels, please'.

Determined to show that I had a better figure than Betty, I began now, with a kind of reckless abandon, to leave off the many layers of clothing my mother had encased me in. First went the hated vest, the following week the liberty bodice joined it, well hidden under the tallboy at the end of the bed. Then the flannelette petticoat, worn because 'May was not yet through' went the same way. Then the cotton petticoat followed suit. I was still wearing a jumper, and I did not feel the cold any more than before. In point of fact, it was wonderful to be free of the many layers of clothing. I had thought that perhaps my breasts would grow more quickly if they were not held back by the unnecessary clothing. Whether I was right or it was simply just a coincidence, I don't know, but it proved effective, just as I had planned.

It did not dawn on my mother for several weeks. Her arthritis was worse and Bopa Sophy was still doing the bulk of our washing. Then one morning my mother called upstairs, 'Have you put your flannelette petticoat out for Bopa Sophy?' I came down the stairs rapidly. 'No, Mam, I haven't worn one for weeks now.'

She looked at me in astonishment, as if seeing me clearly for the first time. 'Weren't you afraid of catching cold?' 'No, Mam. I was wearing too much, it was bad for me.' I held myself as tall as I could, knowing that my hips were still non-existent, and that my waist was no more than 18 inches at the most. I was like a bird showing off her new feathers. I wanted her to notice and she did. She said slowly, 'I think you are going to have a nice figure after all, Mair.'

'I need a bra Mam.'

'I've never worn one.'

I could not say what I had noticed a long time ago, that in common with most of the mothers I knew, her breasts were far too near her waist. 'Rona wears one and she wears rayon petticoats, not cotton.'

'We'll wait until you've put a bit more weight on. Besides, you haven't got any coupons.'

I found myself feeling angry for the first time. I never had the use of my own clothing coupons. Perhaps she read my thoughts because she said, 'Muriel and Derek are going to school, and you know how Derek gets through his shoes.' I felt suddenly deflated. How would things have been if *I* had gone to school and would have wanted, as I knew I should have wanted, to stay on? I was still only fifteen but once again I was reminded that I was not contributing anything to the cost of my keep. Betty, along with all the rest of the girls and boys in my age group, was working. Still, I had proved a point.

Having at last grown out of most of my own clothes, the turquoise coat in particular, my mother asked Bopa Sophy if Eirwen had any 'hand me downs' she could spare. Bopa Sophy turned up one day just as I was drying my hair.

'You've got lovely hair Mair. I wish Eirwen's was like that but it's always been thin with her.' The praise was sweet, I had little enough of it, except from Rona, who described my hair as 'Titian' and who wished that she was as slim as I was. Having thrown away my blue tinted spectacles I enjoyed the feeling that perhaps I was pretty at last . . .

One evening, coming out of the Pavilion cinema in Treorchy, (first house as usual) I found that it had started to rain. Not heavy rain, but the thin, summer drizzle that I loved to feel on my face. However, I had no mac with me, so I began to run. The shoulder bag that had been a joint Christmas present from the family slipped from my shoulder and I stopped to pick it up. 'You look just like a mermaid,' said an amused voice. I looked up quickly. I saw a tall, dark boy of about my own age. It was Paul and I liked what I saw. His eyes were a darker brown than Dat's had been but they were kind. He fell in beside me, unasked.

I told no one about Paul. It was somehow too precious and too new. We would become officially engaged when he had his eighteenth birthday. Afterwards, I regretted that we had not been lovers, but although I could never quite understand the stigma of having an illegitimate child, I knew that I would not have the courage to go against the rules. 'Don't ever bring trouble on the house,' my father had warned, whilst my mother warned me not to have sex until at least I 'got engaged'. This was before I was old enough to conceive a child. Their attitudes had not changed, nor had the mores of the society in which we lived.

Now, I cannot remember his face. And I sometimes wonder if this April love had just been a dream. It was too much like a romantic novel perhaps. It's only when I remember riding pillion on Paul's motor bike down the Bwlch road that I know it happened.

Paul was posted to Aden, and when the airmail letters came, I at last confided in my mother, who grew happily interested. Then, his letters ceased and I began to wonder if he had fallen out of love with me as easily as he had fallen into it. It was nearly three months later, when I was again coming out of the Pavilion cinema, that I bumped into his sister, the only other person to know about me. Rose came close to me, Paul was dead . . .

When I broke the news to my mother, her eyes filled with tears but I could not cry. It had happened three months before. 'Perhaps,' said my mother, 'you'll never marry now!' I looked at her in surprise. It was true that I never came into contact with other boys. I had never learnt to dance and that was where almost everyone found his or her partner, but I was too young to think of myself as a possible old maid like poor Bopa Rina.

Money matters again became pressing. The New Look had come in and I longed for new clothes and high-heeled shoes. It was Aunty Lou who suggested it. There was now something called National Assistance and it was given out to those who were unable to work. My mother became interested and excited. She consulted our local councillor Glyn Davies about it, and he told her that he would get in touch with the department and someone would come out to interview me.

I hated the idea. It pressed on me like a weight. I would be considered feeble-minded or something, certainly 'not normal'. When at last someone did call, all my worst fears were realized. He demanded to see all my underwear and asked highly personal questions, which included the question, 'Are you a virgin?' For the first time I was glad that all Paul and I had done was to behave like innocent children in the ferns on Maindy mountain. I would not sit down in the presence of this obnoxious man but stood glaring at him until he left. I then went upstairs to my bedroom where I shed tears of rage. I had not asked to have asthma or wanted to be kept away from school. I knew that if I had been allowed to attend as both Muriel and Derek were doing, I would not have suffered this humiliation.

The application was successful, and I was duly awarded National Assistance. My mother was greatly relieved and allowed me to keep some of it as pocket money. It was very little but it allowed me to buy new clothing by paying a small amount weekly to Miss Howells. I bought a blue coat with a velvet collar in a darker shade. It was nipped in at the waist but with a fuller skirt and it reached down to mid-calf length. I bought blue shoes with very high heels and with ankle straps to match. I also bought a dirndl skirt, again with a very tight waist, two blouses, one blue, made out of parachute silk and one in white with a frilled collar. The 'New Look' suited me and although I hated the thought that all this had been possible only by 'living off the State', I had enjoyed buying the clothes.

I cut my hair back to shoulder length and curled the edges. Now, I felt myself to be fashionable as well as pretty, and hoped that I fitted in with girls of my own age.

I thought of joining a drama group but on being told that they had no one under thirty, I changed my mind. I asked my father if there was a Labour League of Youth somewhere. There wasn't. I hadn't been particularly keen on joining the Labour movement anyway. At that stage my views were much further to the left. My father was still bringing home the papers taken by the Labour Club and these now included the *Soviet Weekly*. I read it as I read everything that came my way, and one day I read an article about the Young Communists League (YCL). Without even thinking about it, I dashed off a letter to ask where I could find the nearest branch.

I had a reply saying that there was no Rhondda branch at present, but that there was going to be a branch starting in Tonypandy. The letter included the name and address of Annie Powell* and suggested that I contact her . . .

I enrolled as a member of the Communist party at a reduced fee and went along to some of their meetings and met George Baker, Stan Davies and Miriam and Sam Wood, the latter to become good friends. But I found that much of the meetings bored me. I was more interested in the YCL which was due to begin in Tonypandy.

My first glimpse of the special Cadre they were sending up from London was through my bedroom window. I had developed a huge abscess under one of my high teeth, and my face was swollen and ugly. I heard the knock on the door, and I peeped through the curtains. Two boys stood at the door, one very ordinary boy of about seventeen and the other a little older with a shock of curling blond hair. I dived under the blankets. When my mother came hurrying up to tell me, I made her promise to make some excuse. I had flu, I had anything. That good-looking boy should never see me with a swollen face . . .

Eventually, I did meet Roy, at the first meeting of the YCL in Tonypandy. I was introduced and then Roy asked me to wait outside while they voted for committee members. Being a new member, I

---

*Annie Powell (1906-1986) Communist Councillor for Rhondda District Council (1955-1962; 1967-1983), became first communist mayor in Britain in 1979.

was not eligible to vote. I was, however, allowed back in for the counting. I sat there watching and listening, as Roy read out the names. Then he looked puzzled, 'Ginger' and yet another 'Ginger'. Altogether he counted out thirteen 'Gingers'. There was general laughter at his bewilderment, and it was only when he glanced at me that the penny dropped. Being so very fair himself, his blond hair having a slight streak of gold in it, he had not thought my colouring unusual. Nor indeed had I any idea that I had been voted on to the committee at my very first meeting. It was of course the boys who had ganged up to vote me on. I was thrilled.

Weeks later, when I had my very first poem published in 'Daylight' (published and edited by Margot Heinemann) I was even more pleased. At last I was on the verge of an exciting new life.

Kingfisher of Hope

~

Maggie Pryce Jones

Late spring brought great rejoicing throughout the country; the war was over, in Europe at least, the fear of bombs removed, and, although many families grieved for their lost ones and worried about sons and daughters still at war in the Middle East, there was cause for celebration to the fullest extent that rationing would allow.

Every house in the villages of Trelewis and Treharris was decked with red, white and blue bunting, the grey houses on the surrounding hillsides were a mass of colourful arcades of flowers. Street parties were arranged at which men and women danced wildly, the children joining in. A great fear was lifted from us all: we could look forward to a peaceful future.

It was a long time before food and clothes became available without coupons, but now that lights were allowed to shine out again, everyone's spirits soared. There was talk of new baths at the pit-head, available for all colliery workers. When they came, the men would all return home clean, their working clothes left behind in their lockers. No more bathing in front of the fire, no more dirty working clothes in the house.

I was more than happy at the thought: I and the other inhabitants of our small row of cottages fought an everlasting war against the bedbugs and black beetles that crawled everywhere. We would all join in a periodic co-operative effort to supplement our individual attempts to rid our homes of these filthy invaders. We were successful for months at a time, then they would return; now we hoped we could get rid of them forever, for we believed that the insects were brought to the cottages in the men's working clothes. And indeed, when ultimately the pit-head baths were available, we did rid the cottages of their unwanted guests.

Time flew past, so much was happening, locally and nationally . . .

We were all full of hope because a Labour government had been elected and the workers would be given a fair deal and the respect that their labour merited. This came to the colliery on the day when a huge notice was erected on top pit proclaiming that the colliery was now the property of the National Coal Board under the title of Deep Navigation Colliery. There was a new spirit amongst the colliers and the surface workers, soon followed by the first of their many benefits. They became entitled to increased holidays, *with pay*, so that we need no longer dread Easter, Whitsun, and August bank holidays which had been compulsory but unpaid. Holidays, a constant worry to the colliers' wives, became, at last, the pleasure, release and relaxation they always ought to have been, two weeks' annual leave, with full pay.

Many families were now able to go on holiday for the very first time in their lives. How I wished that Mam had lived to enjoy such elementary benefits, which, together with increased pay, made working in the pits more attractive. Safety measures were at last improved, by law, and there was money to pay for the many long-overdue improvements.

It was wonderful. How right Grannie had been, so many years ago, when she said, during a strike, that if a cause was worth having, then it was worth fighting for.

The National Health Service was born, with specialist treatment available to all sick people, not only to those who could afford to pay. Dental treatment became free; soon there would be fewer mouths full of blackened, decaying teeth. 'Mam would still be alive,' I thought sadly, 'if this Health Service had been born earlier.' She would never have envisaged a free ambulance service, on request, or free medicine without a means test, all for a single weekly payment. And if all this had been available when she was alive, she could have looked forward to a university education for Bryn and for me, with generous free grants available to working-class children who had the ability to pass the necessary exams.

If only she had lived just a few years longer. If only . . .

The years immediately after the war brought many changes to the valley, mental as well as physical. The outlook of young people changed to suit their new environment; they adopted a chameleon skill which shocked the older generation. New employments were arriving, and the new factories, such as the Hoover, offered such good wages and conditions that many men left the pit and snatched the chance to work above ground, away from the killer dust. The lives of the women changed dramatically, for it had not been only the freedom from never-ending housework that appealed to them when they were called upon to work during the war years.

The chance to earn money for their families was a great inducement. Previously they had relied upon their men to provide every penny they needed; there was never cash left over for luxuries. Now they could earn enough to pay for the extras for themselves; they could afford to buy the luxury goods which until now had been denied them. After proving their ability to hold their own in a man's world, they were unwilling to return full time to mere domesticity. They demanded, and got, the chains removed.

EPILOGUE

Chrysanthemum is Hard to Spell

~

Maggie Pryce Jones

My passion for education was installed in me at our village's autumn flower show in about nineteen twenty nine, I think. I was there with Mam because Dad was showing his dahlias. The show was held in a large dirty white tent on our local playing field.

The air inside the tent was hot and humid, heavy with the scent of the different flowers. I remember we were admiring the colourful displays. Mam loved flowers but did not like to see them cut from their own environment. 'Poor things,' she said as she touched the velvet petals in the vases and jugs.

We reached the benches where the chrysanthemums in all their magnificent glory were on show, their wonderful colours, red, gold, bronze and blood-red made a wonderful display.

'Oh, chrysantememums,z' exclaimed my Mam in delight. 'No perfume Maggie, but aren't their colours wonderful?' A thin high voice spoke from behind us, 'You mean chrysanthemums Martha, if you could read you would know,' it said spitefully. It had to be my aunt, the toffee-nosed one of course. I saw my quiet mother blush and turn away, and I with all the dignity of a young child, said slowly and loudly, 'My Mam can read anything that you can.' I remember the silence in the tent then Mam took my hand and we left the show and went home. Mam never mentioned the matter afterwards, now I know she was ashamed because I knew of her lack of learning.

Later that week I asked Grannie, who lived with us, why my mother could not read. 'Does it matter, child, as long as there is food on the table and the beds are clean?' she demanded. 'A woman does not need to read or write. Our work is in the home, the men see to all else, and that is how it should be.'

I knew that it did matter. The incident stayed in my mind, fostering a deep rebellion inside me. Unknowingly I hoarded such incidents, asking repeatedly why I had to help in the house while my brothers played outside. The answer was always the same. 'You will have a house of your own to look after one day Maggie, the boys will have wives to look after theirs.'

I began to notice that Mam always saw that Dad had the best food, the most comfortable chair, and new clothes when he went out anywhere with the Legion. She had nothing and never went out unless all our family went as well. The one thing I could not understand as I grew older was – why did she accept it all? Our neighbours, her friends were exactly the same, the men had first claim on luxuries and their wives were happy to accede to this as their due. 'After all they work hard, Maggie,' Mam said one day when I asked her why she spent all her club money on Dad and us children – nothing for herself.

John, our lodger, told me one day when we were discussing the matter on one of our walks, 'I think it is hard on the women, cariad, but nothing will ever change I am afraid, because the women themselves see no wrong in it.' I often sat in the room when one or other of Mam's friends came in, their talk was always about their homes and family, they went nowhere, they saw few people, only their neighbours or families, and as most could not read they had no other topic of conversation.

In those days, voting day was a big event, schools were closed because they were called into use as voting stations. Husbands and wives went to vote together, I remember hearing Mam tell John when he asked her who she thought was the best candidate 'Lew will tell me who to vote for', and so it was, wives voted as told by their husbands.

I was fifteen when Mam died, and how I wished that my brothers had learned to help in the house, they were good and tried hard but it was difficult for them to come to terms with it.

I vowed then that any children I might have would be treated equally, whatever their sex, and more, I would see that they would have the best possible education. If only Mam and her peers had known and recognized the power they held. They were the strong ones, not the men. They had the iron hands in their velvet gloves.

The women of the valleys were forced to use that strength in nineteen thirty nine and in the years that followed. Then, they broke the chains that held them to their kitchens, they thought for themselves, and they changed the history of the valleys, as women elsewhere changed the history of this country.

APPENDIX

PROFILE OF WRITERS

Florence Allen was born in Abergavenny in 1907. When she was 18, she married a pit safety man and moved to Bargoed in the Rhymney Valley. After the war, bringing up her daughter and two sons alone, she began to write. Florence worked as a door to door insurance agent and as local correspondent to *The Merthyr Express* and *The Argus*. She became a prodigious writer of novels, short stories and stage plays. Her plays have been performed all over the Rhymney Valley, whilst her short stories include a *South Wales Echo* 'Saturday Story'. Florence, who is presently seeking a publisher for her two novels 'Black Velvet' and 'Between Heaven and Hell', still lives in the Bargoed home she moved to 70 years ago.

Elizabeth Andrews (1882-1960) was born into a large Welsh-speaking mining family in Hirwaun. Elizabeth left school at thirteen years of age and spent a period at Llandrindod Wells as a dressmaker before returning to South Wales in 1908 to supervise a large sewing workshop at Ystrad, Rhondda. During the First World War she became secretary of the first Rhondda branch of the Women's Co-operative Guild at Tonpentre and was the first woman to be elected to the Executive Committee of Rhondda Borough Labour Party. She gave evidence to the Sankey Commission of Enquiry in 1918. In 1920 she became the Women's Organiser for the Labour Party in Wales, a post which she held until 1948. She was appointed to the Glamorgan Health Executive Committee by Aneurin Bevan and also served as a magistrate from 1924 to 1947. Her autobiography, *A Woman's Work is Never Done*, was published in 1957.

Lucy Arundell (1912-1990) was brought up by her grandparents in Monmouth and later in Cwmparc in the Rhondda. She married and in 1939 moved with her husband to his native Hull. Lucy was kept busy looking after her three sons and helping out in her husband's shop but still felt homesick for Wales. In order to come to terms with her new environment, she learnt about the history of Hull, started writing and became a member of the Hull Writers' Circle. Her work has appeared in numerous publications and she was a regular broadcaster on BBC Radio Humberside.

Gabrielle Capus was born in Swansea in 1931, moving to Newport with her family when she was just eighteen months old. She taught music and general studies in both junior and senior schools until retirement, and was a chorus member of the Welsh National Opera in the 1960s. She is now a member of the Cwmbrân Writers and has had poems and articles published in a wide variety of anthologies including *Poetry Now*. Gabrielle who still lives in Newport, also enjoys watercolour painting and looking after her much loved garden.

Dorothy Craig was born in Penydarren, Merthyr in 1923. She went to school in Merthyr and then on to Cardiff University to study Chemistry and Botany. She taught in Coventry for five years and then in London for 36 years. She returned to Merthyr with her husband in 1985. Dorothy writes articles for the local newspaper, and is an active member of Merthyr Writers' Circle and the Merthyr based women writers/performers group, 'Masquerade'.

Edith S. Davies (1907-1996) was born in Ynysybwl. Her miner father had started work at the Lady Windsor pit when he was twelve. Her mother resolved that her two sons would never go down the pit, but a great believer in equal opportunities, she was also determined that her two daughters should be educated. Edith was educated at Pontypridd Girls Grammar School and at Cardiff University where she read English. Her family's finances were so reduced during her time at University that she had to share a single pair of shoes with her mother, who would remain indoors while Edith attended lectures. Her mother also read every one of her daughter's course books. Edith taught at Senior School, Abercynon until 1939 when she married a fellow teacher. Her daughter, Thora, was born in 1942 and Edith didn't return to teaching until 1954. She taught in several schools in the area including Pontypridd Boys and Girls Grammar Schools, finishing her career at Trerobart Junior School, Ynysybwl. Her childhood memories *The Innocent Years* was published in 1995, just a year before her death.

Menna Gallie (1920-1990) was born in Ystradgynlais and brought up in Creunant in the Dulais Valley. Her background was socialist, Welsh-speaking and nonconformist. She studied English at University of Wales, Swansea and worked as a civil servant during the Second World War. Married to Professor Bryce Gallie, Professor of Philosophy at Belfast and Cambridge, she had one son and a daughter. The family lived in Northern Ireland and in Cambridge before she and her husband retired to Pembrokeshire in the early 1970s. Her six novels, two of which are set in the Swansea Valley, are better known in America than in Wales, although one novel, *Travels With a Duchess* (1968), was republished by Honno Press in 1996. She also published *Full Moon* (1970), a translation of Caradog Prichard's novel *Un Nos Ola Leuad*, and a study of Pembrokeshire folklore, *Little England's Other Half* (1974).

Winifred Griffiths was born in Overton, Hampshire in 1896. She became influenced by socialism following her experiences as a worker in a clothing factory and in domestic service. She worked in the Co-op before and after her marriage to James Griffiths in 1918. He was later to become an M.P. and Cabinet Minister. In 1927, she became a member of Ystradgynlais Labour Party Women's Section, and served as a Poor Law Guardian (1928-30), a District Councillor (1928-36) and a magistrate. From 1932 to 1935, she contributed a series of articles to the *Social Democrat* chronicling her experiences. Her husband's career took the family to London, bringing to an end her personal political activity in South Wales. Her autobiography, *One Woman's Story*, was published in 1979.

Gertrude Harris was born in London and moved to Abercarn as a child. As a young girl, she was in service in Penarth. She was a lifelong socialist, and a member of the Labour Party for most of her adult life. After marriage, she and her husband lived in Barry. She was involved in the 'Spanish Aid' movement in the 30s, The Clarion Club and Youth Hostels Association. She died in 1985, aged 80.

Maggie Pryce Jones was born in Trelewis. She was forced to leave grammar school at fifteen to bring up her younger siblings when her mother died. She returned to education during the 1960s, gained her 'O' and 'A' levels and worked for many years in the Civil Service. She started writing, a long held ambition, when her husband suffered a stroke and became bedridden for six years. Her published work includes poetry and her autobiography *Kingfisher of Hope*. Her latest novel, 'White Doors, Black Memories', is awaiting publication. Maggie has two sons and two daughters and lives in Treharris.

Margaret Lloyd was born in Merthyr in 1930. She trained and worked as a nurse, took breaks to bring up her four sons and finally qualified and worked as a health visitor until her retirement. She became a member of the Merthyr Writers' Circle in 1990 and a founder member of Merthyr's women writers/performers group 'Masquerade' in 1993. An intrepid world traveller, Margaret still lives in Merthyr and has had her poems published in a wide variety of anthologies.

Mair Eluned McLellan was born in Pentre, Rhondda in 1928. Given no formal education on account of her childhood asthma, she became a prodigious writer from the age of six. She had several poems published whilst in her twenties' and was called 'a promising novelist'. Her health once again broke down however, and she was forced for many years to put her writing on the back boiler. As well as her (as yet) unpublished autobiography 'Shadows On The Wall', she has written many short stories, several of which were broadcast as Radio Four 'Morning Stories'. Mair lives with her husband in Colbren, Neath.

Enid Mavis Mitchell was born and brought up on a small farm on the top of the Graig mountain, Pontypridd. Her father split his time between running the farm and working at a local pit, so his children were expected to pull their weight to help him. 'Mitch', as she is universally known, worked as a gas tester during the war years and enjoyed doing a man's job and earning a man's wage, writing about her experiences in Honno's *Parachutes and Petticoats*, a volume of Welsh women's recollections of the Second World War. After the war, she became a clerical worker and only started writing when she retired in 1993. Her stories have been published in the anthology *Short Stories From Mid Glamorgan*. Mitch has two sons and a daughter and lives with her husband in Pontypridd.

Elaine Morgan was born in Pontypridd in 1920. Educated firstly in Hopkinstown and then in Treforest, she went on to study at Lady Margaret's

Hall, Oxford. Her television screen writing credits includes nine episodes of 'Doctor Finley's Casebook', 'Testament of Youth', 'Lloyd George', and dramas based on the lives of Marie Curie and Gwen John. Her ground breaking books on evolution include *The Descent of Woman*, *The Aquatic Ape*, *The Scars of Evolution* and *The Descent of the Child*. Her latest book, *The Aquatic Hypothesis*, was published in June 1997. Elaine has three sons and lives in Mountain Ash with her husband.

Marion Phillips (1881-1932) was born in Melbourne, Australia. The daughter of a Jewish lawyer, she attended the London School of Economics in 1904, before being employed as a research assistant to socialists Sidney and Beatrice Webb. She became involved in both the socialist and the women's movements and between 1913 and 1918 she was Secretary of the Women's Labour League. In 1918 she was appointed Chief Woman Officer of the Labour Party and as such was involved with organising relief in South Wales during the 1926 Lock Out. For many years, she edited *Labour Woman* and became M.P. for Sunderland in 1929.

Katie Pritchard was born in Caernarfon in 1907. Her father came to Gilfach Goch (in the Rhondda) to look for work when she was a child. The monoglot Welsh-speaking family moved there and learnt to speak English for the first time. Her lack of English kept her back in school but she soon made up for lost time by attending night classes. She was teacher for 40 years, finishing her career as headmistress of Hendre Forgan Infants School. She founded the Gilfach Goch Ladies Guild in 1961, an organisation which is still going strong. Her publications include *The Story of Gilfach Goch, Gilfach in Cameo* and other books of local history.

Eunice Hughes Thomas was born in Ogmore Vale in 1929. Her father died when she was twelve and she moved with her mother to Cefn Coed y Cymer, near Merthyr. She left school at fourteen to become a clerical worker. After marrying and having two daughters, she went back to college to train in shorthand and typing. She had enjoyed writing in her youth, and took it up again when she got bored with telling her grandchildren the same old fairy stories. In her mid-50s, she bought herself a motorbike and her wild rides on the Valleys' mountain tops inspired her to poetry. Eunice still lives in Merthyr where she is a member of the Writers' Circle and 'Masquerade', the women writers/performers group.

Iris Roderick Thomas was born in Twynyrodyn, Merthyr. She attended the County Intermediate School and had been accepted for a teaching course at Swansea College when she had a change of heart and opted for a nursing career at the City General Hospital, Gloucester during the Second World War. She went on to work in St Tydfil's Hospital, Merthyr. Iris married, had two daughters and changed career again in 1965, when she became Zone Sales Manager for Avon Cosmetics, retiring after 21 years in 1986. Her books of memoirs include *Thanks for the Memories* – volumes one and two, *Dearest Grandfather*, *To the Top of the Stoney Road* and *Remember When*. She has also published a collection of Welsh-flavoured short stories *Slices of Teisen Lap*. She is presently working on another collection of stories and poems, 'A Little Bit of This and a Little Bit of That' and a novel 'Some Sigh and Some Cry'. Iris became a Writer on Tour for the Welsh Arts Council in 1992 and still lives in Merthyr with her husband.

Barbara Walters was born in Glyncorrwg near Port Talbot in 1926 where her miner father worked at the South Pit. When she left school, she ran a milk round with a horse and cart and was a member of the Land Army during the war. Barbara had always enjoyed writing but took it up seriously when her children, two sons and a daughter, grew up. She has had four 'Morning Stories' broadcast on Radio Four, 'Any Old Dream Will Do' being further broadcasted in Ireland and the Netherlands. Her work has appeared in many anthologies including *Two Valleys*, *Cambrensis*, *Poetry Now* and *Black Harvest*. She is presently working on an anthology of poetry which reflects on life in the valleys from the 1930s until the present. Barbara still lives in Glyncorrwg with her husband.

Heulwen Williams was born in Rhymney, Monmouthshire in 1922. She was educated in Rhymney and trained as a teacher in Swansea Training College from 1940 to 1942. She taught in Shropshire, London and in several Rhymney Valley schools before joining the staff of Ysgol Gymraeg Rhymni (Rhymni Welsh School) in 1965. She became head teacher of the school in 1971 and held the post until her retirement in 1983. Heulwen, who still lives in Rhymney with her husband, remains active in the community. She is a school governor, a chapel deacon and President of the local Welsh Society.

Nessie Williams was living in Builth Wells when *My Childhood in the Valleys* was published in the *Anglo-Welsh Review* in 1973. She later lived in Llandrindod Wells.

Beatrice Wood was born in Dowlais in 1916. She started her working life in domestic service and later worked in both a butter factory and a chocolate factory. When she retired, she started to write for her grandchildren, who constantly asked for stories about the old days. She was a founder member of Merthyr Writers' Circle and has to date written 500 poems. Her autobiography, *Wednesday's Child*, was published after much encouragement from Elaine Morgan. Beatie lives in Merthyr with her husband and has one daughter.